THE ARIADNE OBJECTIVE

THE ARIADNE OBJECTIVE

PATRICK LEIGH FERMOR
AND THE UNDERGROUND WAR
TO RESCUE CRETE FROM THE NAZIS

WES DAVIS

PAUL DRY BOOKS
Philadelphia 2024

For Slim

Contents

I dream'd that Greece might still be free.

LORD BYRON

*It seemed . . . and to me, then, rather shockingly . . .
like a practical joke played on the Germans
in fancy dress.*

A. M. "SANDY" RENDEL

Sea of Crete

Peristeri
Peninsula

Chania

Suda Bay

Rethymnon

C H A N I A

Anogeia

WHITE
MOUNTAINS

R E T H Y M N O N

Asi Gónia

Alones

Amari

Mount Ida

Rodakino

Gerakari

Sphakia

Saktouria

Paximadia
Island

Tymbak

Gavdos
Island

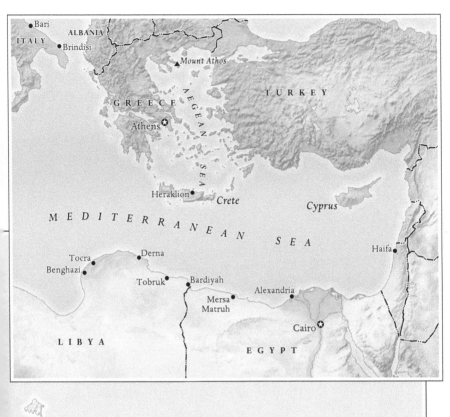

Foreword

THE SEED FOR THIS BOOK was planted during the summer of
1993, when I was working as camp manager on the excavation
of a pair of Iron Age settlements near the village of Kavousi, in
the mountains above the Bay of Mirabello, at the eastern end
of Crete. I had first joined the Kavousi project two years earlier,
as a volunteer, while I was still a classics student. In the time I
had spent there, I had learned a fair amount about the Kavousi
site, which had been occupied as early as 1100 BCE, and I had
gleaned some understanding of the Minoan backdrop to its set-
tlement. But I had taken in less information about the island as
a whole and its modern history.

That changed in a significant way one afternoon in July or
August, as I drove the director of the excavation, Geraldine
Gesell, to meet a colleague of hers at Knossos, the Bronze-Age
palace site south of Heraklion where Arthur Evans had first
uncovered the remains of the civilization that he came to call
Minoan. The drive to Knossos from Pacheia Ammos, where
the excavation team was based, took a couple of hours in those
days, and the conversation along the way unfolded like an informal seminar on the archaeological sites we passed. The main
road that runs along the north coast of the island passes by, for
instance, the site of Gournia, the best-preserved Late Bronze
Age town yet uncovered on Crete. But I also received a primer
on some more modern aspects of Cretan history, including

commentary on how the island had changed over the previous decades and how some things, like the Cretan mistrust of Germans in the wake of WWII, remained the same.

Snaking our way down from the coast in a loop that avoided the capital city of Heraklion, we overshot Knossos by a few kilometers and came to a juncture where the Knossos road branched off from one coming from the village of Archanes, to the south. A striking, abstract monument, composed of a fractured stone column crowned with barbed wire, was set back from the intersection. As I made the turn toward Knossos, Professor Gesell, gesturing out the window, said "That's where they kidnapped the general." It was an offhand comment that invited a flood of questions. Who were "they," what force did the general command, and why was he kidnapped?

After the visit to Knossos, we drove into Heraklion to pick up supplies. An archaeological excavation, I had learned by this time, depended as much on cardboard boxes and office supplies—notebooks, drafting tools, glassine envelopes—as on spades, trowels, and surveying equipment. So our first stop was at a grocery store where I tracked down the manager to ask if we could take some discarded boxes off his hands. These were used to store artifacts in the dig's *apothiki*, or warehouse, and were always in short supply. (The most durable boxes, I recall, were those used to ship a certain brand of coffee creamer; the discovery of a trove of those generated nearly as much excitement around the dig house as an important find in the field.) Next came a stationery shop that, in addition to the pens and journals we were seeking, displayed a dusty collection of paperbacks, among which Professor Gesell pointed out Patrick Leigh Fermor's books. It turned out that it was Leigh Fermor—a writer I knew for his lyrical travel memoirs—who, as an officer in the British Special Operations Executive (SOE), had parachuted onto Crete and organized a unit of Greek Resistance fighters with whom he had abducted the commander, General Heinrich Kreipe, in charge of the German division that had occupied the island during the Second World War.

As I dug deeper into Leigh Fermor's wartime exploits in the years that followed, I found that his story combined the drama and danger of the resistance with elements that were more familiar to me: literature and archaeology. As an erstwhile classics student, I was fascinated to learn that it was their study of Ancient Greek at school that put many of the SOE commandos on the island, since the knowledge of the ancient language gave them a clearer path to learning Modern Greek. It also turned out that another ancient language, Latin, played a key role in bringing about a kind of understanding between enemy combatants at a dramatic moment in the story.

The story's cast of characters could not have been more agreeable to someone with an interest in archaeology. There was the eccentric Cambridge archaeologist John Pendlebury, who had written the guide to the archaeology of Crete that I had carried in a dogeared copy as I explored the island. I hadn't known at the time that soon after the book was published in 1939 its author, under cover of an appointment as British vice-consul in Heraklion, had begun secretly organizing a resistance network ahead of the German invasion that was beginning to look inevitable. Tom Dunbabin, who later collected intelligence for SOE in and around the Amari Valley in central Crete, was an Oxford-trained archaeologist who had been serving as director of the British School of Archaeology at Athens when the war broke out. A third SOE officer, Sandy Rendel, had studied classics alongside Dunbabin at Oxford.

Strong as the lineup was, the archaeologists and classicists in the story were rivaled by the literary talent. Three of the central figures were burgeoning writers: Leigh Fermor; his second in command, William Stanley Moss; and Xan Fielding. After the war, Leigh Fermor would establish a reputation as one of Britain's finest travel writers. Moss would go on to write a number of novels and nonfiction books, as well as a spellbinding account of the abduction of General Kreipe, while Fielding produced accounts of his wartime activities, travel memoirs, and translations, including an English translation of the French novelist Pierre Boulle's *The Bridge over the River Kwai*. During the war the three funneled their literary energy into the descriptions of German operations that they composed in caves and shepherds' huts all over Crete. It is impossible to imagine a wartime theater of operations from which emerged more delightfully-written field reports.

The resistance story itself, unfolding on a landscape steeped in myth and legend—including both Mount Ida and Mount Dicti, each a purported birthplace of Zeus—seemed to link the heroic age of the ancient world to the bravery and resolve of the modern Greek population, as represented by men like the resistance fighter Manoli Paterakis, who faced every risk the war threw at him—he was "ready for anything," Leigh Fermor wrote—and would still be clambering through the high mountains hunting wild goats into his seventies. Added to all that was the cosmopolitan world of Cairo, which served as wartime headquarters for SOE operations in the Mediterranean and had become home to noncombatant figures like the enchanting Sophie Tarnowska, an expatriate Polish countess who presided over the house Moss and Leigh Fermor shared there. Taken all together, it was a tapestry that entirely captivated me and captivates me to this day.

It is my hope that this new edition will have a long life and carry the story of the resistance to the wide audience that its remarkable protagonists deserve.

A Note on Names

IN THE NARRATIVE that follows I have referred to British officers most often by their surnames, usually dispensing with the formality of rank in order to maintain the sense of immediacy with which the story unfolds in the primary documents—mostly field reports—on which the book draws. For the same reason, the Greek partisans who bore the brunt of the risk in the dangerous work described here are referred to by their first names or nicknames, as they generally are in the field reports. Greek names can be transliterated from the Greek alphabet in a variety of ways, and I have relied largely on spellings that appear in field reports, in part for consistency with other historical accounts but also to capture the tone of the action as it unfolded. These spellings generally reflect the casual pronunciation used in the field: thus Manoli, for example, rather than the more proper Manolis, or still more formal Emmanouil. In a few cases, I have preferred code names where they are particularly descriptive or colorful, as in the case of Mihali "Micky" Akoumianakis, who is here called "Minoan Mike," using the code name derived from his familial association with the Palace of Knossos. Greek resistance leaders who commanded their own organizations, the *kapetans,* are generally referred to by surname or code name—Bandouvas or Bo-Peep—or both. In actual practice in wartime Crete, names used in the field were fluid and flexible. Patrick Leigh Fermor was frequently called "Mihali," the Hellenized version of his middle name, Michael. But in field reports he is just as often referred to as "Paddy." Tom Dunbabin was either "Yanni" or "O Tom"; Harry Booke was "Mihali" or sometimes "Mihalaki," to distinguish him from "Mihali" Leigh Fermor. Names also evolved over time, as is seen in the case of George Psychoundakis, whose code name shifted from "Changeling" to "Changebug."

The organization that became known as the Special Operations Executive also bore different names at various stages of the war. For the sake of consistency I have used SOE throughout.

PROLOGUE

Whimsical

IT WAS JUST AFTER five thirty in the evening when a four-engine Halifax bomber lumbered off the runway of the RAF aerodrome in Brindisi. Climbing through thickening cloud cover, it banked toward the southeast and roared away along the heel of Italy. The crew's scheduled mission was routine. Or what passed for routine in a squadron dedicated to special operations. They were making a run down to a mountain range midway along the northwestern fringe of the Greek mainland, to drop supplies for British agents working with the Greek Resistance to undermine the now nearly three-year-old German occupation. This ongoing operation, code-named Tingewick, had been under way for months. But on this evening, February 4, 1944, an unfamiliar operation appeared alongside Tingewick on the Halifax pilot's duty list. Its code name—a designation that would prove unusually fitting over the coming weeks—was Whimsical.

According to the orders sent down to the 148th Squadron, Operation Whimsical consisted of four men who would be dropping into Crete by parachute. Two of them were British officers, the other two Greek partisans. The commander of the operation was a handsome, gap-toothed young major named Patrick Leigh Fermor. He was called "Paddy" by the other Englishman, a captain named William Stanley Moss, himself a tall, debonair figure who moved with an unhurried confidence. When the two officers loped aboard the Halifax that evening, they looked less like commandos embarking on a covert mission than like a pair of dashing young aristocrats on a Mediterranean lark. In contrast, the two Greeks traveling with them had the authentically fierce appearance—sun-narrowed eyes and bristling mustaches—of Cretan shepherds. Or sheep rustlers. In neither case would these first impressions have been exactly right. But they would not have been far off the mark either.

The Whimsical party brought some five hundred pounds of equipment on board with them. Marlin guns, revolvers, and ammunition were packed away in cylindrical containers, along with more exotic supplies: from Benzedrine and knockout drops to lumps of plastic explosive fashioned to resemble goat droppings. Much of their gear was for all practical purposes invisible. The magnetized buttons of their trousers were designed to be used as compasses. They had maps, printed on fine silk, which could be tucked into the linings of their jackets, the lapels of which also concealed caches of cyanide, to be bitten as a last resort if capture looked inevitable. In addition, each man carried a surprisingly large quantity of gold sovereigns. For all the unexpected riches there was nothing extravagant about their attire, however. Under their down-filled jumpsuits all four wore plain clothes that, ragged as they appeared, might have been stolen from a shepherd's hut. Moss wore a black beret.

Their destination was an upland plain ringed by the Lasithi mountains in eastern Crete. In theory the Katharo plateau, as it was called, would be an ideal drop point. Although the northeastern fringe of the plateau was only twenty miles or so from the sea, it stood at an elevation nearly four thousand feet above sea level. The steep ascent from the Bay of Mirabello in the northeast was made, when it could be made at all, on a primitive trail riddled with switchbacks and narrow passes. And reaching Katharo from the south coast was no easier. All in all it was inhospitable terrain for German patrols. Yet the same topography might actually aid the parachute drop itself. The name "Katharo," which meant "clean" or "cleansed" in Greek, referred to the way the surrounding mountains served as a weather break, sheltering the plateau itself from the full force of winter storms. When the ring of mountain peaks was darkened by clouds, the plateau remained clear. That was the theory anyway.

By seven o'clock the Halifax had reached the mountainous area of northwestern Greece where the first drop was to take place. The pilot, who bore the portentous name Cyril J. Fortune, circled the area pinpointed in his flight plan, scanning the rugged terrain below for landmarks. But there was little to be seen through the blanket of cloud. Over the course of the next fifteen minutes, Fortune corkscrewed the Halifax down to seven thousand feet and at last found a break in the cloud cover. He spotted two lights that might have been signal fires but saw no sign of a third fire that would have confirmed the location of the drop. The crew flashed a prearranged Morse code pattern—the letter of the day was *K*—as a signal to agents on the ground. But no reply was seen. At 7:19 Fortune put Tingewick on hold and set a course for the Whimsical area.

Two hours later the plane was off the coast of Crete. The navigator, a sergeant named Cowell, pinpointed the target area, and Fortune brought the Halifax in for a reconnaissance run. But the Katharo name proved inappropriate for the plateau on this night. Clouds engulfed the mountains and plain alike. Fortune was forced to descend to 4,500 feet before he found any break at all. A brief glimpse of the ground revealed that they had come in north of the target. The crew fired a white Verey light as a clearer signal to the waiting ground force, and Fortune banked the Halifax to approach the drop zone on a westerly heading. At last he was able to verify that the appropriate signal had been lit. A single fire could be seen burning inside a triangle formed by three others. This was the right spot and all was in order on the ground. But the cloud base was a mere three hundred feet above ground level. Fortune explained to Major Leigh Fermor that "if he wished to drop, it would be necessary to make a low drop."

A parachute jump was hazardous business in the best of circumstances, but dropping from a lower altitude multiplied the risk considerably. Add to that the darkness and cloud cover, and it was anyone's guess what the outcome might be. Leigh Fermor, though, was unruffled. He would go, he said, and once down he would signal by flashing four times if it was safe to drop the rest of the party.

Fortune banked again and guided the Halifax in from the east at 4,700 feet above sea level, less than a thousand feet above the plateau itself. As it neared the drop zone, he brought the plane up another three hundred feet to give Leigh Fermor a slight margin of safety. Sergeant Rowland, the bomb aimer, spotted the target from inside the cloud bank while Leigh Fermor, perching on the edge of the jump hole, peered at the ground below. He had just caught sight of the triangle of signal fires when Rowland shouted, "Go!" An instant later he was somersaulting through the aircraft's backwash.

Moss watched as his friend disappeared through the drop door, knowing his turn would be next. "There was some terrible finality about seeing Paddy go through that hole," he felt. "One moment he was with us—then gone, utterly and irretrievably gone."

The Halifax circled back for another run, again approaching from the east. By now the clouds were closing in even more thickly, and it proved impossible to spot either the signal fire or Leigh Fermor's go-ahead signal. And there was no opening to get down for a better view. As the aircraft continued to circle, it slowly dawned on Moss that he and his two Greek friends would be unable to join Leigh Fermor. At 9:46 Fortune announced that they would have to abandon the Whimsical mission.

He would, however, give Tingewick one more try. Another two hours of flying time took the Halifax back to the mainland. But conditions there proved no better than in Crete. The drop area was blanketed by unbroken cloud cover. Fortune was unable to get below eight thousand feet, and it took him no longer than a minute to recognize that it was fruitless to continue circling. By 11:42 they were winging their way back to Brindisi.

As the weather continued to deteriorate, Fortune began to have difficulty controlling the aircraft. The wings were icing over. The trouble began at thirteen thousand feet, but the icing dogged the plane all the way down to four thousand feet. At that altitude Fortune was able to regain control of the Halifax. About the same time, however, a break in the cloud revealed that the aircraft had dropped below the level of the surrounding mountains. As the rugged terrain of the mountainside rushed into view, the situation looked perilous, but Fortune, apparently unruffled, eased the plane into an impossibly steep climb and slipped over the looming ridgeline with a hairbreadth of altitude to spare. As the sortie report he filed later calmly phrased it, "Captain found he was below level of the mountains and had to make a rapid ascent to avoid disaster."

The Whimsical flight touched down safely in Brindisi at 1:15 in the morning. But the foul weather had trailed it back. For the next three nights all missions scheduled to fly out of Brindisi were grounded.

ON FEBRUARY 9, Leigh Fermor, at least, believed he would soon be reunited with his comrades. Holed up in a cave east of the Katharo plateau, he took the time to compose a letter to a lady friend he had met in Cairo. A hand-sketched map of Crete at the top of the page marked his "window" with a cross, as if he were sending a postcard from a resort hotel. "Well," he wrote, "here we are in the old home, at least I am at this moment as the second I left the . . ."—here, in a nod to wartime circumspection, he crossed out a word and inserted "car"—"the second I left the car a horrid cloud appeared that stopped Billy and Manoli and George from jumping. We are expecting better tonight. Then up and AWAY!"

The storm that closed in after his jump had left its mark on the countryside. "It's very cold and snowy," he told his friend, "and rather beautiful. Wish you were here." His enthusiasm for Crete was undiminished by either the chill or the risk he was taking in venturing behind enemy lines. "It's great fun being back, and, of course, life is just one big whisker as usual."

A runner was waiting to carry away the letter, so he had to close. But he took the time to sketch a cartoon scene that was sure to amuse his friend. It showed a Prussian-helmeted German officer crawling from a cave in an attempt to reach the sea. A swastika flag flapped nearby. Two slender figures were bearing down on the German from the other side of the island. One, armed with a machine gun, called out, "Don't you dare move," while the second, wearing a tunic and dark forage cap, brandished what looked like a wooden sword and exclaimed, "Rather not." The wide-eyed German, knowing he was about to be captured, cried out, "Himmel!"—*Heavens!*—"I am undone." The caption read: "Life on the Island."

It was fortunate that the Germans failed to intercept the letter. The fanciful plan that had brought Leigh Fermor to Crete was all there in the cartoon. The two swashbuckling British officers closing in on a hapless German general—it was like a thumbnail sketch of the improbable mission Leigh Fermor intended to carry out as soon as his friends could join him.

PART ONE

DEPOSITED ON THE LIMESTONE

CHAPTER 1

Shanks's Mare

ON THE AFTERNOON of December 9, 1933, a London taxi traveling from Shepherd Market lurched to a stop on the north end of Tower Bridge. Three young men and a girl in high heels got out. Rain was beating down. "Nice weather for young ducks," the driver remarked. The four passengers hunched against the downpour as they ran toward a flight of steps leading down to Irongate Wharf on the Thames below. One of them wore an army greatcoat and carried a faded rucksack and a walking stick made of ash. Once they had reached the wharf, the party huddled by a gangway leading to the Dutch steamer *Stadthouder Willem* and said a hasty round of good-byes. Then the boy with the rucksack dashed aboard.

When he looked back, he saw his friends disappear into the stairway, then reemerge for a moment on the bridge above. He waved to them and noticed that the girl had pulled the mackintosh she was wearing over her head to protect her hair from the rain. A tremor of loneliness shivered through him, then faded away.

Patrick Leigh Fermor was eighteen years old. He was sailing for Rotterdam, on his own. When he reached the city's port, known as the Hook of Holland, he planned to make his way across the whole of Europe to Istanbul, in his mind still Constantinople, the capital of Rome's empire in the East. The idea

3

had seemed simple when it burst into his head on a similarly sodden evening a few weeks earlier. "I would travel on foot," he had decided, "sleep in hayricks in the summer, shelter in barns when it was raining or snowing and only consort with peasants and tramps." Looking back later, he gave the plan a lighthearted name: "Europe by Shanks's Mare." The old Scottish expression for walking—"riding Shanks's mare"—lent a hint of romance to the hard work of trekking across the continent.

The real peculiarity of the enterprise had struck him only the previous day, at the passport office off Victoria Street, where he had gone to apply for the document that would be his ticket across a succession of national borders. Under the eye of the clerk on duty, he had filled in the application form by rote—"height 5'9¾"; eyes, brown; hair, brown; distinguishing marks, none"—but had faltered when it asked for his profession. Whenever he imagined what he was setting out to do, it was in fanciful terms you couldn't spell out on an official document. Not, at least, without embarrassment; "pilgrim" and "errant scholar" were not exactly recognized professions. Without thinking, he had begun humming to himself as he considered what to write down. The tune that had floated out was one that had been in the air lately, and the passport official had recognized it: "Hallelujah I'm a Bum."

"You can't very well put *that*," he had said. Leigh Fermor had hesitated. Then the man suggested he "should just write 'student.'" That had settled it. Leigh Fermor scribbled the word on the proper line and handed over the form. Now, with the stamped passport in his pocket, the student was shipping out for the continent.

The rain let up about the time the *Stadthouder* slipped from the wharf, and the young traveler watched the stone towers and steel framework of the bridge slide away overhead. Rainwet and glistening, the riverside backdrop of the city began to scroll past. Nearly as noticeable as the scenery was the procession of maritime smells. Mud, salt, seaweed, smoke, and ashes gave way gradually to "a universal smell of rotting timber" and even—or maybe this was a romantic whim set free by the start of a voyage—the faint hint of spice. By the time the steamer reached Greenwich a few miles downstream, the sun was down. Leigh Fermor could see the lights of the Royal Observatory hanging in the darkness, and it occurred to him that he was about to cross the great imaginary line that had helped make the age of exploration possible. Yes, "the *Stadthouder* was twanging her way inaudibly through the nought meridian."

In the ship's saloon he rifled through his pack for an as-yet-empty journal. The rucksack—on loan from a friend who had carried it around Mount Athos in the company of Robert Byron, whose book about their adventure had inspired Leigh Fermor's plan to walk to Byzantium—held everything he would need in the coming months. A tattered copy of *The Oxford Book of English Verse* was in there somewhere, along with a Loeb edition of Horace that his mother had given him as a farewell gift. Inside she had inscribed a poem translated from Petronius's Latin, which began, "Leave thy home, O youth, and seek out alien shores." There were pencils and erasers, notebooks and drawing pads. The clothing he had packed was rustic and simple: gray flannel shirts for everyday, white ones if he needed something more presentable, a light leather jacket, hobnailed boots, and a gray set of puttees to keep the snow out of them. He recorded his first entry in the journal and wondered what story it would tell by the time he returned to England. Similar questions churned through his thoughts later on when he tried to get some sleep. Despite the excitement, he finally drifted off. When he woke some time later and went on deck, he found that the steamer was now alone in a black sea. "The kingdom had slid away westwards and into the dark," he realized. "A stiff wind was tearing through the rigging and the mainland of Europe was less than half the night away."

LEWIS LEIGH FERMOR, Paddy's father, was an unusually tall, lean man with deep-set eyes, a booming voice, and an Edwardian penchant for scientific paraphernalia. On excursions his kit might include a magnifying glass, a butterfly net, field glasses, a mineral hammer, a vasculum for collecting wildflowers, and a set of watercolors and brushes. In his son's eyes he was "an out-and-out naturalist"; though as the boy admitted, "we hardly knew each other." He had joined the Geological Survey of India in 1902, and by the time Paddy was born he was already its superintending director. The post allowed him a furlough only every few years.

His specialty was the rocks of the Archean period—some 2.5 billion years ago—and he made a name for himself among geologists, while still in his twenties, with a monumental thousand-page study of the manganese deposits of India. To his colleagues the elder Leigh Fermor's work had big implications. One award-winning paper was among the first to speculate about the way continental plates move and what causes deep earthquakes. But to his son his findings seemed to involve only minute slices of the natural world. What Paddy remembered years later was that his father had identified a novel sort of worm and described a particular crystalline structure that occurred in snowflakes. The snowflake discovery seemed to Paddy especially ephemeral.

Muriel Ambler, the woman Lewis Leigh Fermor married, appeared to breathe a different atmosphere. Her father was a captain in Britain's Indian navy and her grandfather had been an officer on the HMS *Bellerophon* when Napoleon Bonaparte surrendered to the ship's captain off the coast of France in 1815. When Paddy thought of her past, he pictured her as the belle of a British hill station in India, the "Rose of Simla" twirling across a ballroom floor to the tune of "Tararaboomdeeay." Muriel was imaginative and funny. Her knack for performing could conjure real amusement out of just reading aloud. Given the chance she might try her hand at anything. At one period, while living in a cottage in Northamptonshire, her zest for activity had her "simultaneously writing plays and, though hard up, learning to fly a Moth biplane at an aerodrome forty miles away." She was also a prodigious reader, and her excitement about the arts was infectious. When she moved to a London neighborhood that was also the home of Arthur Rackham—whose illustrations for books like *Alice in Wonderland* and *Grimm's Fairy Tales* were widely celebrated—she persuaded him to decorate her apartment. Leigh Fermor remembered the results: "navigable birdsnests in a gale-wind, hobgoblin transactions under extruding roots and mice drinking out of acorns." It was a fanciful and humorous decor that suited her. Years later, when her son confided his plan to walk across Europe, her show of maternal resistance quickly melted into laughter, followed by enthusiasm for the preposterous idea.

Leigh Fermor's parents eventually divorced, but even before the marriage crumbled they left the boy largely in the care of others. Not long after he was born, in the second dark year of the First World War, his mother and older sister went out to join his father in India. "I was left behind so that one of us might survive if the ship were sunk by a submarine," Leigh Fermor recalled. For the next few years he lived with a family in rural Northamptonshire, "more or less as a small farmer's child run wild." By the time he was reunited with his mother, he was not just wild but reluctant to be tamed. "Those marvelously lawless years," he later told himself, "had unfitted me for the faintest shadow of constraint."

His father could not have been more different. When Lewis Leigh Fermor was a boy his strong suit was self-discipline. Once, when faced with a difficult scholarship examination, he devised a rigorous plan to supplement what he was already learning at school. It required him to "rise at 5 o'clock each morning, take a cold bath, do two hours' work before breakfast, work another two hours in the evening, and always be in bed by 9.30 p.m." He kept to the plan for two years and won the scholarship he wanted to attend the Royal School of Mines. Later on, he took advantage of a summer vacation to teach himself Latin. Paddy, it seemed, had inherited his father's curiosity and his knack for languages but not, as yet, his restraint. The boy ran into trouble at one school after another.

The one that gave him the most leeway was a bohemian establishment called the Priory Gate School. It occupied an out-of-the-way manor house, Walsham Hall, in the Suffolk village of Walsham-le-Willows, not far from the ruined abbey at Bury St. Edmunds. Here wildness was not just accepted; it was the norm. The school was run by Theodore Faithfull, a former Veterinary Corps major and author, who wrote and lectured on sexuality and psychology. (When Leigh Fermor wrote about the experience years later, he disguised Faithfull, calling him Major Truthfull and the school Salsham Hall in Salsham-le-Sallows.) Faithfull's educational philosophy blended a Freudian mistrust of repression with a pacifist brand of naturalism. As soon as they arrived at the school, students and faculty were inducted into the Order of Woodcraft Chivalry, an organization with mystical overtones founded during the First World War as a coed alternative to the martial tradition of scouting. Leigh Fermor's fellow students were a mixed band of eccentrics, savants, and well-to-do ne'er-do-wells. Among the teachers, the men wore beards, the women bangles. The boys and girls were dressed alike in homespun jerkins and sandals. When they were dressed at all, that is. Faithfull encouraged nude sunbathing, and for recreation the faculty and students performed naked eurythmics exercises and country dances together in a barn on the premises. For his part, Leigh Fermor fell for the gardener's "fearfully pretty" daughter. It seemed a sylvan paradise. Needless to say, it was not long before scandal shut the place down, and Paddy was thrown back on the treadmill of more conventional education.

Finally, in 1929, he wound up at King's School in Canterbury. In some ways it was an ideal match. The medieval temperament he had soaked up in fits of boyhood reading—"a mixture of a rather dog-eared romanticism with heroics and rough stuff"—primed him to thrive in the atmosphere of Canterbury. It was said that the school had been founded at the end of the sixth century by Saint Augustine of Canterbury—a legend that, if true, made King's the oldest public school in England. The place certainly had the trappings of long tradition. To Leigh Fermor, the crumbling arches and stately elms that lined its precincts produced "an aura of nearly prehistoric myth." The ghosts of Thomas Becket and the Black Prince Edward—one murdered in the cathedral, both buried there—hovered in the air. "There was a wonderfully cobwebbed feeling about this dizzy and intoxicating antiquity," he thought.

The cluster of gray stone buildings that made up the campus sat next door to Canterbury Cathedral and reflected back its Gothic architecture. The boys wore starched white shirts with wing collars and black jackets and ties that would not have looked out of place a century earlier. Even the food served at the school had stood the test of time. Boiled beef, boiled vegetables, and stale bread: it was a menu that drove the young scholars to a candy shop tucked under one of the Gothic arches. The more self-sufficient of them fried up eggs and sausages on Primus stoves in their rooms. Bicycling a few miles into the countryside brought the relief to be found in pubs. The best of them served a dark ale called Gardner's Old Strong.

Leigh Fermor was soon befriended by a boy in the year ahead of him, a young classics scholar named Alan Watts. Watts was an eccentric figure at the school. He grew up on a rural lane in Chiselhurst, on the southeast side of London, in a cottage filled with Asian ornaments—vases from China and Korea, hangings from Japan, a mandala table from India—that were the legacy of his missionary grandparents. He came to King's with an almost mystical affinity for the natural world. (As a child, he once said, "I knew that plants, moths, birds, and rabbits were *people*.")

But he could also shoot the tobacco out of a cigarette from twenty feet away, and he knew how to handle a bow and arrow. He relished games that tested his unusual abilities nearly as much as he enjoyed testing the boundaries of school decorum. Although he was an excellent Latin student, he got himself into hot water on one occasion by inscribing the assigned exercise in Gothic script, replete with an illuminated initial capital. He liked to make up ditties to mimic the way certain teachers walked. To his ear, the headmaster, "in his black gown and mortarboard, went 'Damson, damson, damson, damson.'" Watts cemented his reputation as a cerebral sort of renegade when he announced to the school authorities that he had become a Buddhist. The declaration turned out to be serious, and before he left King's he had been elected secretary of the London Buddhist Lodge. Not long after that, he published a book, on Zen, that would be the first of many.

Although there was an unwritten taboo against forming friendships with younger classmates, Watts was drawn to Leigh Fermor as "the only really interesting boy in the House." He seemed a kindred spirit, "a fine poet, a born adventurer, a splendid actor." Watts noticed the traits that served Paddy well at a place like King's—"an Arthurian and medieval imagination," for instance—but he also saw the preoccupations that might lead to his friend's downfall. In particular, he thought of Leigh

Fermor as "a gallant lover of women." Watts recalled watching the younger boy flirting with one of the kitchen maids, a "dowdy blonde" whose appeal he chalked up to "sheer desperation" in the monkish setting of a boys' school.

For a while, Leigh Fermor thrived. He soaked up books and languages and succeeded—although fitfully—in most of his subjects. Poetry, for better or worse, leaked out of him "like ectoplasm." He and Watts took long walks together and spun their bicycles over the countryside, sometimes traveling with the idea of poking around a musty Norman church, but just as often to visit a pub. The forests and fields of Kent became a kind of sanctuary for them. But their retreat of last resort was right next door. "When utterly oppressed by the social system of the school," Watts recalled, "we would sneak off to Canterbury Cathedral—which because of its colossal sanctity, could never be made out of bounds—to study the stained-glass windows, to explore the Anglo-Saxon crypt, or to read books in the serene and secluded garden adjoining the Cathedral library."

In the long run, the same romantic streak that sought out dusty corners of the cathedral started to work against him, as if something were pushing him to make his life more like the books he read. He was often lost in thought, but the trouble was more than simple absentmindedness. Whatever he could imagine he tried. If it meant breaking a rule or slipping outside the school's boundaries, he would worry about the consequences later. The worst offenses resulted in floggings. He remembered these as "swift and flexible sanctions which came whistling shoulder-high across paneled studies and struck with considerable force." Watts had tried to have the practice banned at the school, but that failed effort did his friend no good. He was distressed to see that Paddy "was constantly being flogged for his pranks and exploits—in other words, for having a creative imagination." By Leigh Fermor's third year, the chain of misdeeds exhausted the patience of his housemaster. The report the master wrote made it clear that Leigh Fermor's days at the school were numbered. "He is a dangerous mixture of sophistication and recklessness which makes one anxious about his influence on other boys," it read.

The final act unfolded just as Watts had foreseen. Leigh Fermor fell for the daughter of the local greengrocer. She was some seven years older, "a ravishing, sonnet-begetting beauty," who looked after her father's store in the cattle market. Her wide-eyed features reminded him of the sylphs whose illustrations adorned the storybooks he had read as a child. Just her presence in the shop turned that workaday setting into a "green and sweet-smelling cave" straight out of a pastoral poem. To Watts she was simply "a comely brunette." In the end Paddy was caught holding her hand—"we were sitting in the back-shop on upturned apple-baskets—and my schooldays were over."

IT WAS JUST over a year later that Leigh Fermor hatched the plan to walk across Europe. Now, at last, the adventure had begun. The *Stadthouder Willem* glided into the port of Rotterdam before dawn the next morning. Snow was falling as Leigh Fermor found his way to a café, where he ate a breakfast of coffee and fried eggs and watched the sun come up. When he rose to leave, the owner, noticing the rucksack and walking stick he was carrying, asked him where he was headed. He answered "Constantinople," and the man lit up. He filled small glasses for each of them from a salt-glazed stone bottle marked "Bols" and toasted the young traveler. "It was the formal start to my journey," Leigh Fermor felt.

As the morning brightened, he followed a straight road out of town. Over the next few days he made his way, fueled by hunks of bread and cheese, through towns with names like Dordrecht, Sliedrecht, and Gorinchem. One night he slept in luxury in a cell at the local police station. "Thank God I had put 'student' in my passport," he thought; "it was an amulet and an Open Sesame." Back in England he was slated to become a student in earnest. After the disaster in Canterbury he had spent a year cramming for an examination that would allow him to enter the military college at Sandhurst, and he had passed the test. The housemaster from King's had even given him a favorable recommendation.

When he thought about life as a peacetime soldier, forced to live in England on the army's meager pay, the prospect soured quickly. But sometimes he imagined serving in India, like his mother's people. He pictured himself singled out, "thanks to an effortless mastery of a dozen native tongues and their dialects, for special duties: unrecognizable under my rags I would disappear for months into the lanes and the bazaars of seething frontier cities." It was an uncanny premonition of what lay in store for him. But for now he was happier to be a student—if in name only.

The river Waal cut a path across Holland. He trailed it eastward through a gently rolling landscape of meadows and plowed fields that reminded him of the pictures Brueghel painted in the sixteenth century. At Nijmegen he found a room over a blacksmith shop. The German frontier was only a two-hour walk away. He reflected on the beauty of the countryside he had crossed much more quickly than he had expected. He also wondered what he would find when he crossed the border the next morning.

He could vaguely recall seeing German prisoners of war in Northamptonshire during the war. Since then, movies and magazines had layered on depictions of German soldiers that were equal parts sinister and alluring. What came to mind were scattered images: "atrocity stories, farmhouses on fire, French cathedrals in ruins, Zeppelins and the goose-step; uhlans galloping through the autumn woods, Death's Head Hussars, corseted officers with Iron Crosses and fencing slashes, monocles and staccato laughs." In fact, his most vivid early memory swirled around the image of Kaiser Wilhelm. In the summer of 1919, when he was just four, the older daughter of the family he lived with in Northamptonshire took him to see a bonfire villagers had built to commemorate Peace Day, marking the formal end of the war.

It was a Saturday afternoon, and the townspeople were gathering around a huge mound of wood and dry brush. On top of the pile someone had placed effigies of Wilhelm and his eldest son. "The Kaiser wore a real German spiked helmet and a cloth mask with huge whiskers," young Paddy noticed. The crown prince sported a monocle fashioned out of cardboard and wore a hussar's hat. When it was dark enough, the fire was lit, and the boy watched the blaze climb toward the two dummies. At last they burst into flames and there was a drumroll of explosions as the fireworks stuffed inside detonated. A little while later one of the village boys was terribly injured by a Roman candle and Paddy was whisked away. What he saw when he looked back was etched into his memory in a dreamlike tableau. He could still make out the two scarecrow effigies, hauntingly illuminated by the leaping flames and both beginning to crumple.

IN HIS ROOM at Nijmegen the sound of a hammer clanking against iron on the blacksmith's anvil woke him at six the next morning. Snow was falling again as he walked along the road leading toward the border. When he reached the Dutch guard post, an official there stamped his passport and he trudged on through the drifts toward the German frontier. "Black, white and red were painted in spirals round the road barrier," he noticed, "and soon I could make out the scarlet flag charged with its white disc and its black swastika. Similar emblems had been flying all over Germany for the last ten months. Beyond it were the snow-laden trees and the first white acres of Westphalia." By nightfall Leigh Fermor had covered seventeen or eighteen miles and arrived at the town of Goch. Here Nazi flags hung wherever he looked. He stopped in at a tobacconist's for cigarettes and on the way out paused in front of the shop next door. The window, he saw, was filled with Party regalia. The centerpiece of the display was a wax figure dressed in the uniform of an SA storm trooper. Uniforms for women and children lay stacked alongside. Arrayed around the clothing and equipment there were photographs depicting Nazi luminaries. In one shot Hermann Göring, chief of the newly formed Luftwaffe, offered a bottle of milk to a lion cub; another showed a fair-haired little girl handing Hitler a fistful of daisies. A third photo presented the Führer shaking hands with SA leader Ernst Röhm. Leigh Fermor couldn't know at the time that Hitler, turning on his former ally in an effort to consolidate his own power, would order Röhm's murder the next summer.

The clacking of boots on the cobbles nearby turned his attention from the display. In the muted light of the streetlamps he watched as a formation of brown-shirted SA troopers marched into the square and assembled to hear an address by a man who appeared to be their commander. Leigh Fermor had not yet picked up enough German to make out what the man was saying. But his manner was ominous in itself.

That night, with the SA marching song still reverberating in his thoughts, Leigh Fermor found a room at an inn where the portraits on the wall looked back to an older Germany. But even here the likenesses of Frederick the Great and Baron von Hindenburg shared wall space with Hitler. Once settled at an oak table in a timber-framed hall warmed by a wood-burning stove, he was busy recording the events of the day in his journal and drinking beer from a pewter-lidded stein when a party of men in SA uniforms traipsed into the inn and gathered around a nearby table. Watching their good-humored manner as they drank that night only muddled the emotions he had felt earlier in the evening. "They looked less fierce without their horrible caps," he thought. "One or two, wearing spectacles, might have been clerks or students." He overheard them singing a song about a woodsman's beautiful daughter. It might as well have been written for the pretty girl tending the greengrocer's shop back in Kent. "It was charming," he felt. "And the charm made it impossible, at the moment, to connect the singers with organized bullying and the smashing of Jewish shop windows and nocturnal bonfires of books."

From Goch, Leigh Fermor struck out toward the southeast, passing through Krefeld and Düsseldorf. One night he took shelter at a workhouse where the crowded sleeping room reminded him of his school days. When the route looped its way back to the Rhine—he remembered this was really the same waterway as the Waal that had been his thoroughfare across Holland—he tracked the river upstream and arrived at Cologne on December 20. His first stop, characteristically, was the celebrated Gothic cathedral. The second was a bar. At a crowded place on the quay, just a short, steep walk downhill from the cathedral, he fell in with a rough crowd of bargemen and sailors who were chasing shots of schnapps with beer. He wound up dancing with a girl who drifted into the party late in the evening. "She was very pretty," he thought, "except for two missing teeth." He soon learned that she had lost them in a brawl.

When his head cleared the next day, he sought out a bookshop, in order to buy a paperback copy of *Hamlet, Prinz von Dänemark*. Maybe he could pick up some German by reading Shakespeare in translation, he thought. As he explained what he wanted to the bookseller, the word "student" once again worked its magic. Before he left the shop, Leigh Fermor had been invited to spend the night with the owner's friend, a student at Cologne University. Over dinner that evening the two young men discussed literature. Later, while they drank tea laced with brandy, the talk turned to recent events in Germany. The student and his landlady—she was the widow of a university professor—both despised Hitler. But when they spoke of the Nazis their conversation grew morose, as if they felt helpless to resist the changes Hitler was bringing to their country. It was more pleasing to dwell on books.

Before bed Leigh Fermor had his first bath since leaving England. When he drifted off to sleep, it was under a clean down quilt in a study lined with volumes of Greek and Latin literature.

On top of the evening's hospitality, the university student also wangled a lift for his new friend on one of the barges that plied the Rhine between Basel and the North Sea. When Leigh Fermor had said his good-byes the next morning, he lit out upstream on a diesel-slicked tub crewed, he was surprised to see, by a gang from the bar where he had spent his first night in Cologne. It carried him as far as Koblenz, where the river Moselle, cascading off the Ballon d'Alsace through a vineyard-flanked valley, rushed into the Rhine. The clear new stream presented an enticing fork in his route, but he pressed on along the Rhine. Christmas morning found him at an inn in Bingen. He was the only guest, and the innkeeper's daughter gave him a tangerine and a tinsel-wrapped packet of cigarettes.

In Heidelberg he was adopted by the elderly proprietors of an inn known as the Red Ox, Herr and Frau Spengel, who treated him to clean laundry for the first time since he left home. He found himself wondering whether a German vagabond would be cared for as well in England. The Spengels' son Fritz took him into the hills above the town the next day to see the ruins of Heidelberg Castle. Pooling their memories from long-lost history lessons, they pieced together its story and remembered that this was one place—the palace of the "Winter Queen" Elizabeth, daughter of James I, who married Frederick V—where the stories of Germany and England intertwined. But the happy spell was soon broken. Returning to the inn just after sunset, they passed by a gang of boys who were whistling the "Horst-Wessel-Lied," which had become a favorite marching song of the Nazis. Later that night, while the two new friends drank to the coming year, Leigh Fermor found himself berated by a pale, rime-eyed young man seated at a nearby table. He demanded to know why Germany should be made to suffer as she had since the end of the last war. His angry voice rang out a dismal envoi to 1933. "Adolf Hitler will change all that," the stranger barked. *"Perhaps you've heard the name?"*

THE WEEKS PASSED in a whirlwind, but the whirlwind had a rhythm to it. A night in a baroque palace in Bruchsal was followed by another in a barn outside Pforzheim, where Leigh Fermor slept under his greatcoat on a makeshift bed of cut hay. At each town he visited he nailed a small metal plaque bearing its name to his walking stick. The ash-wood *Wanderstab*, as the Germans called it, soon bristled with commemorative medallions.

One evening in Stuttgart, a windblown shower of sleet and hail chased him into a café across the street from the city's best hotel. He could not spare the price of a room, he knew, but a better option turned up. Two girls settling their account at the counter caught his eye. They were about his age. Both were pretty. One had dark tousled hair and wore horn-rimmed glasses; the other had blond braids twisted into buns over her ears like a heroine out of Wagner. "They were amusingly dressed in Eskimo hoods, furry boots and gauntlets like grizzly bears which they clapped together to dispel the cold." Before Paddy could concoct a way to meet them, the girl in glasses edged toward his table and asked, "How do you do, do, Mister Brown?"

He recognized the line from a silly foxtrot that had been last year's novelty sensation. The girl must have noticed the German-English dictionary splayed out on the table in front of him. Although the song's catchphrase used up more or less all of her English, Leigh Fermor had by now learned enough German to strike up an acquaintance. It turned out the two girls, Lise and Annie, were music students. Just as important, Annie's parents were away in Switzerland. The three of them hit it off, and the next morning the girls added a new word to his growing German vocabulary: *Katzenjammer.* It meant hangover. Fortunately the weather remained unsuitable for travel; Leigh Fermor was forced to linger with the girls in Stuttgart another evening.

When he finally tore himself away, he picked up a road veering away from the Neckar River outside of town and took it as far as Ulm, where he crossed the Danube. The route then angled toward the east. In Munich he ditched his rucksack at an empty youth hostel and sought out the famous Hofbräuhaus—the city's cathedral to beer. Winding his way through darkening streets in search of the place, he was alarmed by the growing numbers of SA and SS uniforms in evidence. At the beer hall the menace felt suddenly more visceral. "Halfway up the vaulted stairs," he saw, "a groaning Brownshirt, propped against the wall on a swastika'd arm, was unloosing, in a staunchless gush down the steps, the intake of hours."

Dodging the foul-smelling mess on the stairs, Leigh Fermor slipped inside. The drunk storm trooper's companions were crowded into one of the hall's numerous rooms, and black-clad SS officers occupied another. It was no surprise to find them here; Hitler, after all, had convened the first meeting of the Nazi Party in a room on the third floor. Leigh Fermor settled at a table downstairs, surrounded by more affable farmers and laborers.

As the tall mugs of beer arrived and were drained, it seemed to him that the boisterous scene grew more and more to resemble a mead hall out of *The Ring* or *Beowulf.* At some point he quietly crumpled across the table. He woke up the next morning on the couch of a couple who lived nearby. His *Katzenjammer*, he was sorry to find, was as heroic as the drinking had been. To make matters worse, when he returned to the youth hostel he discovered that his rucksack had been stolen during the night. Lost along with it were his passport, what money he had, the medallion-encrusted *Wanderstab*, his journal, and—except for the German *Hamlet,* still safe in his pocket—his books.

At the British consulate a sympathetic official issued a new passport and spotted him a five-pound note. Leigh Fermor spent the next five days with a family outside of town who had been expecting him, thanks to a friend's letter of introduction. Their household delivered a welcome antidote to the Hofbräuhaus. The patriarch was a baron whose family had fled to Munich when the state seized their castle in Estonia after the war. He was a font of literary knowledge. When Leigh Fermor asked him whether he thought the German translation of *Hamlet* deserved its lofty reputation, he conceded that the original was best, then read aloud from Russian, Italian, and French versions to illustrate their inferiority to the German. He may have exaggerated the national styles as he went along, Leigh Fermor thought, but the rich, unhurried music of the German startled him; "in those minutes, as the lamplight caught the reader's white hair and eyebrows and sweeping moustache and twinkled in the signet ring of the hand that held the volume, I understood for the first time how magnificent a language it could be."

The baron and his son rummaged through the house and attic to find a rucksack and other gear to replace the equipment he had lost. The baron also wrote letters of introduction that gave the young traveler aristocratic contacts stretching across eastern Europe. On the day Leigh Fermor left, the baron, apologizing that his library was inadequate to replace all of the books that had been stolen, handed him a priceless duodecimo edition of Horace. He looked at this pocket-sized heirloom with wonder. "It was the Odes and Epodes, beautifully printed on thin paper in Amsterdam in the middle of the seventeenth century, bound in hard green leather with gilt lettering. The leather on the spine had faded but the sides were as bright as grass after rain and the little book opened and shut as compactly as a Chinese casket." It was a gift that would prove strangely providential before the impending war was over.

PUSHING ON to the southeast led Leigh Fermor deeper into Bavaria. Beyond the village of Rosenheim he followed telegraph lines and resorted to footpaths when the country roads gave out. At the inns where he sheltered here in the countryside, the obligatory photograph of Hitler sometimes got lost among religious pictures and the intricate wood carving that seemed to be worked into every corner of the rooms. He attributed the carving to a geographical accident—"long winters, early nightfall, soft wood and sharp knives"—that ran around the world at this elevation.

At a bar in one small town he fell in with a factory worker who offered to put him up for the night. When they clambered up to the young man's attic room, Leigh Fermor saw that the walls were covered with Nazi flags and posters. He noticed an SA uniform and an automatic pistol. The man explained that he had been a Communist just a year earlier. The walls of his room then had been papered with red stars and portraits of Lenin. "I used to punch the heads of anyone singing the 'Horst-Wessel-Lied,'" he said. "Then suddenly, when Hitler came into power, I

understood it was all lies. I realized Adolf was the man for me."
The alarming thing was that all his friends had fallen into step
with the Nazis too—"Millions!"

Skirting eastward to the north of the Chiemsee—the great
freshwater lake that was sometimes called the Bavarian Sea—
Leigh Fermor reached the village of Traunstein on January 23.
When he left the next morning, the weather had cleared and
he could see the Alps rising in front of him. Hitler's mountain
retreat, the Berghof, lay hidden away near Berchtesgaden, just
above. He continued east and reached the Austrian frontier at
the river Salzach late in the day. At the border station the official who stamped his passport wore a red armband emblazoned
with a black swastika. Leigh Fermor hoped it would be the last
one he ever saw.

IN AUSTRIA life fell back into the pattern he was growing accustomed to. At St. Martin, another castle; a cowshed near Riedau.
Fading photographs of Emperor Franz Joseph, dead now for
nearly two decades, replaced the portraits of Hitler. By the end
of the month Leigh Fermor was nearing the Danube once again,
and the alteration in the landscape made it feel like walking
into a different world. A bracing glass of *Himbeergeist* he drank
at an inn near Linz seemed to reflect the change. It tasted to him
like "a thimble full of the cold north."

On the afternoon of February 11, after trudging all day
through a gusting snowfall, he marked his nineteenth birthday in a count's lamp-lit *Schloss*, "lapping whiskey and soda
from a cut-glass tumbler." The next morning he hurried on
toward Vienna, holing up in a barn for an hour when the snow
gave way to a thunderstorm. For once he was glad to hitch a
ride when a truck pulled alongside later in the day. He rode into
Vienna nestled under a tarpaulin in the back, sharing the makeshift shelter with a bright-eyed fifteen-year-old girl named Trudi

who was transporting a basket of eggs and a large duck to her grandmother's house.

Leigh Fermor spent a fanciful few weeks in Vienna. At the workhouse where he lodged first, he met the itinerate son of a Frisian pastor, with whom he cooked up a plan to sell sketch portraits to the locals. Later he was taken up by a creative circle of students and expatriates. "Wildish nights and late mornings set in, and after a last climactic fancy dress party, I woke in an armchair with an exploding head still decked with a pirate's eyepatch and a cut-out skull and crossbones."

One of his new friends was Einer von der Heydte. He was twenty-seven, a baron, and a devout Catholic. His father was a retired Bavarian army officer whose family fortune had declined along with the falling value of German war bonds. The studious son was expected to follow his father into the army. But the world had changed since the older Heydte's heyday. The war had ended when the boy was eleven, and Germany had been transformed into a socialist republic. When he was twelve, Einer had helped a gang of boys tear the red flag down from a building in Traunstein—the same Alpine village where Leigh Fermor had stopped earlier in the year. Although he later entered the army as a cavalry officer, he had been granted leave to study at the university—first at Innsbruck, then at Berlin. Now in Vienna, he was enrolled at the Consular Academy, which trained students for diplomatic service. Just about the time Leigh Fermor met him, he got himself tangled up with the Gestapo by beating up a Nazi who was badmouthing the Church. Returning to his old cavalry regiment was the only way he could think of to evade the secret police.

The two young men talked endlessly about literature and history. They also shared a fascination with the ancient Greek world. Even as an adult Heydte recalled how, as a schoolboy, he had been moved by Greek mythology, in particular the story of the Minotaur, the monstrous bull-man who was imprisoned in a labyrinth beneath the palace of King Minos at Knossos and fed on the blood of Athenian youths. Heydte remembered how Theseus, a brave young Athenian, had traveled to Crete and overcome the monster, escaping from the labyrinth with the help of Minos's daughter Ariadne, who gave him a thread by which he could find his way through the maze's twists and turns. And how Daedalus, who engineered the labyrinth, had flown from Crete on wings made of feathers and wax. Heydte could still recall hearing the story for the first time. When he talked about the myth, it all came back: the dimly illuminated schoolroom, the schoolmaster's pinched voice as he spoke, even the graffiti scratched into the desks in front of him. According to Heydte's teacher, the myth was a tale of human triumph—"how the progress of the human mind in technical science had mastered the animal in mankind!" This was an idea he had trouble accepting. Even as a boy Heydte had sensed that the story held something darker at its core. Many years later he would come to believe the Minotaur's real name was "War." But the mysterious world the schoolmaster had described nevertheless drew him in. He imagined himself traveling to Crete one day—"perhaps as a scholar," he thought, "or a treasure-seeker, or an investigator to try and fathom its secrets."

On Saturday, March 3, Heydte and a few others drove Leigh Fermor to a village outside Vienna. After lunch and rounds of *Himbeergeist* at an inn, they took a walk through the snow-blanketed forest. The talk that day was of Europe's heroic past and the waning days of chivalry. When they said good-bye, Leigh Fermor had no way of knowing that he and Heydte would cross paths again.

IN THE FOLLOWING MONTHS Leigh Fermor drifted through the last outposts of an aristocratic world that was rapidly disappearing. He crossed the Danube into Czechoslovakia the next day. Nearly a month later he entered Hungary. As he rambled across what had once been the Austro-Hungarian Empire, the introductions that flowed from the baron who had outfitted him in Munich led him from one aristocratic estate to another. He was getting a glimpse of life as it might have been when Franz Joseph was emperor. But the news of the day that filtered in along the way was ominous.

He was in Transylvania when he heard that Hitler had ordered a bloody purge of the SA. Ernst Röhm, whose photo he had noticed in a shop window months earlier, was among those killed. A month later word came that the Austrian chancellor, Engelbert Dollfuss, had been shot to death by Nazi gunmen in Vienna.

In a remote corner of the Carpathians he met an elderly rabbi who, with his sons, was visiting his brother at the logging camp where the younger man was foreman. The foreman wanted to know why Leigh Fermor was traveling. He fumbled for an answer and finally said, "For fun." The foreman responded with something in Yiddish that made the others laugh. Then he explained—"Es is ist a goyim naches" meant it was something only a gentile would enjoy. "It seemed to hit the nail on the head," Leigh Fermor thought.

When the conversation turned to Hitler and the Nazis, they all spoke of them as if they were "a nightmare that might suddenly vanish, like a cloud evaporating."

BY DECEMBER 1934, a little more than a year after he left home, he had reached Varna, on the Black Sea, and was making his way south along the coast toward Burgas. Constantinople now lay a mere four or five days' trek to the southeast. The track he had been following all day wandered along between the sea, to the east, and a span of foothills that mounted like rounded stairsteps toward the Balkan and Rhodope ranges in the west. In the distance he could discern signs of life—smoke rising from hillside villages and the red patchwork of plowed fields—but an old Tartar fisherman puffing on a narghile outside his hut was the only person he encountered along the trail.

As the day wore on, the landscape grew emptier, as if the country itself were petering out as his journey approached its end. Maybe it was the solitude that made it feel as if the world itself were darkening and dwindling, or perhaps it was the foreboding of winter, which was about to close its grip on the countryside. But at the same time the shafts of bright sunlight that broke through in the clearings hinted at vistas that lay beyond his original destination. "A promise of the Aegean and the Greek islands roved the cold Bulgarian air," he felt.

On one of the hills he glimpsed a cluster of beehive huts that must have belonged to a Sarakatsani band. These were nomadic Greeks who trailed their flocks to each season's best grazing. Their summer haunts were likely high in the Rhodope Mountains. Walking across the plains and valleys, Leigh Fermor would sometimes come across the decaying circles of thatch— like the gravestones of their huts—that marked the makeshift hamlets where they had spent the winter months.

Late in the afternoon he found himself descending into a rock-strewn cove. When the last of the daylight faded, he fished a flashlight from his pack and pressed on. But the trail seemed to disappear as the terrain fell away in a steep pitch toward the water below. All at once his grip on the rock let go, and the next instant he landed in the water. "Jarred and shaken," he hauled himself from the pool, "shuddering with cold." He could see his flashlight emitting its now-useless beacon on the bottom of the deeper end of the pool.

He tried to shout for help, but the word was not there in the Bulgar he had learned. What came out instead were cries of "*Dobar vecher!*"—"Good evening, Good evening!" Feeling his way along in the darkness, he inched across the pool until he came to a sandy stretch of shore. Here he noticed a light coming from the rocks nearby, and when he got closer he saw that there was a door, which he pulled open.

He could make out that it was a long, shallow cave, with stalactites studding the ceiling that arched high overhead. Someone had built up a front wall by filling spaces between the natural rock formations with rubble. A group of men were sitting around a fire. As he stumbled inside, several of them rushed to help him. They did what they could to dry him and clean the cut he had received in the fall.

When his eyes adjusted to the flickering light, he surveyed the company he had fallen in with. "They were wild looking men," he thought. All were dressed in ragged clothing, some in brownish hues, others in shades of blue. A handful wore peaked caps. It took Leigh Fermor a moment to understand that his lot had been cast with a mixed company of shepherds and fishermen. He was reminded of Polyphemus and Sinbad—the most remarkable of shepherds and sailors.

He could see the tools of the men's work heaped around the cave: on one side, spears, fish traps, and bait baskets; on the other, wicker baskets and goatskin bags used in making cheese from goat milk. Hidden away in the deeper shadows were the goats themselves. He watched their eyes glowing whenever a flare of firelight reached them.

The men rustled up a dinner for him of lentils and mackerel-like fried fish. Leigh Fermor found the fish delicious and asked what they were called. When one of the fishermen replied, "*Skoumbri*," the shepherds protested. "No, no, no," they exclaimed, the word was "*skumria*." The shepherds, it turned out, were Bulgars, the sailors Greek.

As the hours wore on, his first night in the company of

Greeks turned into a full-blown bacchanalia. One of the shepherds broke out a goatskin bagpipe. A sailor picked out a tumultuous tune on the bouzouki. Digging into his pack, Leigh Fermor pulled out two bottles of raki and passed them around. The fiery clear liquor the locals distilled from grape skins and pulp—a far cry from the anise-laced Turkish variety—soon had the party in full swing. At the height of the revels a ferocious-looking sailor called Dimitri began to career around the cave in a mock belly dance, which was soon taken up by one of the shepherds.

For Leigh Fermor the camaraderie he felt with the Greeks in particular seemed to corroborate his growing attraction to Greece. It was Dimitri, the dancer, who finally gave voice to the feeling by naming the special connection that tied them together. "*Lordos Veeron!*" he said. Seeing that the sailor had "raised his bunched fingers in a gesture of approval," Leigh Fermor eventually understood that the oddly pronounced name referred to his own countryman Lord Byron. Even here in the middle of nowhere the poet, who died of fever while preparing to attack a Turkish fortress, was remembered as a hero of the Greek struggle for independence.

Leigh Fermor had a difficult time getting to sleep that night. Over the sounds that reverberated through the cave—the men's snoring punctuated now and then by the clink of a goat bell—he could hear the undulations of the Black Sea washing against the shore. Its whispering hinted at still-more-distant shores. "There was much to think about," he told himself, "especially Greece and the Greeks, which were drawing nearer every day."

IT WAS NEW YEAR'S DAY when Leigh Fermor arrived in Constantinople. He had been traveling for just over a year and had covered more than 1,500 miles as the crow flies. But a footloose vagabond made for a haphazard crow. With the twists and turns thrown in by chance along the road, he had easily traveled twice that far. And he was not ready to stop. Constantinople, or Istanbul as it was called in the recently established Turkish republic, had been the eastern hub of the Greek world for centuries. Fascinating as it was to be here after so many months of traveling, the sights and sounds of the exotic city only made him yearn more to set foot in Greece itself. He mailed off five pounds to repay the consul who had helped him in Munich. Then, early in the new year, he struck out toward the west.

The first spot he wanted to visit was the one that had hovered in the back of his mind since the idea for this journey first occurred to him more than a year earlier. The young travel writer Robert Byron's description of his trip to Mount Athos in *The Station*—and the image of Byzantium that Byron's book had planted in his head—had provided the spark for Leigh Fermor's own adventure. Now he wanted to see its famous monasteries for himself.

The holy mountain, as the Greeks called it, was nearly four hundred miles away, opposite the Dardanelles, on the far side of the Thracian Sea. Getting there by land meant trailing the coasts of Thrace and Macedonia. He knew that in ancient times innumerable ships bound from Asia Minor to Greece had foundered trying to round the peninsula formed by the mountain. Herodotus told how Xerxes, when he was preparing to invade Greece early in the fifth century BC, put great armies of men to work digging a channel across the isthmus northwest of the mountain, so that his ships could avoid rounding the Athos cape. In Herodotus's view Xerxes had done it out of sheer egotism—because he could. "For though it was possible, without any great labour, to have drawn the ships over the isthmus, he commanded them to dig a channel for the sea of such a width that two triremes might pass through rowed abreast." It took the Persian leader three years to get his navy to the far side of the isthmus. By February Leigh Fermor had made his way there.

What he discovered when he reached Mount Athos was a world apart. A rugged finger of land jutting forty miles out into the Aegean, the peninsula was cut off from the mainland by Xerxes' channel. It had its own culture, even its own constitution. Legend held that the Virgin herself had once come here, though later on such a visit would have required a special dispensation: for nearly a thousand years a strictly enforced rule prohibited "all women, all female animals, eunuchs or beardless boys." Monks and hermits had maintained legal proprietorship over the peninsula since the tenth century. But holy men had scratched out an existence among the rocks even before that. One of them, Euthymius of Salonica, who retreated to Athos in the ninth century, was said to have spent his first years here foraging on all fours like a goat.

The earliest of the monasteries, known as the Great Lavra, had been founded by Athanasios around 960. Since then the fortunes of Athos had risen and fallen. At its peak the population of monks may have reached as high as ten thousand. Now there remained a small fraction of that number, scattered across twenty monasteries. For Leigh Fermor, who was still in the thrall of Robert Byron's book about the place, a visit to Athos offered a glimpse of what the great monastic tradition of the east had been like at its apex. To Byron, who had been here in 1926 and 1927, Mount Athos was the Byzantine Empire itself, frozen in amber—a "station," he once said, "of a faith where all the years have stopped." You could see the truth of that just by watching the sun come up . . . at eleven. Even the clocks still ran on Byzantine time.

Leigh Fermor found life on Athos relaxed. He grew fond of the monks, with their "fierce-whiskered, brigand-faces." You could watch their lively eyes "smoulder and flash and twinkle under brows that are always tied up in knots of rage or laughter or concentration or suddenly relaxed into bland Olympian benevolence." The monks rose early, and they were often called upon to fast, but by Western standards their discipline was lenient. The monastic rule they followed went back to the fourth-century system of laws organized by St. Basil, whose idea of the contemplative life favored peaceful contentment over deprivation. As Basil described it in his letters, the monastery he founded in the hills above the Black Sea was a spiritual arcadia. The mountain plain on which it sat was hedged in by a forest "of many-coloured and various trees" and watered by cool running brooks, "so that even Calypso's isle, which Homer seems to admire beyond all others for its beauty, is insignificant compared to this." Reading Basil's letters later on, Leigh Fermor was struck by the joyfulness that ran through their depiction of monastic life. "'Light,' 'peace' and 'happiness' are the epithets, often recurring, that St. Basil finds most fitting to capture the atmosphere of his cloister." Life at Athos, untouched as it was by many of the changes in the outside world, hinted at the spiritual and pastoral pleasures Basil and his fourth-century monks had once enjoyed—with the brilliant Aegean supplying a watery hedge. Abundant wine and the occasional stinging thimbleful of raki were added benefits.

Settled on Greek soil for the first time in his life, Leigh Fermor spent his weeks on Athos basking in the mountain's monastic tranquillity and preparing himself to plunge deeper into the Greek countryside. The first job, he knew, was "to convert imperfect ancient Greek into the rudiments of the modern." On February 11, with the grounds of the monastery muffled by a heavy blanket of snow, he turned twenty.

THE TIMELESS RHYTHMS of monastic routine on Mount Athos obscured the unrest that was brewing in Greece. But the conflict soon became impossible to ignore. Late in the afternoon on the first day of March 1935, a group of conspirators led by retired naval officers slipped into the Greek naval base on Salamis and took control of a pair of cruisers—the *Helle* and the flagship *Averof*—along with two submarines and a handful of other vessels. Once at sea, the leaders radioed the garrisons of other Greek bases, calling for the military to rise up and overthrow the government. The coup aimed to throttle what the rebels feared was a growing monarchist sentiment in the regime that had recently assumed power. Eleftherios Venizelos, a Cretan revolutionary and former prime minister of Greece, would soon emerge as the rebellion's de facto leader.

In Athens, rebels occupied the military college and the barracks of the presidential guard. In Macedonia they seized installations in several towns. Meanwhile, the *Averof* made for Crete, where Venizelos—who had retreated to the island after an attempt on his life the previous summer—assumed command of the movement.

On the other side, the remainder of the Greek army, now commanded by the minister of war, pushed toward Macedonia to confront Venizelos's rebels. A week of sleet and snow had held the fighting to a minimum, but now that the weather was clear the two armies were clashing along the Struma River.

Since leaving the monastery at Mount Athos, Leigh Fermor had traveled up the Chalcidice peninsula. Near Madytos, nearly seventy miles northwest of Athos, he borrowed a horse and struck out to explore Macedonia and Thrace. As he traveled along, he found that the countryside was buzzing with news of the rebellion. And by the time he met up with a light cavalry unit that had gotten separated from the main body of the Greek army, the excitement seemed to be sweeping him along. There was nothing to do but spur his own horse into a gallop to join the column as it trotted by.

As the day wore on, the unit made its way northward, and soon they were galloping toward the sound of musket fire and shelling. When they reached the Struma at a town called Orliako, north of Nigrita, there was real fighting under way. They heard firing from both banks, but the rebellion had already cracked. At one point Leigh Fermor followed the cavalry troop into the river. "It was the most extraordinary thing," he thought. "The water comes up to your waist, and the horse's head sticks out like a chessman." Once the shooting stopped, the horsemen drew their sabers and "thundered fast but bloodlessly across the wooden bridge." It was Leigh Fermor's first taste of war. It was also, he knew, "the nearest any of us would get to a cavalry charge."

BUT THERE WAS more of Greece to explore, so Leigh Fermor pulled up short once the excitement of the charge had settled. He shouted farewell to his new comrades, and after pledging to meet again, he "watched them jingle away, their spurs clinking against the steel scabbards of their sabers; then pounded off towards the hills and the far-sounding goat-bells."

He eventually made his way to Athens, where he met a Romanian girl named Balasha Cantacuzene. A few years older than he, Balasha was a painter from an aristocratic family who had gone to school in France and England. She was, to Paddy's eye, also extraordinarily beautiful, and she shared his enthusiasm for literature and the arts. They spent the summer together living in a disused watermill on the Peloponnese, the mountainous peninsula that juts out into the Mediterranean on the southwestern arm of the Greek mainland. As autumn began turning to winter, they traveled by steamer and train to Baleni in northern Romania, where her family owned a house. That winter the snow "reached the windowsills and lasted till spring."

Wherever he went for the next two years—all over Romania, then home for a spell in 1937—Baleni was where he returned. He would always remember the meals eaten in the shade of oak trees, the food and jugs of wine spread on trestle tables. It was here, after the idyllic summer of 1939, that he got word that Germany had invaded Poland. On September 2 the whole household assembled for a picnic in the forest. They gathered mushrooms under the oaks. They ate and drank and talked. At the end of the afternoon they made their way—some in carriages, others on horseback—home to the estate. "It had been a happy day, as we had hoped," Leigh Fermor thought, "and it had to last us for a long time, for the next day's news scattered this little society for ever." On September 3 Britain and France declared war on Germany.

Not long after, he said good-bye at the train station in Bucharest. He was on his way back to England to join the army.

ALTHOUGH LEIGH FERMOR had once set his mind against the life of a peacetime soldier, the war changed things. Soon after his arrival in England, he enlisted in the Irish Guards and reported to the Guards' Depot at Caterham for training. The depot was only a twenty-mile train ride south of London in the hilly Surrey countryside, but it might have been another world. When Leigh Fermor passed through the entrance gate, he knew he was in for a change from the freewheeling life he had enjoyed in the castles and cowsheds that had been his home for the last few years. The spit-and-polish discipline the camp was known for earned it the name "Little Sparta."

Leigh Fermor did not make an immediate splash with the guards, among whom he cut an eccentric figure. One day the drill sergeant pinpointed the trouble. "Recruit Leigh-Fermor!" the flinty old soldier growled. "Why're you walkin' about like some strange bird? Where d'you get them bird-like ways?"

The young recruit might have replied that this bird walk had carried him all the way to Constantinople. But before he had a chance, the sergeant major as much as threw up his hands.

"Put 'im in the book, Corporal Driscoll. For walkin' about like some strange birrrd!"

AS IT TURNED OUT, the strange, birdlike recruit did not remain a guard for long. His experience in Greece before the war soon drew the interest of the War Office, and before long he wound up in intelligence and was on his way to the Mediterranean. As Leigh Fermor saw things, "it was the obsolete choice of Greek at school which had really deposited us on the limestone." Modern Greek was a difficult language to learn in a hurry, but even a schoolboy familiarity with ancient Greek lightened the load considerably. The shortcut to fluency, he thought, accounted for the "sudden sprinkling of many strange figures among the mainland and island crags." By the next fall he was in Egypt. Soon he would find himself once again in Greece.

Patrick Leigh Fermor.
© *Imperial War Museum*
(HU 98922)

CHAPTER 2

Sword Stick

AT THE END of October 1940, when news reached Crete that Greece had entered the war, John Pendlebury took a British army captain's uniform out of the box it was hidden in and pulled it on. Until this moment he had been, publicly at least, nothing more than a civilian employed by the British consulate. But as he admitted to a friend, he was undoubtedly "the most bogus Vice-Consul in the world."

A Cambridge-trained archaeologist, Pendlebury had been living in Crete off and on since 1928. His book about the island's ancient past was on its way to becoming the standard guide for anyone interested in Cretan archaeology. For a number of years in the early thirties, he worked as the curator of Arthur Evans's excavations at Knossos. Evans, the celebrated pioneer of Minoan archaeology who had unearthed the Palace of Minos at the turn of the century, came to think of Pendlebury as "the heir apparent to the archaeological kingdom of Crete." Given his choice of inheritances, this was just what Pendlebury would have selected. From the beginning he loved the island. To his mind everything about Crete, even the dialect of Greek he heard here—its aspirated *k* and *x* sounds reminding him of Italian— was a notch above the mainland. It struck him as "a wonderful country—much richer than Greece—the peasants finer men."

During his first season of excavation at Knossos in 1930, he had gone so far as to begin dressing in traditional Cretan clothing. He got himself up in a high-collared white shirt, dark blue vest, and matching breeches—their balloon legs tucked into tall boots made of white leather. The fine Cretan cloak he wore was particularly impressive. "It was a soft darkish blue on the outside," a friend recalled, "embroidered in black braid with a hood folded back and all lined with scarlet." A tasseled black kerchief wound into a squat turban topped off the outfit. Pendlebury was thrilled with it. "Have just got a Cretan costume," he wrote to his father; "perfectly gorgeous, a great show."

Even in Egypt, where he excavated later that year, the sumptuous cloak remained his regular evening dress. For Pendlebury the costume was more than simply appropriate clothing for the climate—it was a kind of uniform, a symbol of the affinity he felt for Crete and its people.

Dressed now in the drab pea green trousers and tunic of the British army, he cut a less striking figure, but he appeared capable and confident. At thirty-six, he was tall and lean, with broad, athletic shoulders and a keen, weather-roughened face. His brown hair fell to the right, and you could see, if you looked closely, that his left eye was made of glass, the token of a childhood misadventure involving—he said family stories differed—either a pen or a thorn bush. Whenever Pendlebury left the consular offices in Heraklion for long treks through the mountains, often on business he was not at liberty to disclose, he favored an eye patch. The unusual accessory only added to the romantic aura that seemed to hang over him. Rumor had it that on such occasions he left the glass eye on his desk as a signal of his whereabouts.

Never one to be constrained by regulations, even if there *was* a war looming, Pendlebury took a few poetic liberties with his British uniform. He tucked a silver Cretan dagger into the

John Pendlebury takes target practice.
Col. Stephen Rose, courtesy of Imogen Grundon

government-issue Sam Browne belt and added a leather-covered sword stick to season the ensemble. On October 31 he sent a telegram to his wife, Hilda, that read, "Greece behaving grandly. Very proud of Crete. Reverted to my proper rank."

A YEAR EARLIER Pendlebury had taken his family on a vacation to the Isle of Wight. Hilda had settled for the time being in Cambridge with the couple's two children, so the excursion gave the family a rare chance to be together. But the news reports that reached them on the island cast a shadow over the holiday. On the way home on September 3, they stopped at a pub for lunch. As he was settling the account after the meal, Pendlebury heard that Britain and Germany were now at war. When the Pendleburys reached Cambridge that night, John handed each member of the family a gas mask and they retreated to a room that had been turned into a makeshift bomb shelter. Pendlebury and his son passed the first evening of the war rolling a tennis ball back and forth across the floor of the shelter.

The next day Pendlebury began searching for a way to join the war effort. He had already been in touch with naval intelligence, but now he cast his net wider. He would sign up with any department that might benefit from his unique knowledge of Crete. On October 14 he got word that the War Office could use him in intelligence. By January he had been ordered to report to Weedon in Northamptonshire for a cavalry-officer training course, which would give him a basic military education.

When time for the course rolled around, Pendlebury felt anxious about the welfare of his family while he was away, but he was also exhilarated. As a boy he had relished pretend war. Even as an undergraduate at Cambridge, whenever his attention wandered, he was known to fill the margins of his notebooks and letters with sketches of crusading knights and Muslim warriors. Years earlier, at the height of the First World War, he had written an urgent letter from boarding school asking his mother to make toy pistols and tomahawks for him. "Send everything as quick as you can," the letter had implored her, "as we want to raid the other dormitory." Now that the war was real, he sounded equally enthusiastic. "I went up to town on Monday to get a few things at the Army and Navy including a gigantic sword," he told his father. "I am taking Gibbon's 'Decline and Fall' with me. It seems a good opportunity to read it right through which I have never done."

On January 19, he reported to the 110th Officer Cadet Training Unit in Weedon. The conditions when he arrived were atrocious, even for Northamptonshire in winter. A cold, pounding rain had already turned the training ground into a mud pit, and there was more wet weather on the way. But Pendlebury was pleased with his prospects. "I think it is going to be great fun," he wrote to Hilda. By the end of the month the intensive training in horsemanship and soldiering already had him feeling like a military officer. It was as if his life had taken a new direction. He soon told his father, "I've forgotten all about being an archaeologist."

In May, with the cavalry course behind him, Pendlebury was ordered to London. The war was now heating up, after months of escalating tension but little actual combat. There were reports of heavy fighting in France, and German forces were known to be barreling through Belgium and the Netherlands. When Pendlebury arrived at the stubby, turreted building in Whitehall that housed the War Office, he learned that he was being put to work immediately.

He found his way to a room he had been directed to in the basement. As he entered, he recognized an old friend from the British School of Archaeology in Athens. Like Pendlebury, Nick Hammond had studied classics at Cambridge. Later, at the British School, where both young men held fellowships in the 1920s, Hammond had developed a reputation as "an especially resolute traveller." His work on the archaeology of the Greek world's northern fringe had sent him on long journeys through parts of Albania and Epirus where travel was notoriously demanding.

Seeing Pendlebury stride into the dreary basement office, Hammond brightened. He was disillusioned with the "hocus-pocus" he had encountered so far in military intelligence, and seeing the familiar face of another hobnailed adventurer like Pendlebury promised to dispel the "mists of unreality" that hung over the War Office operations.

Not only was Pendlebury good at cooking up schemes, Hammond remembered; he also could pull them off. In December 1929 he and Hammond and two other students at the British School had decided to walk to Thebes, some forty miles away. They got started around three o'clock in the morning and fol-

lowed moonlit roads from the peaceful Kolonaki neighborhood, where the school was located, skirting the coast of the
Saronic Gulf and then heading northeast across the mountains. The plan was to reach Thebes in time to hop the Orient
Express on a spur off its long-distance run that would carry
them back to Athens. But none of the young men could match
Pendlebury's pace. At Cambridge he had broken track and field
records that had stood for half a century, and he had once won
a race against hurdler David Burghley—the future gold medal-
ist whose exploits would later inspire the film *Chariots of Fire*. A
comfortable pace for an athlete like Pendlebury was deadly for
anyone else. Hammond kept him in sight until the last miles,
when Pendlebury dashed ahead to hold the train. By the time
the others finally reached the station, they found him waiting
patiently, looking "fresh as a daisy," Hammond recalled. He had
already "consumed most of the beer in sight."

Reunited now in London, the two old friends spent the next
several days preparing for the missions they had been assigned
by the military-intelligence branch of the War Office—"learning
the tricks of the trade" of covert operations, Hammond called
it. They were given a whirlwind course in explosives that left a
quantity of mangled angle iron in its wake. Hammond soon saw
that Pendlebury, more than the other intelligence officers he
had met, had a practical sense of what a resistance movement in
Crete required. But there was also a romantic streak in his zeal
for the mission. "He talked to me of swordsticks, daggers, pistols,
maps," Hammond remembered; "of hide-outs in the mountains
and of coves and caves on the south coast." It was clear, however,
that there was more to Pendlebury's talk than leftover schoolboy excitement. Hammond was convinced that much of what
Pendlebury had learned in Crete could be put to practical use.

He knew the island's geography as well as anyone and he
was comfortable with the peculiar modes of travel—he men-

tioned "mules and caïques"—that the topography necessitated. From experience he could identify the twists and turns in the island's mountain roads where outsiders would expose themselves to attack. Most important, he had forged relationships in far-flung villages that would be invaluable once the war put a premium on trust. As Hammond watched his friend "poring over the latest maps of Crete," he began to sense the hard reality of the work ahead of them.

Near the end of the month the War Office arranged for Pendlebury to fly over France. The carnage he witnessed there firsthand—as a pathetic wave of refugees fled the advancing German army—fired his commitment to Crete. When he returned, he wrote to Hilda asking her to bring his luggage to London. He asked her in particular to pack the sword stick, which he had concluded "would be the ideal weapon against parachute troops." Hilda arrived the first week of June. When they were at last together again, she was moved to see her husband's face harden as he told her what he had observed in France. He "could hardly wait," he told her, "to take his personal vengeance." They ate dinner together at the Oxford and Cambridge Club and then, on the street outside, they said good-bye.

BY JUNE 12 Pendlebury was back on Crete. He took up residence in the guesthouse of the Villa Ariadne, the estate Arthur Evans had built for himself at Knossos just south of Heraklion. Posing as the vice-consul for the island, he set about accumulating lists of allies and potential traitors. He called on old friends from his earlier expeditions for help. Kronis Bardakis, who had often supplied the archaeologists with mules, became his first lieutenant. With the help of the "Old Krone," as the grizzled Bardakis was called, Pendlebury enlisted the leaders, or *kapetans*, of key clans around Heraklion. They made an imposing crew. Antonis Grigorakis from Krousonas was a compact man with a determined face and a white Vandyke beard. He was known as Satanas, more for the tenacity he had shown against the Turks in 1897 and more recently during the same Venizelist uprising in 1935 that had swept up Leigh Fermor on the mainland than for his day-to-day demeanor. But he was violent enough in outbursts to have shot off his own finger for rolling a losing number in a game of dice. "He is a very dignified old gentleman who looks like an Elizabethan pirate," Pendlebury told his father.

Pendlebury next recruited Manoli Bandouvas, a hardheaded ruffian from Asites, in the middle of the Heraklion region, with an impressive black handlebar mustache, a deep, dramatic voice, and a short temper. He had made his fortune on sheep and had "the restless furtive eyes of the rich peasant," one British officer thought. "Bandouvas is a good man," Pendlebury confided to Satanas, "but judgement and discretion he does not possess." Most dependable was the black-bearded Giorgos Petrakogiorgos, a successful olive oil merchant whose loyalty to the British never wavered. Together these three men would come to be known as "Pendlebury's Thugs."

In October, when Greece declared war on Italy, Pendlebury—now Captain Pendlebury—put aside his cover as vice-consul, but he remained secretive about preparations he was making. In November, with elements of the British army landing on the island, he acquired an assistant, a corporal in the commandos, who was impressed by his new boss's relaxed attitude. He was surprised to be presented with clean sheets for the camp bed the Old Krone set up for him—unheard-of luxury to a soldier—and even a Cretan cloak like the captain's own. When the corporal called Pendlebury "un-Captainlike," it was a compliment.

There was nothing regimented about the office either—a disheveled room, one visitor observed, furnished with "a somewhat rickety wardrobe filled with guns of all sorts, piles of paper money bundled in with every sort of other paper." Pendlebury gave the corporal the job of answering the office phone. Years later the number would remain etched in the man's memory— "*pente dodeka*, 512." He was also put in charge of monitoring shipping at the harbor in Heraklion. The hardest part, the corporal soon discovered, was fending off the harbormaster's hospitality—a slug of raki to get the day started. "It took a few visits," he found, "before I managed to explain that coffee was preferable at nine o'clock in the morning."

With his new assistant managing the office, Pendlebury was free to roam the island. Because he spoke Greek he was sometimes pressed into service by the army. On one occasion the medical officer of the commando unit based in Heraklion asked Pendlebury to translate for him while he conducted examinations for venereal diseases in the city's brothels. For the most part, though, Pendlebury was on his own, tramping through the mountains to survey and map spots that might be defended in the event of a German invasion. It was brutal work. One officer posted to the British headquarters in Heraklion noticed, "Pendlebury would sometimes saunter in, exhausted and bedraggled, and after a chat and a drink he would go fast asleep on the floor. He would have disappeared by the time I woke up in the morning."

At first Pendlebury told his new assistant little about the work he was doing in the hills. Gradually, though, he took the young man into his confidence. "He told me about his hill men," the corporal recalled, "how he was trying to organise them into fighting groups and train them, explaining that since the Cretan Division was in Albania, the island's defenses were pretty thin on the ground."

In December Pendlebury enlisted a sailor known as Agios Georgios—Holy George—to help him survey coast defenses. Sailing from Heraklion on George's caïque with a crew of three fishermen, Pendlebury inspected the shoreline to the east and west of the harbor. "We also checked out look-out points," his assistant, the commando corporal, recalled. "They were supposed to be manned and most of them were fairly alert. On some occasions Holy George insisted that they were drunk and asleep and wanted to borrow my rifle to wake them up."

The most troubling difficulty they encountered was with the engine on George's caïque, which had come from a Leyland truck and still growled as if it were hauling freight up a mountain road. The racket made the boat a liability when it came to covert operations. But Pendlebury soon came up with a solution. He told the Old Krone to collect metal scouring pads from wherever he could find them, and when he had gathered enough, Pendlebury packed them into an empty oil drum. He then piped the engine's exhaust through the improvised device, turning it into an effective muffler. "It worked quite well," the corporal thought, "except that it 'sooted up' easily and every now and then it blew a pan-scrubber out of the pipe."

One thing Captain Pendlebury could not improvise was a way to arm the Cretan bands he had recruited. Bandouvas and the others had been forced to relinquish their weapons in the wake of the Venizelist rebellion in 1935. Pendlebury knew they would soon face a very well-armed foe. Again and again he put in requests to Middle East Command in Cairo asking for as many as ten thousand rifles. He had still received no reply.

Pendlebury's confidence in the Cretans themselves, however, remained high. When he read that Benito Mussolini had been heard complaining about the savage ferocity of Cretan troops who were mobilized against the Italians on the Albanian front, he had to laugh. In the Christmas letter he sent home to Hilda he ventured that the Cretan fighters the Italians had met with so far were "nothing to the savages that can be sent."

EARLY IN THE NEW YEAR Pendlebury took part in an unsuc-
cessful commando raid on the island of Kasos to the northeast
of Crete. That the naval commander in charge of the operation brought along Italian maps no one involved could read
was only one of the slipups that ensured the mission's failure. Pendlebury's assistant found himself mixed up in a similar fiasco on Kastellórizon late in February. As a result of the
two failures, the commando unit to which the corporal was
still attached was sent back to Cairo in March. The young commando was reluctant to leave. "The Uncrowned King of Crete,"
as he thought of Pendlebury, "proved that, soldier or not, he was
a leader, and real leaders are rare, especially among soldiers." On
March 7 Pendlebury wrote a letter to Hilda reporting that all
was well, for the moment. "At present we seem as safe as you,
though by the time this gets to you we may not be so!" In a cable
sent ten days later he sounded a more ominous note. "Love," the
message concluded, "and adieu."

NEAR THE END of March 1941, Pendlebury struck out on foot
for the eastern end of the island, coincidentally retracing the
route of a trek he had made more than a decade earlier. This
time, instead of surveying the ruins of the island's Minoan past,
as he had done on that occasion, he inspected observation posts
and set up communications networks that would one day be
used to relay information about enemy movements. From Heraklion he headed east along the coast to Áyios Nikólaos; then,
turning south, he climbed up to the hill town of Kritsa and continued over the mountains to the southeast, making for the port
town of Ierápetra on the southern coast. From there he traveled
north across the narrowest part of the island to Kavousi, which
looked down on the beautiful blue water of the Bay of Mirabello.
Above the town were the ruins of an Iron Age stronghold where
the ancient Cretans had once fled to escape raiders from the sea.

It might make a good radio outpost, he noted before continuing east along the north coast to Sitea, at the island's eastern tip. From Sitea he looped south and west back through Ierápetra and continued westward along the south coast, as far as Tsoutsouros, where there was a beach that could be used for landings. From there it was a strenuous climb over the mountains to return to Heraklion. Though Pendlebury had no way of knowing, it was a journey that ranged across the same territory Paddy Leigh Fermor and Billy Moss would disappear into some three years later.

Everywhere along the route Pendlebury met Cretans who were determined to fight for the freedom of the island—"Keen as mustard," he thought. Nevertheless he was discouraged by much of what he saw. In his notebook he observed that the beaches were patrolled by a makeshift group of policemen, youths, and older former soldiers. And the ex-soldiers were mostly aging veterans of Crete's struggle to drive out the Turks. At the very least this ragtag defense force would have to be supplied with arms. If weapons were stockpiled at the police stations, Pendlebury believed, they could be distributed when the time came. "May be against rules of war but otherwise there will be a massacre, since men, women and children will fight without arms."

While Pendlebury was still making these rounds, news came that Germany had invaded Greece on April 6. He rushed back to Heraklion. On April 9 German tanks captured Thessaloníki, and the British soon pulled back to the Thermopylae Line, a defensive position stretched along the line where the Greeks had fought the Persians in 480 BC. Newspapers reported on the eighteenth that the Greek prime minister, Alexandros Koryzis, had died of heart failure, but everyone suspected suicide. (It came out later that he had in fact shot himself.) Two days later the commander in chief in the Middle East gave the order to evacuate British forces from the mainland. On the twenty-third the Greek government, along with King George II and the royal family, fled Athens for Crete.

Already German dive-bombers were staging daily attacks against the island's harbors. Suda Bay near Chania was "under more or less perpetual air attack during daylight hours." On the twenty-fourth two tankers were hit near the mouth of the bay; one was still burning a week later. Entering the harbor under these conditions was so terrifying that men being landed by troop transports ferrying them from the mainland were said to have leaped overboard and attempted to swim ashore rather than brave the ferocious attacks leveled against the ships. Corpses floating in the water may have dissuaded some from taking this approach.

ON MAY 14 Nick Hammond found his way to Pendlebury's office in Heraklion. Since leaving London along with his friend almost a year earlier, Hammond had been riding a wartime whirlwind. His original mission was to enter Albania through Greece and help organize resistance against the Italian occupation. But when the Sunderland flying boat he and Pendlebury traveled aboard touched down in Athens, Nick—who lacked even the feeble cover Pendlebury's bogus vice-consulship provided—was refused entry into the country. He spent a dispiriting month in Alexandria, attached to a regular-army regiment whose most hazardous engagements at the time involved a string of cocktail parties. Soon he moved on to Haifa, where he helped T. E. Lawrence's younger brother Arnold Lawrence set up a covert training camp for Jewish guerrillas. One of his students was a twenty-five-year-old named Moshe Dayan. By October 1940 Hammond was training covert agents at a nearby camp. His specialty was demolitions, which earned him the nickname "Captain Guncotton."

The organization that employed Hammond, the Special Operations Executive, "SOE" for short, had been formed earlier that summer. Combining a number of earlier intelligence units, SOE was charged with conducting espionage and sabotage operations in occupied Europe. Some referred to the group as "Churchill's Secret Army," because SOE worked under a direct injunction from the prime minister to "set Europe ablaze." In the coming years the unit would play a crucial role in the Greek Resistance.

When the situation in Greece began to fall apart that spring, Hammond rushed to Athens. There was no time left to organize a full-scale resistance network, but with the German army advancing down the Greek peninsula throughout the month of April, he busied himself blowing up equipment and facilities that might prove beneficial to the enemy war effort—creating what a fellow intelligence agent called "havoc of a spectacular and enjoyable kind." On the twenty-sixth he managed to destroy a warehouse full of cotton at Haliartus, a spot northwest of Athens where the armies of Sparta and Thebes had once tangled. In Athens the next morning, just after daybreak, Hammond gathered his remaining stock of explosives and escaped to the Peloponnese aboard a vessel sailing from the yacht harbor. From there he intended to make his way to Crete. Athens fell that same day.

After months of working in secrecy, Pendlebury was eager to show Hammond the highlights of the resistance network he had prepared. He introduced his old friend to a handful of his *andartes*, as Greek guerrilla fighters were termed. Hammond was especially struck by one "bald-headed giant with a ferocious moustache and a large family of sons." If this man was typical of Pendlebury's allies, the Germans were in for a fight. "He breathed blood and slaughter and garlic in the best Cretan style," Hammond thought.

Hammond's arrival gave Pendlebury a chance to solicit advice about demolitions. He had already made arrangements for destroying the telegraph office and planned to do the same at the power station. Key roads and bridges would have to be demolished. Pendlebury drove Hammond into the mountains along the main road linking the north and south coasts, to show him where hairpin turns and narrow gorges created vulnerabilities. "He had already driven some bore-holes for camouflet charges," Hammond observed, "and he had trained men in the neighbouring villages."

There was also some concern that the Germans might land aircraft on the Nidha plateau, a great alpine plain that sat nearly five thousand feet high in the Ida range. Pendlebury knew the area well. He had spent a night there in 1932 while on an expedition to the summit of Mount Ida that included a stop at the Idaean Cave, where Zeus was said to have been raised. Ringed by limestone crags that hid it entirely from the lowlands below, the plateau would make a nearly impregnable stronghold for any force that occupied it with sufficient numbers and supplies. It was a spot writer Lawrence Durrell would later visit; it seemed to him "like the roof of the world." Pendlebury had his men strew massive boulders across flat stretches where an airplane might be able to land.

Hammond had his own plans under way too. Since arriving in Crete, he had been teamed up with another SOE operative named Mike Cumberlege, a bright, well-informed man who wore a gold earring in one ear. When Paddy Leigh Fermor met him later, he thought him "an amazing buccaneerish figure." Cumberlege skippered the HMS *Dolphin*, a caïque that had been refit in Haifa with a forty-millimeter "pom-pom" cannon and two twenty-millimeter antiaircraft guns. Middle East Command had sent Hammond on a mission aboard the *Dolphin* to blow up the Corinth Canal, and he took an immediate liking to Cumberlege. When the *Dolphin* sailed from Chania for Heraklion, Hammond was on board. Now the two were plotting further raids in the nearby Dodecanese islands. Not long after Hammond introduced Cumberlege to Pendlebury, the three men hatched a plan to attack the Italian garrison on Kasos, where Pendlebury had watched the commando raid fall apart earlier in the year. They hoped to launch the mission on May 19, but the navy unexpectedly sent the *Dolphin* to Ierápetra, on the south coast, where an operation was under way to salvage munitions from a sunken transport vessel. Kasos would have to wait until the twentieth. "It was going to be a terrific party," Cumberlege thought.

Around dusk on the evening of May 18, Pendlebury went down to Heraklion harbor and climbed aboard the *Dolphin*. He wanted to get in some practice on the ship's machine gun before dinner. When the usual evening air raid came, Pendlebury opened fire on the low-flying Stukas from the deck of the little ship. Although he failed to bring one down, the gesture impressed a party of Greeks who were watching the fireworks while waiting to gather fish that would be blasted to the surface by the German bombs. That evening Pendlebury took the crew of the *Dolphin* to dinner at the officers' club near the harbor. They drank wine and ate fish provided by the Stukas. His mood was buoyant. "Pendlebury was confident," Hammond felt, "that if Crete were lost his Cretans could be depended upon to carry on guerrilla warfare in the hills."

ON THE MORNING of the twentieth, the attack Pendlebury had been waiting for came at last. And it was bigger than he could possibly have imagined. Starting near the Maleme airfield in the west, German paratroopers began to plummet from the sky in extraordinary numbers, their color-coded parachutes blossoming across the horizon, with still more troops and matériel landing by glider. What Pendlebury, his Cretans, and the Allied forces on the island now faced was the first full-scale airborne invasion in history.

HIGH ON THE EASTERN SLOPES of the White Mountains, still far from the fighting, a young Cretan shepherd named George Psychoundakis was standing watch over his family's meager flock when he heard the thrum of aircraft engines in the distance. He wondered whether the Germans were making another of the bombing runs that had come almost daily in the last weeks.

At twenty-one, Psychoundakis was the eldest of four children, but he might easily have been mistaken for a boy—his youthfulness a matter of character as much as appearance. He had a small, slender build and he moved over the craggy terrain as nimbly as a sprite. His delicate face, shadowed by coal black hair and the beginnings of a mustache, looked sad, until he grew animated in conversation, when it sparkled with equal parts intelligence and mischief.

He lived just down the hill in Asi Gonia, a mountain village hemmed in on three sides by soaring outcrops of the Lefka range. His family occupied a dirt-floored one-room house near the village spring; the place where water was drawn and clothes were washed, it amounted to the town center. Unusually for a student in a remote village school, he had learned to read, and he borrowed what books he could from the village doctor and the priest.

Word soon reached Asi Gonia that the planes Psychoundakis had heard that morning were not just bombers but transports. German parachutists were dropping around Chania in the west. Men from the village hurried to dig up weapons buried years earlier, and Psychoundakis left his sheep and followed them to a nearby village where a larger contingent was forming.

From there they could see the German planes streaming overhead, coming and going, he thought, "like bees in a bee-garden, each time bringing more bombs and more troops."

When the men reached the main road that ran along the north coast from Chania to Rethymnon, young Psychoundakis asked anyone traveling from the west for news about the fighting. It stirred him to hear the invariable reply—"We've eaten them up!"

But when he looked around at the Greek fighters who had assembled in the village, it was hard to imagine them fending off airplanes and soldiers armed with machine guns. Few of them were armed, and those who were carried weapons that might have come from a museum. "For the villagers had kept them hidden for many years in holes and caves," he knew, "and now, all eaten up with rust, they were really almost archaeological specimens." On one occasion when the men fired on a damaged German plane that had landed nearby, he watched one of them struggling with an old Martini rifle. Each time the man fired, he had to open the breech and force the spent casing out with a ramrod. An old saying from his grandfather's day flashed through Psychoundakis's mind—"Stand still, Turk, while I re-load."

ALL OVER THE ISLAND civilians turned out bearing whatever weapons they could lay their hands on. One New Zealand soldier noticed a Greek bearing "a shot-gun with a serrated edge bread knife tied on like a bayonet." Most were older men and boys, because the men of fighting age had joined the Cretan Division of the Greek army and been sent to fight on the mainland. Their absence gave the fighting a bitter edge. "You cuckolds!" Psychoundakis and his friends yelled at the German planes overhead. "If only we had our aeroplanes and our troops here. If only the Division were here."

In at least one village, the women took to the fields carrying sticks and the sickles ordinarily used to harvest their crops. They would not have known that the goddess figures archaeologist Arthur Evans had discovered at Knossos carried the same primitive weapon. Elsewhere armed women in Greek uniforms were reportedly captured by the Germans. At Rethymnon, where the police force was equipped with rifles, the invaders encountered fierce resistance, just as Pendlebury had predicted.

A young Greek surgeon who had recently made his way home from the Albanian front, where the Cretan Division was still tied up, witnessed the attack on the morning of May 20 from his village twenty-five miles south of Chania. His sixty-year-old father walked into the family garden and dug up a Mannlicher rifle that had been buried there for nearly a decade. "He too wanted to go and fight," the surgeon saw. "It was only when I told him that I too had to enlist, even without a weapon, that he gave it to me. Clutching both my doctor's kit and the gun in one hand, I put 20–25 bullets in my jacket pocket. I was not even sure they were unused." As the surgeon made his way toward the fighting, he fell in with a group of some forty others, and together they surrounded a party of paratroopers and wiped them out. When the shooting stopped, the young man quickly resumed his role as a surgeon. He had the wounded from both sides taken to a schoolhouse nearby, where he and another pair of doctors gave them what medical care they could manage under the circumstances. "Unfortunately I didn't have many bandages on hand," he recalled later. "The first German I bandaged, I myself had shot."

PADDY LEIGH FERMOR suffered his first wound on Crete before the fighting even began. Near the end of October, the previous autumn, Middle East Command had received orders from London to organize a military mission to Greece. The prime minister wanted to know what was going on there, and he recommended sending officers from Cairo to observe the action firsthand. As Churchill's cable put it, "Let them go and see the fighting and give us some close-up information about the relative merits of the two armies. I expect to have a good wire every day or so, telling us exactly what is happening, so far as the Greeks will allow it."

Soon after the telegram arrived, Leigh Fermor found himself among the handpicked group of officers who sailed from Alexandria for Athens on the HMS *Ajax*. When the cruiser made a stop at Suda Bay, on the northwest coast of Crete, he and a companion slipped ashore for the evening. After drinking their fill in nearby Chania, they hitched a lift back to the docks on a ration truck driven by a soldier from the Black Watch, the famous Highland regiment that had distinguished itself in wars stretching back two hundred years. As they rounded a bend along the rocky coastal road, the driver, who turned out to be no more sober than his passengers, managed to flip the truck into a ditch. Paddy was still in the hospital with a head injury when the *Ajax* sailed for Athens.

When he finally reported for work with the British mission a week later, he joined the mission staff at General Headquarters in Athens, which was housed in the luxurious Hotel Grand Bretagne, off Syntagma Square. The Greek king had a private office in the building. And his young cousin, Prince Peter, served as liaison to the British mission. Leigh Fermor and the other officers took a liking to Peter, an anthropologist who had traveled in Tibet and studied the Toda herdsmen in the Nilgiri Hills of southern India. On top of his ethnographic interests, Peter had collected what one of the officers called "an astonishing repertoire of bawdy songs." Peter's good humor aside, though, Leigh Fermor found the atmosphere at the Grand Bretagne stifling. Whenever an opportunity arose, he took to the field.

One assignment sent him into Albania, Nick Hammond's old stomping grounds. Leigh Fermor remembered what Gibbon had said about this isolated stretch of the Balkan peninsula in *The Decline and Fall of the Roman Empire*. It was "a country within sight of Italy which is less known than the interior of America." A lot of water had trickled under the bridge since Gibbon's time, Leigh Fermor knew. But in some ways little had changed. Albania had been "flung open" after the last war, but few outsiders had ventured in even then. When he got there himself, he discovered a rugged country that he would be reminded of many times in the coming years. "It was a fierce mountain state," as he saw it. And the Albanians themselves struck him as "hardy and courageously independent."

As he trekked along the Albanian front, he noticed that some of the foreign soldiers had adapted surprisingly well to the harsh terrain. They did not seem to mind the bone-chilling mountain weather and they moved over the upland crags with little effort, carrying their rifles across their shoulders like shepherds' staffs. This, it turned out, was the Fifth Cretan Division. In January a single regiment of these fierce Cretan fighters routed an entire enemy division in the Trebeshina Mountains in southern Albania.

BUT IN THE END, even the tenacity of the Cretan Division could not stop the Axis advance across the Balkans. It was not long before word came to evacuate the Greek mainland, and Leigh Fermor and the others in the Athens mission set about destroying the mission's documents and equipment. On April 22 a group of them climbed aboard a truck and drove southeast out of the city toward Cape Sounion. The truck came to a stop not far from the ruined temple of Poseidon, where you could still see Lord Byron's name cut into the base of one of the columns. The men clambered out and began pushing the truck toward the cliffs that dropped off into the Aegean. Legend had it that King Aegeus had leaped to his death from here when he saw his son Theseus's ship returning from Crete with a black sail—the signal that his son was dead. Theseus had defeated the Minotaur in his own lair and had even managed to escape from the labyrinth that held the monstrous bull-man, following the thread Ariadne had given him to trace the way out. But then one moment of thoughtlessness had cost him a terrible price. When Leigh Fermor and the others got the truck to the edge, they gave one final push and watched it tumble toward the sea.

They then boarded the armed caïque *Ayia Varvara* and set out for the Gulf of Argos. Four days later they put in at Myli on the northwestern shore of the gulf. Abandoned British vehicles could be seen lining the roadways. After picking up a few British stragglers and some vital supplies—including several bottles of champagne—the *Ayia Varvara* put back out to sea. The next day, forty miles to the south, near the mouth of the gulf, the caïque was sunk by German bombers. Everyone on board managed to escape the wreckage. Leigh Fermor and the other men soon bought another vessel and made it past the island of Antikythéra, nearly halfway to their destination, before the engine gave out. They limped back to the island and transferred to a schooner that carried them, exhausted but in relatively good condition, to Crete at last.

The schooner landed at Kastelli Kissamou, a sleepy town with a Venetian harbor, twenty-five miles west of Chania. There Leigh Fermor bumped into Prince Peter and another member of the British mission, and together they traveled to Galatas, in the hills outside Chania, where Prince Peter had a house. After a few days of rest there, Leigh Fermor was attached to the Fourteenth Infantry Brigade as an intelligence officer. At the end of April the unit moved to Heraklion and the commander, Brigadier Chappel, set up his headquarters in a deep cave set back in a rocky hillside between the town and the airport to the east.

ON MAY 18 Leigh Fermor went into town for a drink with another officer from the British mission. Two days later the invasion began. The Junkers transport planes that dropped German paratroopers in the west had returned to the mainland to reload and refuel twice since the morning. Heraklion was hit by the third wave. It was nearly four thirty in the afternoon when the attack there began. First came an hour of the most destructive bombing the city had yet suffered.

Soon after the bombing subsided, Leigh Fermor again heard the drone of aircraft and looked up to see the near horizon dotted with transport planes from which parachutes were already emerging by the dozen. Because Brigadier Chappel had ordered the crews of the anti-aircraft guns to stand down during the initial bombardment, the emplacements had gone unnoticed by German bombers during the initial attack. Now they opened fire on the lumbering transport planes. "When the roar of our guns broke out," Leigh Fermor saw, "many invaders were caught in the olive branches and many were killed as they fell; others dropped so close to headquarters that they were picked off at once."

It was not long after the attack began that a British soldier rushed a captured German document to Brigadier Chappel's command center. Because Leigh Fermor had picked up some German in his travels, he was called on to translate. What he discovered as he read was the entire German order of battle. It laid out the distribution of German units and included their troop strengths and the names of the unit commanders.

One item in particular stopped him cold—"the spearhead of the attack," he noticed, "was under the command of a Captain von der Heydte." It hit him immediately that this must be Einer

Heydte, the young baron who had befriended him in Vienna. At home Heydte had confronted Nazis, and now he had been swept up in their war. Reading on, Leigh Fermor gathered that his friend's battalion had dropped by parachute near Galatas at the western end of the island. He was astonished to think that the spot indicated, which lay between Chania and the airfield at Maleme, was close to where he had enjoyed the hospitality of Prince Peter just days earlier.

That evening, when the brigade's Black Watch piper let loose a twilight blast from his bagpipe, Leigh Fermor was still ruminating on Einer Heydte's unexpected reappearance. "The short May night was illuminated by destroyed planes burning fitfully among the olive trees and during these hours of respite, I couldn't stop thinking of this strange coincidence." He felt a wave of nostalgia for the era when opposing warriors who had moved in the same social circles might exchange a greeting during a lull in the fighting. But he knew that times had changed. In the chaos of the battle raging on Crete, such antique gallantries were impossible. He was thankful that he and his friend, now fighting in far-flung reaches of the island, were unlikely to run into each other.

Still, his memories of the carefree days in Vienna flooded back. The death and destruction all around him now gave the recollection a new poignancy.

LEIGH FERMOR was occupied at Chappel's headquarters the next afternoon when suddenly there was someone at the mouth of the cave. When he looked up, he saw a tall man stooping as he descended the stairs at the entrance. "He had a Cretan guerilla with him, festooned with bandoliers," Leigh Fermor noticed. Unlike the other officers, who carried only service revolvers, the tall man had a rifle slung across his back. And he carried a sword stick. As soon as he saw him, Leigh Fermor felt "enormously impressed by that splendid great figure." When the man introduced himself as John Pendlebury, Leigh Fermor realized that this was someone he had heard about already. "He had a great reputation for knowing Crete and the Cretans backwards, being an indestructible force in the steepest mountains."

Seeing the man for himself, Leigh Fermor thought "Pendlebury made a wonderfully buccaneerish and rakish impression, which may have been partly due to the glass eye." The man's jaunty demeanor was enough to buoy the others, despite the grave circumstances. It was not long before the "dismal cave was suddenly full of noise and laughter."

Pendlebury had come to ask Brigadier Chappel where he and his guerrillas would be most useful in the fighting. After some consideration, the two men focused their attention on the Chania Gate, to the southwest of the city center. There was a freshwater spring just outside the gate, where intelligence gleaned from a captured German map suggested the paratroopers would gather. Chappel then agreed to supply Satanas's men with a few rifles.

As Pendlebury rose to leave, one of the officers asked, perhaps in jest, to see his sword stick. Neither the gravity of the moment nor the hint of mockery in the officer's request fazed Pendlebury. Leigh Fermor watched as he "smiled obligingly, drew it with comic drama and flashed it round with a twist of the wrist. Then he slotted it back and climbed up into the sunlight with a cheery wave."

NEAR GALATAS, Leigh Fermor's old friend Einer Heydte had begun to feel that the tide of the battle was turning the German army's way. Paratroopers had taken control of the Maleme airfield outside Chania, allowing transport planes to land reinforcements and supplies, despite the continuing barrage of anti-aircraft fire from British guns in the surrounding hills. But it was not yet decided. There was no word from Rethymnon, and reports from Heraklion, which had briefly been in German hands, told of British and Greek fighters driving German units from the city.

In the afternoon on Friday, the twenty-third, a soldier dressed in a German uniform dashed out from behind the British line and scrambled across a stretch of open ground to reach Heydte's position. Heydte at first feared a trick, but once he had established that the man was not an impostor, the bedraggled soldier was allowed to tell his story. His platoon had landed by caïque near Chania with orders to attack the antiaircraft emplacements on the Akroteri heights overlooking Suda Bay. After a rough landing that knocked a number of men out of action, the remainder had tried to fight their way through the New Zealand forces that defended the Akroteri peninsula. In the end the entire German unit had been killed or captured, except for this man, who was forced to make his way alone to the German lines. Heydte had him escorted to the relative safety of his headquarters, where the soldier broke down and wept. Later that day the man learned that his two brothers, who were also paratroopers, had been killed soon after the invasion began.

On Sunday afternoon, the twenty-fifth, Heydte received orders for what he expected to be the final attack on Chania and the surrounding highlands. He gathered his company commanders and told his young orderly that he was taking them up to a stretch of high ground called Great Castle Hill, which commanded a view of the entire Chania plain below. From there he would be able to point out landmarks as he gave them their orders for the coming attack. In order to keep the number of men moving together small enough to avoid attracting attention, the orderly was to follow later.

The sun was setting when Heydte finished laying out the plans for the attack, and his orderly had not yet appeared. As the battalion's officers started back for headquarters in small groups, only a sliver of light still brightened the western horizon. He waited for a while near the ruins that had given the hill its name, listening to the sound of fighting in the nearby Galatas heights. Something must have held up the usually dependable orderly, Heydte concluded at last, and started back toward his headquarters.

When he reached the camp he found it strangely quiet. One of his men, the unit's adjutant, explained why. Heydte's orderly, the young man he had grown closest to in the months leading up to the invasion, had been seriously wounded three hours earlier on his way to Great Castle Hill. A bullet that might have been a stray round or might have come from a sniper's rifle had struck him in the chest and pierced his lung. The boy would not survive. "I could not see the adjutant's face in the darkness," Heydte remembered, "and I was glad he could not see mine, with tears welling into my eyes."

That night, as he settled into the trench he had shared with his young orderly since the battle began, Heydte was unable to sleep. "What was the point of ordering my soldiers to kill human beings whom they did not know and who had not done anything to them," he wondered, "and what was the point in allowing those same human beings to kill us, who meant nothing to them?" With the star-dotted Cretan sky looming above his trench, Heydte felt very small and alone. On the warm wind, known as the *meltemi*, that was blowing up through the gorge, he could detect the odor of corpses.

EVELYN WAUGH was the intelligence officer in Number Eight Commando, a secret raiding force commanded by his friend Robert Laycock. Already a successful writer with a well-deserved reputation for biting satire, Waugh had joined the Royal Marines in December 1939 but had seen little action.

In November 1940, when a friend told him, "You ought to be with Bob Laycock's tough boys," he wasted no time requesting a transfer to the new unit.

Near the end of May, the unit now known as Layforce was in Cairo. When the invasion began, Waugh sailed with Laycock from Alexandria bound for Crete on the destroyer *Isis*. Rough seas made the crossing difficult, and when the *Isis* made landfall on the southwestern end of the island, it was impossible to land troops. After an hour the ship returned to Alexandria. The next evening the commandos sailed on the cruiser *Abdiel*, and they landed at Suda Bay, near Chania, at eleven o'clock the following night.

Laycock and Waugh had been led to believe that British forces were getting the upper hand in the fighting on Crete. Their job would be to launch raids against German strongholds. But soon after the *Abdiel* dropped anchor, they saw evidence that this was untrue. While Waugh stood waiting in the captain's cabin for the arrival of landing barges that would carry the unit's men and gear ashore, a shell-shocked naval commander burst into the room. "He was wearing shorts and a greatcoat," Waugh noted, "and could not speak."

"My God, it's hell," the man exclaimed. "We're pulling out. Look at me, no gear. O My God it's hell. Bombs all the time. Left all my gear behind." His best friend had just been killed, he said, and the army was in full retreat. "Crete is being evacuated!"

The brigade major in Waugh's unit told the man that they were going ashore and asked him the password of the day, but he could not recall it. Once on dry land, Waugh learned that German troops had entered Chania. The New Zealand brigade that had been defending the airfield at Maleme had been forced to retreat. Australian, British, and Greek units were also pulling out. All Laycock's commandos could do was provide cover for the evacuation.

The next morning Waugh began to make his way inland against a steady stream of bedraggled men headed in the other direction. Around eight o'clock he noticed that German dive-bombers had begun crisscrossing the sky, but their attacks were focused to his west. Later in the day, he saw their fury at closer range. "Just below us was a very prominent circular cornfield in a hollow and they used this as their pivot so that they were always directly overhead flying quite low, then they climbed as they swung right, dived and let their bombs go about a mile away." Waugh assumed that the target was the headquarters of the British commander, General Freyberg, just off the nearby Suda-Heraklion road. Whatever the target, the dive-bombers attacked it savagely. "At first it was impressive," Waugh thought, "but after an hour deadly monotonous. It was like everything German—overdone."

By the following day the Allied forces were in a chaotic rush toward Sphakia, on the southwestern coast, where the evacuation effort was now under way. With the help of a Maori unit, the commandos managed a brief counterattack. But the situation now looked hopeless. Soon Laycock ordered his men to Sphakia, where they boarded one of the last departing ships.

WHEN EINER HEYDTE'S battalion of the Third Parachute Regiment entered Chania on the morning of May 27, the city might have been a ghost town. During the preceding days of Luftwaffe bombardment, the Greek population of the town had fled into the countryside, and now the British garrison had withdrawn to the western end of the city. A party of wounded Germans left behind when the British pulled out appeared to be the town's sole residents.

Much of the city was in ruins, its buildings gutted and the cobbled streets sloping down toward the waterfront strewn with rubble. Heydte and his men were in little better condition.

His own uniform was in tatters. The legs of his trousers had been hacked off at the knees, and in place of a cap, he now wore a sweat-soaked handkerchief with its corners tied in knots. He had not shaved since the night before the invasion began. When a perspiring bald man in glasses presented himself as the mayor and asked to speak with a German officer, Heydte had a difficult time convincing him that the disheveled figure standing before him *was* the battalion commander. He led the man into the nearby hospital, and there the mayor eventually explained "that he wished to surrender the town and, in the name of the Greek authorities, to ask for clemency and, if possible, help for the civilian population." Heydte accepted the terms and offered the mayor a tin cup filled with wine. When he walked outside again, he saw that the German flag was being raised on one of the town's minarets—the Islamic architecture of the building itself a reminder that the Turks had once taken over the city in similar fashion.

Heydte set up his battalion headquarters in a villa near the sea, not far from the British consulate where John Pendlebury had his office. Then he and his staff officers stripped off their uniforms and took the opportunity to wash themselves with fresh water drawn from a well in the garden alongside the villa. As the cold water sluiced away the week's accumulation of dirt and grime, the men's spirits rose, as if the tension of the past days had been washed away too. While they were cavorting like schoolboys, a British soldier suddenly appeared and gaped at them. In an instant he was gone. Heydte later learned that the villa had been a British command post, and he surmised that the soldier had come carrying a message for headquarters, not realizing that the city had been captured. "He was the last British soldier I saw in the battle for Chania," Heydte would later remember.

But the next day an incident occurred that, in hindsight, offered a warning that the fight for Crete had hardly begun.

Heydte's commanding officer ordered him to investigate reports that a nearby monastery was sheltering an armed band of partisans. It was a job that called for the strength of one of his companies, but because a similar report had proved to be a red herring, Heydte decided to look into the allegation on his own. He and one other soldier sped out to the Akroteri peninsula above Suda Bay—where the monastery was located—on a pair of captured British motorcycles. When they arrived, they found the site abandoned. But as they roamed from room to room, opening and closing doors, a Greek boy appeared and led them to a cell where a white-bearded monk seemed to be waiting for them. When the man greeted him in French, Heydte, feeling embarrassed at making the accusation, asked if there were any armed men in the monastery.

"In a monastery one should seek God, not human beings," the monk replied. "Here there can be no soldiers." Heydte, still as devout a man as when he defended the Catholic Church against a Nazi's insult in Vienna, had felt a surge of religious sentiment when he first walked into the sanctuary. Now he wanted to believe what the monk said.

The old man raised his arm as if to offer a blessing and muttered, "May the saints protect you." Heydte decided to take him at his word. The two Germans remounted their motorcycles and rode back to Chania through the growing dusk. "Only a few days later did we learn that over a hundred heavily-armed Greek soldiers and partisans had been hiding in the monastery while we had searched it. The very thought sent a shiver down my spine," Heydte admitted. He wondered whether the old monk had lied to protect the partisans or to save the pair of foolhardy German soldiers. Either way, the struggle was clearly far from over. In Crete, he realized, "we had encountered for the first time an enemy that was prepared to fight to the bitter end."

IN THE FIGHTING around Heraklion, eighty or ninety miles east of Heydte's area, the British felt they had the upper hand. On the morning of the twenty-eighth—the day after the withdrawal through Sphakia began on the western end of the island—Brigadier Chappel delivered the evacuation orders to a stunned group of officers. A company commander in one of Chappel's most storied regiments had proclaimed some days earlier that "the Black Watch leaves Crete when snow leaves Mount Ida." Unaware as they were of the heavy losses in the west, the officers felt betrayed by the decision to pull out.

That evening Leigh Fermor was busy at the cave, where the brigadier's staff officers were engaged in burning documents. Outside, soldiers worked hurriedly to bury some equipment and destroy the rest to prevent its falling into enemy hands. Line soldiers had not yet been informed of the planned withdrawal. Neither had the Greeks. But it was not hard to see that the British were pulling out.

"All at once," Leigh Fermor observed, "an old Cretan materialized out of the shadows. He was a short, resolute man, obviously a distinguished *kapetan*, with a clear and cheerful glance, a white beard clipped under the chin like a Minoan and a rifle butt embossed with wrought-silver plaques." It was Pendlebury's friend Satanas, who had come to speak with Brigadier Chappel.

Leigh Fermor watched as the man approached Chappel and took the much taller English commander by the shoulder. "My child," the old *andarte* leader said in Greek, "we know you are leaving tonight; but you will soon be back." A hush fell over the cave as he continued. "We will carry on the fight till you return. But we have only a few guns. Leave us all you can spare."

Chappel was visibly stirred by the veteran fighter's request. He turned to Leigh Fermor and the other officers and directed them to gather what weapons they could find.

At eight o'clock orders to withdraw went out to the men. There was a final flurry of sabotage. Stores of food were distributed and the surplus was destroyed. One regimental commander threw an impromptu party as a way of using up supplies. Men opened the oil reservoirs on their trucks and filled them with sand, then raced the engines until they rattled to a halt. Other equipment was rigged to explode if anyone tampered with it.

Then the units began making their way toward the harbor. Marching along the empty streets of Heraklion was like passing through a wasteland. Familiar buildings lay in ruins and there were signs of destruction everywhere. One Australian soldier was struck by the "stench of decomposing dead, debris from destroyed dwelling places, roads were wet and running from burst water pipes, hungry dogs were scavenging among the dead. There was a stench of sulphur, smouldering fires and pollution of broken sewers."

At the harbor the men boarded Royal Navy destroyers, which ferried them out to larger cruisers—*Dido* and *Orion*—waiting offshore. Leigh Fermor and the rest of the headquarters staff went aboard last. By a quarter to three in the morning, the two destroyers carrying them had slipped beyond the submarine net at the mouth of the harbor. So far the operation had run like clockwork.

But then everything began to go wrong. The steering mechanism on the destroyer HMS *Imperial*, which had suffered damage from a Stuka attack the day before, now malfunctioned. Another vessel, HMS *Hotspur*, pulled alongside to allow the passengers from the *Imperial* to leap aboard. Then torpedoes were fired into the battered ship, sending her to the bottom, along with a party of Australian soldiers who had been too drunk to rouse. Now, with *Hotspur* limping along under an extraordinary weight of passengers, the hours of darkness were quickly slipping away. When the sun rose the next morning it caught the

British convoy still in range of Stukas based at Kárpathos, the island lying between Crete and Rhodes. Soon after 6:00 a.m. the ships were attacked by more than a hundred aircraft. Within half an hour the destroyer *Hereward* was so badly damaged it had to turn back toward Crete. When the ship finally sank in shallow water, two Stukas closed in to attack the lifeboats but were kept off by an Italian Red Cross seaplane.

By the time the surviving vessels reached Alexandria at eight o'clock that evening, hundreds of men had been killed, including the captain of the *Orion* and 260 of her passengers. Nearly half of the Black Watch soldiers who had sailed aboard the *Dido* were dead. The overcrowded conditions pushed the casualty count higher than it might have been otherwise, with men dying not just from bomb explosions and gunfire but also from fire and drowning when they could not escape from damaged compartments. Altogether more than a fifth of the troops who had fought to what seemed like a victory in the Heraklion area had now been lost. Leigh Fermor was among those who arrived safely in Alexandria.

NOT MUCH LATER, on a bright morning in June, Einer Heydte also left Crete. As the transport plane carrying him to Athens climbed into a sunlit Mediterranean sky, he reflected that he was now soaring away from this storied island "just as Daedalus had done so many centuries ago." If he recalled his old schoolmaster's argument that the myth of the Minotaur presented a tale of human triumph, the notion must have seemed more wrongheaded than ever. What mattered in the end was not Theseus's victory in the land of the Minotaur but that Daedalus was forced to carry on his famous flight alone, after the death of his beloved son Icarus. Such a lesson was not lost on Heydte as his plane winged its way farther and farther from the spot where his young orderly had lost his life.

JOHN PENDLEBURY, Leigh Fermor later learned, had also re-mained behind on the island he loved. After leaving Brigadier Chappel's command center in the cave outside Heraklion, he and Satanas led a group of men toward the Chania Gate, at the western edge of the city. There they joined another group of Cre-tan recruits and a Greek army unit that had taken up positions along the massive Venetian wall that formed the gate. From their fortified position this ragtag band fought off a battalion of paratroopers from the German First Parachute Regiment. The German commander was surprised to find that "the western edge of the town was magnificently defended."

The next day the Cretans still had control of the Chania Gate. The German unit had retreated over a quarter of a mile west. Pendlebury sent Satanas to his home village of Krousonas, fif-teen miles southwest of Heraklion, where he was to mobilize his men and distribute the weapons contributed by Chappel's unit. Pendlebury then made his way back to his office. From there he dispatched another runner to the village of Skalani, south of Knossos, with orders for the *andartes* based there to hold the high ground overlooking the airfield and the main road lead-ing south out of Heraklion. He then took another gun from the cabinet in his office—he now had a pistol on each hip and a rifle slung across his back—and drove with one of his men through the Chania Gate and up into the hills southwest of the city.

Meanwhile, Nick Hammond, on the return voyage from Ierá-petra aboard the *Dolphin*, put in at Sitia on the eastern tip of the island and from there tried to phone Pendlebury at his office. Hammond knew nothing yet of the attack and was surprised to find the phone lines out of commission. The *Dolphin* motored on toward the west and reached Heraklion around dusk.

As the caïque approached the city, it began drawing fire, so skipper Mike Cumberlege put Hammond ashore on the breakwater near the mouth of the harbor. Armed with a pistol and accompanied by one of Cumberlege's men, Hammond made his way into the city to assess the situation. He had not advanced far when the scene stopped him in his tracks. Nearby were the bodies of dead British soldiers. "We saw that machine-guns were covering us from the embrasures. To our right we could see nothing, being bounded by a high sea wall: then we saw the Nazi swastika flying on the electric power station not far off." Had he waited, Hammond would have seen the swastika flag torn down again. But at the moment the state of affairs seemed clear. Pendlebury, if he was alive, would by now be in the hills with his *andartes*. Hammond slipped back aboard the *Dolphin*, and Cumberlege turned the little ship out to sea.

Over the next several days Hammond and Cumberlege looked for Pendlebury along the coast, hoping to establish a communication link that would keep him and his *andartes* supplied once the British pulled out. At last they joined the evacuation convoy steaming out of Heraklion harbor. When the steering gear on the destroyer *Imperial* went haywire in the pre-dawn hours on the twenty-ninth, the *Dolphin* narrowly escaped being rammed by the larger vessel.

Cumberlege later heard that Pendlebury had abandoned his car outside the city and continued on foot with one of his men. His plan was to make contact with guerrillas on the Nidha plateau, high in the Ida range, where he had once feared German planes might land, and then join Satanas at his home in Krousonas. But as they made their way along the Chania road, the two men walked into a firefight between a Greek unit and German parachutists who had taken shelter in a farmhouse. Pendlebury volunteered to lead an attack on the farmhouse. In the battle that followed he was severely wounded. It was said that he killed several Germans before being struck in the chest. Whether he was hit by rifle fire or a round fired by one of the Stukas providing air support to the besieged parachutists was unclear.

Reports of what happened next were jumbled. But Pendlebury appeared to have been captured by the parachutists and taken to the house of a Greek woman, who happened to be the wife of one of his *andartes*. Some said a German doctor treated his wounds. The next day a German unit arrived and arrested the woman for harboring an enemy soldier. Some accounts maintained that Pendlebury wore his British uniform, others that he had changed into a Greek shirt. It was thought that his uniform might have become soaked with blood.

According to one eyewitness, the Germans then propped Pendlebury against a wall and barked a question at him. He answered, "No." The same question was put to him again and then a third time. Each time the answer was the same, "No." Something else was then spoken in German, and Pendlebury responded by lifting himself to attention. Then shots rang out. He was struck in the head and chest and slumped to the ground.

The story of his death that began to circulate on Crete maintained that Pendlebury had led his final charge brandishing his famous sword stick in the face of the much-better-armed enemy. It was a gesture that rang true to everyone who had known him.

Even in their brief encounter in the cave outside Heraklion, Leigh Fermor had been impressed by the heroic vigor Pendlebury radiated. "The great thing was that his presence filled everyone with life and optimism and a feeling of fun," he remembered. "Everyone felt this, and it hung in the air long after his death."

The legend of John Pendlebury would not die. At the end of August—some three months after he was killed—the chief of military intelligence in Cairo sent a confused message to command in London which read: "We also tried to drop a wireless set by parachute to Pendlebury, who at the moment is largely controlling the guerilla activities in the Crete hills."

It would be a hard job to fill the knee-high Cretan boots Pendlebury had once favored. Leigh Fermor could not know for the moment that he would be one of the men sent to try.

CHAPTER 3

Oak Apple Day

AROUND THE BEGINNING of July 1942, a little more than a year after the fall of Crete, a runner turned up at the camp in the hills above Alones, southwest of Rethymnon, where a fresh-faced young SOE officer named Xan Fielding had established his headquarters. As Fielding watched the man approaching along a jagged goat trail from the valley below, he recognized the nimble figure of a villager named Yianni Tzangarakis, "a silent sad-eyed man of about forty, tireless on the road and expert at rolling cigarettes." He came carrying a message from Tom Dunbabin, the SOE officer who was Fielding's counterpart in the Heraklion area, to the east. Together with their wireless operators and a cadre of Cretan allies, Fielding and Dunbabin had assumed the role John Pendlebury had always imagined would be his. It was now their job to collect intelligence about the German occupation force and to coordinate the activities of Resistance groups across the island. Dunbabin's letter was the first communication Fielding had received from the outside world in weeks. It reported that a new radio transmitter had been smuggled onto the island, along with a third SOE officer, and it asked Fielding to come to Dunbabin's hideout at Gerakari above the Amari Valley as soon as he could, in order to meet his new colleague.

When Fielding finished reading the message, he noticed the

sad-eyed messenger standing nearby with an uncharacteristic grin on his face. Fielding sensed that the ordinarily somber villager had something to say. There was *one* thing more, the runner admitted, clearly pleased to hold information not disclosed in Captain Dunbabin's letter. With a little prompting, Yianni revealed that the third British officer now waiting to meet him at Gerakari was in fact an old friend of Fielding's. His name, Yianni said, was Mr. Leverman. Fielding scanned his memory, but he had no clue whom the man might be referring to.

Captain Fielding had been on the island since the beginning of the year. In the hours before dawn on January 12, with the sea running high and wind screaming in the rigging, he had paddled away from the submarine *Torbay* in a rubber dinghy and slipped ashore at Tsoutsouros on the south coast. It was his second attempt to reach Crete. The first try, on New Year's Day aboard a small armed caïque called *Hedgehog*, had introduced him to the explosive weather that often cut Crete off from SOE headquarters in North Africa. When the *Hedgehog* left Alexandria, the sea was completely calm, but by the time the vessel reached Crete, a gale-driven swell forced the skipper to jettison all the gear stowed on deck and limp back to port. On the night the *Torbay* surfaced near Tsoutsouros, again in a gale, pounding waves smashed the folding canoe Fielding had intended to employ and prevented him from landing all of his equipment. He came ashore in an unwieldy dinghy with only his personal gear: "an electric torch, a small automatic pistol, a map of Crete printed on linen for discreet portability but of so small a scale as to be virtually useless, and a sum of money in currency so inflated that I found my total assets on landing amounted to little more than £16."

In place of his British uniform he wore a black suit, with a white sweater, and hobnailed leather boots. Paddling in from the *Torbay*, he experienced a moment of regret that he had not stayed in uniform for the landing itself, since there was no telling who might be waiting onshore and a British officer caught out of uniform by the Germans would be shot as a spy. Fielding had been told at SOE headquarters in Cairo that few Cretan men went about clean shaven, so he had tried to cultivate a mustache. But when he looked at himself in the mirror he thought the fringe that had appeared above his lip, combined with the threadbare clothing, "only succeeded in making me look like an unemployed Soho waiter."

Landing not just in winter but in the first winter of the occupation, when the Cretans' own resources were strained to the breaking point, Fielding received an abrupt initiation in the hardships of a spy's life on the island. In those early months he got used to living on next to nothing. Raisins, when he could get them, snails, and a kind of bread made from carob beans were his mainstays. Soon he learned to eat and sleep whenever there was an opportunity. You never knew when the next chance would come, though the Cretans were as hospitable as their own poverty would permit.

By summer the island had come to feel oddly like home. If anything felt like home to him. Fielding was born at a eucalyptus-shaded hill station in the Nilgiri Hills—Prince Peter's former stomping grounds in southern India—where his father was an officer in a Sikh regiment of the British Indian Army. His mother died giving birth to him, and Fielding grew up in France, where his grandparents lived. With his compact build, dark hair, and hooded eyes, he could still pass for a Frenchman. And before the war was over he would have to.

Now twenty-three, he still had a boyish look. But beyond the youthful demeanor Fielding was sturdy as iron. His arms, although thin, were corded with muscle. In the years before the war he had tramped his way across Europe, roughing it the whole way on almost no money. He slept in haylofts and ditches.

When he was lucky, he spent the odd night in what was for him the height of luxury—on a park bench.

He settled in British-ruled Cyprus, where he found a job as an editor on a local newspaper, but he soon realized he did not fit the imperial mold. In an atmosphere of colonial snobbery he rubbed his countrymen the wrong way by refusing to refer to the Cypriots as "Cyps"—"an absurdly pejorative term," he thought, "considering these people were members of a civilized society when we were still painting ourselves with woad." It did not help that he wrote articles decrying the mistreatment of Cypriot villagers. But Fielding was unpopular for other reasons too. "I had little money," he recalled, "and 'poor whites' are never welcome in British colonies." Worse still, he actually spoke Greek with the islanders and he was eager to soak up more of the language. His attitude eventually got him fired. By the time Britain entered the war, he was making a rough-and-ready living tending bar.

When he heard the news, Fielding's first thought was that the time had come to leave Cyprus. Not to enlist but to avoid being trapped on an island ruled by the same colonial mob that had ousted him from his newspaper job. "I might have made a decent escape by rushing home at once and joining up," he reasoned; "but even if I had felt a romantic inclination to do so, I could not afford the fare back to England." Instead he wound up on a minuscule island in the Bay of Khalkís—St. Nicholas—which was owned by an old friend of his, a frail Oxford-trained anthropologist who lived there alone, surviving on a diet of brandy and bread supplemented by a weekly dose of beef tea. Fielding recalled that this man had made a name for himself in 1925, when he discovered a fragment of Neanderthal cranium in a cave near the Sea of Galilee. But within a few years he had drifted away from anthropology, working for a while with a sexologist in Berlin before retreating to his island hermitage.

Fielding spent the first year of the war on the remote island. In the evenings the two men discussed the war news and Fielding wondered what to do about it. As BBC reports of Britain's early disasters came crackling across the radio, he felt flickers of guilt. But only flickers; he had trouble putting a human face on suffering that was taking place on such a massive scale. It all felt impersonal and somehow unreal. Conscience never overcame the disinclination he felt toward joining up. "I was not afraid of fighting," he maintained, "but I was appalled by the prospect of the army." The idea of enlisting triggered his "antisocial instinct." When Fielding's feelings wavered, his friend was the voice of dispassionate reason, stammering out, "But what good do you think *you* could possibly be?"

Finally, in August 1940, Fielding learned that the British military attaché in Athens was recruiting Greek-speaking officers. Maybe he could be of use after all. Before the month was out Fielding had received a commission. Not long after, he was back in Cyprus to take up a post in the First Cyprus Battalion, which was based in what had once been an American copper-mining camp thirty miles west of Nicosia. It was there, the next spring, that he heard about the invasion of Crete.

At first the fighting on the island held for him only the same abstract interest as the war news he had listened to in the first years of the conflict, which told of nameless units clashing with other nameless units. But by the time survivors of the battle began turning up on Cyprus, Fielding had started to see things differently. "Now, for the first time," he said, "I heard accounts of men fighting men and even, in several cases, of one man fighting another. This was a form of contest I could understand." He could picture the battle—the struggle for the Galatas heights or the chaotic withdrawal to Sphakia—in a way he had never before been able to envision the war. Most of all he was captivated by what the Cretans themselves had done. "Bearded men wielding breach-loading muskets or shotguns, barefoot children behind them carrying the outdated ammunition, hooded women in support with kitchen knives and broom-handles—the image of these people kept recurring."

Those images were still in his head a few weeks later when Fielding was offered an opportunity to work undercover in Crete. He leaped at the chance, partly to escape the claustrophobic life of the regular army but also to throw his lot in with those bearded men and hooded women who had come to inhabit his thoughts. By the middle of December, he found himself in Cairo, meeting with a man named Jack Smith-Hughes at the headquarters of the Special Operations Executive. Fielding had imagined the headquarters of an undercover operation would be hard to find, but it turned out that any taxi driver in Cairo could take you straight to what they had come to call "Secret House."

Smith-Hughes was an enormous man with a smooth, round face. He had been in charge of a field bakery on Crete at the time of the battle and been taken prisoner by the Germans. He eventually escaped from the prison at Galatas and was picked up ten weeks later by a submarine off the south coast. When he reached Egypt, he volunteered to return to Crete to help organize the resistance movement he had seen forming during his weeks on the run. He had just returned from his first tour there and was now head of SOE's Crete section. Fielding took all this in with interest as he sized up Smith-Hughes. With his thinning hair and sparse mustache he was not exactly dashing, but he had a quick-witted presence that Fielding attributed to his being a genuine secret agent, the first Fielding had ever met. He also had a notable ability to home in on the salient point, which may have come from studying law at Oxford before the war.

"Have you any personal objection to committing murder?" Smith-Hughes asked Fielding before the conversation had hardly begun.

If this unsettling question was meant to be a test, Fielding must have passed it. The next thing he knew, he was on his way to the Middle East Commando Depot for a course in sabotage. "For three days I was initiated into the mysteries of plastic high explosive, slow-burning fuses, detonators and primer-cord, and was given detailed instruction in the most effective method of blowing up a railway line," he recalled. "The knowledge that no railway existed in Crete did not dampen my immediate ardour for demolition work, and each morning I happily destroyed an increasingly longer stretch of the metals laid out for us to practise on in the desert around camp." Just after Christmas he was summoned back to Cairo, and less than a month later he was wading ashore on Crete.

Irregular warfare, Fielding discovered once he went into action, suited him just fine. If anything he found it too amusing. He rarely felt afraid in the field. But when he did, it was a giddy, almost manic sensation that washed over him. On one occasion, when an ill-planned nighttime landing shipwrecked him and two other men on an unfamiliar stretch of the island's south coast, not more than a few hundred yards from a German outpost, he knew he ought to have been breathless with caution. "We were in enemy country," he recalled, "and beyond that we had no idea of our whereabouts. But for fully two minutes we could not stop laughing. This mood of hysteria was only dispelled by the cold, which reminded us of the need for immediate action."

At times, though, it seemed that the bloodiest struggle during the early months of the Resistance was waged against an insidious enemy that certainly outnumbered the Germans on the island—lice. When he first tangled with these vermin, Fielding was awed by their numbers. On one occasion he pulled more than two hundred from his undershirt alone. After that, he recalled, "I lost count of them."

The other enemy was monotony, a hazard that came with the territory, since the SOE agents were often holed up in caves or shepherds' huts in the mountains for weeks on end. The only book in Fielding's camp was a volume of Shakespeare's sonnets on which the code he used for wireless transmissions was based. And talk did not offer much in the way of distraction

Xan Fielding sights a
Lee-Enfield rifle.
© *Imperial War Museum*
(HU 66049)

either. As much as Fielding liked and admired the Cretans who volunteered their services as guides and runners, he lamented the single-mindedness of their conversation. Now, he told himself, the journey to Gerakari to meet Dunbabin and this new officer promised an opportunity "to talk to people whose conversation was not limited to discussing the merits of one make of pistol compared with another or the advantages of rubber boot-soles over soles made of leather and other similar concerns."

Gerakari lay some twenty miles to the east on the flank of the Amari Valley, an area so pro-British and so fertile that SOE agents referred to it as "Lotus Land." When Fielding arrived there, he found that the cherry harvest was over—the region was known for its cherries—and the grapes were beginning to ripen. He made his way to the vintner's hut where he was to meet Dunbabin. There he was finally able to solve the mystery of "Mr. Leverman." Yianni had managed a reasonable approximation of the Englishman's name. The new officer Dunbabin introduced to Fielding was Paddy Leigh Fermor.

"To say that we were old friends was an exaggeration," Fielding realized, "though I had already met him once, for five minutes in a Bloomsbury café years before the war. Since then I had heard about him in various parts of the world." Fielding knew that Leigh Fermor had followed a path similar to his own. Now the two former vagabonds felt an immediate kinship. For his part Fielding was struck by the panache evident even through Leigh Fermor's disguise.

"Though we all wore patched breeches, tattered coats and down-at-heel boots, on him these looked as frivolous as fancy dress," Fielding thought. "His fair hair, eyebrows and moustache were dyed black, which only added to his carnivalesque appearance, and his conversation was appropriately as gay and as witty as though we had just met each other, not in a sordid little Cretan shack, but at some splendid ball in Paris." It was an effect Paddy cultivated.

In the vintner's hut that evening it was decided that Leigh Fermor would take over Fielding's area, allowing Fielding to return to Cairo for leave after more than six months on occupied Crete. Dunbabin would continue to monitor the Heraklion region. Fielding traveled straight back to his hideout to radio the plan to headquarters, and a few days later Leigh Fermor joined him there. He showed up carrying a liter of raki, so Fielding rounded up empty cigarette tins to serve as cups. After toasting the operation—"wishing success to the mission of the new arrival and fair winds for those about to depart"—Leigh Fermor and Fielding took the bottle to an outcropping and sat down in a pool of moonlight to work on the rest of the raki. Looking out over the valley, they talked about their travels and remembered mutual friends. For Fielding it was a relief to talk about something other than boots and pistols.

Nevertheless, it was also a good opportunity to exchange information about the mission. There was one audacious idea in particular that Fielding had been mulling over. What about kidnapping General Andrae and holding him hostage?

Waldemar Andrae was commandant of "Fortress Crete," as the Germans called the island garrison. From his headquarters in Chania he oversaw a particularly harsh occupation. Among other things, the British believed he was responsible for the execution of fifty hostages in Heraklion on June 14, in reprisal for a commando raid on the nearby airfield. Among the dead were

Leigh Fermor in civilian disguise on Crete.
© Imperial War Museum (HU 66084)

a former mayor of the city and the former governor of Crete. When General Andrae had made a tour of the rural southwestern corner of the island not long afterward, the notion had occurred to Fielding that it would be possible to hijack his staff car. With the general held hostage, the Germans would be hard pressed to carry out their usual round of reprisals. It was certainly a plan worth considering.

Leigh Fermor and Fielding talked through the night. As the moon moved across the sky, they inched along the outcrop to keep themselves in the moonlight. "By the time the raki was finished we had moved by successive stages almost the entire length of the shelving cliff," Fielding recalled, "and as I fell asleep on my narrow ledge of twigs I could not be sure whether it was the strong spirit, Paddy's company or the prospect of Egyptian fleshpots that was responsible for the happiest night I had so far spent in Crete."

THE NEXT DAY Leigh Fermor pressed on to Vaphes, some twenty miles to the northwest, not far from Suda Bay, where he was to await an airdrop of supplies. He felt uneasy because he had expected to take over Tom Dunbabin's area near Heraklion. Although it had been agreeable talking with Fielding about the Chania and Rethymnon area he was now to assume responsibility for, it was not a substitute for a full briefing. And Fielding's zone was known to be the more difficult and dangerous of the two. Fortunately, he had the next month to acclimate himself during what he came to think of as "a holiday between Tom's and Fielding's areas."

Leigh Fermor had sailed for Crete from Mersa Matruh on June 21, the same day, he would later learn, that Rommel's forces overran the British garrison at Tobruk. It took him nearly forty hours to reach Crete, traveling aboard a motor launch commanded by John Campbell, the *Hedgehog* skipper, who with

Mike Cumberlege, onetime commander of the *Dolphin*, now ran what amounted to the naval arm of SOE's Crete operation. When they put ashore on the south coast, Leigh Fermor was astonished to see nearly two hundred *andartes* waiting on the beach. To the radio operator traveling with him the crowd appeared "a motley rabble."

Once supplies from the launch were landed, the *andartes* led Leigh Fermor a mile or so inland to a cave that served as a staging area for landings. Here, over the next few days, he got to know some of the key figures in the Resistance. They included two of Pendlebury's former henchmen, the *andarte* leaders Manoli Bandouvas and Giorgos Petrakogiorgos, along with members of their respective gangs. In SOE jargon the two *kapetans* now bore the code names "Bo-Peep" and "Selfridge"— the one because of his extensive sheep holdings, the other for his success as a merchant. Bandouvas, in particular, seemed to be thriving in the role of rebel leader. Fielding had described him aptly: "a dark burly man with sad ox-eyes and a correspondingly deep-throated voice in which he was fond of uttering cataclysmic aphorisms such as 'The struggle needs blood, my lads.'"

When he had made arrangements for guides, Leigh Fermor struck out toward Mount Ida, where Tom Dunbabin was wait-

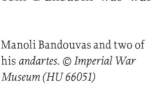

Manoli Bandouvas and two of his *andartes*. © *Imperial War Museum (HU 66051)*

ing. With a sturdy Cretan leading the way and carrying the new radio transmitter, it required four days of hard travel to reach the village of Platanos on the slopes of the mountain. The terrain itself made the going rough, and while traversing the exposed Mesara plain, the party crossed paths with a German motorcycle patrol, which they avoided by a hairbreadth. At last, on June 29, they arrived at Dunbabin's shelter in the hills above the village.

Like John Pendlebury, Tom Dunbabin was an accomplished archaeologist. In 1936, at the age of twenty-five, he became the assistant director of the British School of Archaeology in Athens. When the war broke out, he was employed by the British legation. Born in Tasmania, he had spent the better part of four years studying in Greece and could speak, read, and write Greek fluently. And having lived for parts of two years in Italy and traveled in Germany on holidays, he had a working knowledge of Italian and German, both languages that would come in handy on an island occupied by Germany in the west and central regions and Italy in the east.

At first glance it might have appeared that there was little else to recommend Dunbabin as a secret agent. Although he was in good health, he did not claim to be a ready-made soldier. In the interview intended to assess his suitability for assignment to SOE, he explained, in answer to the standard list of questions, that he did not shoot, box, ski, or ride a bike, though he had done some mountaineering and he could ride a horse. He professed no knowledge of wireless operation and could not transmit Morse. Nor could he yet drive a car, motorcycle, or truck, let alone sail a boat or fly an airplane. (There was no answer to whether there was "any coast you can 'smell out' in darkness with lights and buoys removed or altered.")

Even in the final assessment of his performance at Beaulieu, the SOE "finishing school" in Hampshire, the commandant, clearly unsure what to make of an "academical type," did not yet paint an altogether encouraging picture of a future spy. But he noted the quality that would in fact prove most important: "A very keen and penetrating mind."

Dunbabin had completed the Beaulieu course in September 1941. And in October he sailed from Britain for the Middle East. By the end of the year he was at the SOE training camp near Haifa, where he was given parachute training. The next April he was infiltrated by boat into Crete.

Once he was in the field, the reports on his performance, now highlighting his intelligence and resourcefulness, began to show just how well suited to the job Dunbabin actually was. "He has an excellent knowledge of Greek and physically is able to pass as either a Cretan or Greek," read one assessment. As the war progressed, his capability became still more evident. The man Leigh Fermor met was not the absentminded professor the officers at Beaulieu believed they had seen. He was certainly thoughtful but also cool and cheerful. The former academic had by now become the linchpin of SOE operations on Crete.

Leaving the radio operators behind to exchange information about their mission, Leigh Fermor and Dunbabin had made their way west to Gerakari, where they met Fielding on July 8. After those early encounters, Leigh Fermor was soon on his own. It was a hard life initially. "When I arrived the food situation was poor," he reported to headquarters in Cairo, "though I cannot claim ever to have gone seriously hungry." As the months went on, the situation improved. "In the summer one ate beans, lentils, tomatoes, potatoes, cheese and bread (sometimes scarce), meat sometimes, and oil. Now there is nearly everything one could wish, washed down by plenty of wine and *raki*, from a good vintage autumn."

The potentially touchy work of making contacts among the Cretans—to Leigh Fermor the most important requirement if he was to gather useful intelligence about the island—was made easier by his forerunner, John Pendlebury. When, one day that first year, he rode a bicycle past Pendlebury's grave disguised as a cattle dealer, he noticed that fresh flowers had been placed there, and as time went on, he saw that this was a daily occurrence. Wherever Leigh Fermor went, Cretans welcomed him as a comrade of Pendlebury's. "His memory turned all his old companions into immediate allies," Leigh Fermor sensed. "We were among friends, Pendlebury—Pedeboor—Penbury—however it was pronounced, eyes kindled at the sound."

The rugged landscape of the island presented challenges of its own. But Leigh Fermor was enthralled by what he saw around him. "Little in these crags and ravines had changed for centuries," he imagined. "One felt that each village must have existed in Minoan times." In the houses of the villagers he could discern the pattern of the lives they led. It was woven of subsistence and violence. "Onions, garlic and tomatoes hung from the cobwebbed beams; faded pictures of Venizelos"—the rebel whose uprising Leigh Fermor's cavalry friends had put down in 1935—"looked down from the walls and enlarged sepia photographs of turbaned grandsires armed to the teeth." Rifles and cartridge belts were as natural a part of the mountain villager's household as the hens scratching in the doorway.

The history of Crete under Turkish rule, Leigh Fermor came to learn, "was a sequence of insurrections, massacres, raids, pursuits and wars almost without break." But the tumultuous events of the past had only fortified the people's resolve. "However often these villages had been sacked and burned they were always built again," he reminded himself. One night Paddy found himself sitting on the flat roof of a small house, or *spiti*, in the mountain village of Anogeia. As he looked out at "the moonlit jigsaw of roofs and houses all around," he thought of Aristotle's notion that the capital city in a democracy should be no bigger than this—"cities small enough to hear the voice of one herald."

During the Turkish occupation Anogeia had been a center of rebellion. It had been destroyed in 1822, then rebuilt. When the Turkish army trapped a band of insurgents in the nearby monastery in 1866, the abbot ordered the rebels to set fire to the powder magazine, causing an explosion that, as the American consul at the time put it, "changed what was before but profit-less slaughter into a deed of heroism," killing some 450 of the assailing Turks in the explosion. Leigh Fermor could recall the story from a Swinburne poem. Now, though, he knew there was more to it than that. Incensed at having victory snatched away, the Turkish pasha had next turned on Anogeia and attacked the village. But this time the villagers had fought the Turks off, and here the village stood, he saw, on a pattern that Aristotle him-self would have recognized. At the time, Leigh Fermor could not guess that before the end of the war, the village would be utterly destroyed once again.

For the most part the SOE officers kept to the mountains to avoid endangering the villages that would gladly have shel-tered them. The accommodations were Spartan at best—"goat-folds and abandoned conical cheese-makers' huts and above all, in the myriad caverns that mercifully riddled the island's stiff spine." Even the caves came in different grades, however. "Some were too shallow to keep out the snow, others could house a Cyclops and all his flocks."

In this setting their only real companions were shepherds. These men were nothing like the pastoral figures in poetry, Leigh Fermor thought. They reminded him of wolves or eagles— "active, lean, spare, hawk-eyed men, with features scooped and chiselled by sun, wind, rain, snow and hail." Most of their lives were lived beyond the reach of the law, and some were outlaws in the more literal sense. Sheep rustling was not only common; it was looked on with a kind of pride. But however they might run afoul of the law, these were the best possible companions when the shooting started. "They are virtually weaned on powder and shot; every shepherd goes armed, and a worship of guns and great skill in handling them dominate the highlands." When it came to the Germans they were wary of reprisals aimed at their families, but they showed no fear whatsoever on their own account. Their long memory of earlier struggles turned the occupation into just another, if more terrible, battle they would eventually win. In one firelit cave after another he heard the same sentiment repeated. "Never fear, my child," he would catch some grizzled old mountaineer saying. "With Christ and the Virgin's help, we'll eat them."

LEIGH FERMOR SAW this fierce spirit in action on more than one occasion. Near the end of January 1943 it was to prove especially welcome. By this time he had been on the island for nearly seven months, largely on the move. He spent a good deal of his time accumulating intelligence about such matters as German troop movements and numbers, shipping traffic in the ports, and activity at the airfields, all of which offered clues about the enemy's plans on Crete as well as elsewhere in the Mediterranean. As he told headquarters, he was intent on "seeing as much of the Huns as I could, listening to their conversations, etc."

When the fighting in North Africa was at its peak, he had been eager to launch sabotage attacks against shipping in Suda Bay. "I feel that if I had managed to sink a few tankers last autumn it would have had tremendous point, and a strong influence on the desert battle," he wrote to Cairo. One impediment to that plan was the reluctance of the Cretan guerrillas to cooperate in sabotage. "Their hair stands on end the moment the word is pronounced," he reported. The Germans exacted too high a price in reprisals. "They won't play." Lack of time was another factor, since there were also airdrops to manage. These operations were usually at inconvenient locations that took days to reach, given the difficulty of traveling on foot through the mountains, and their timing was unpredictable due to the weather.

With outright sabotage off the table, Leigh Fermor put a subtler plan into action. Early in December he and Dunbabin began training a few of their Greek friends to chalk short slogans in German on the walls of garrison towns. The idea was to make it look like graffiti scrawled by disgruntled soldiers: "We want to go home. Down with Hitler! Where is our airforce? The Führer is swine!" Paddy himself laid it on thicker whenever the opportunity arose. "I always write up elaborate slogans in bold gothic type when I get a suitable place, and nobody is watching." He thought it might have done some good, and he proposed a similar campaign using leaflets that could be airdropped over the island. "Play on their homesickness and sentimentality," he advised headquarters.

So far, evading the enemy in the course of all these covert routines had not proved difficult.

By the end of December, the SOE operatives on the island felt relaxed enough to gather for a Christmas celebration at Gerakari. Before Leigh Fermor met up with Xan Fielding so they could travel together to the friendly village in Lotus Land, he spruced up for the occasion. When Fielding arrived with George Psychoundakis, the young villager from Asi Gonia who was now his guide and runner, he noticed the debonair twirl Paddy had given his mustache and the jaunty set of his black turban. He was especially envious of the new Cretan vest his friend wore—"of royal blue broadcloth lined with scarlet shot-silk and embroidered with arabesques of black braid." Leigh Fermor's panache seemed to be a symbol of the romantic attitude they both had toward their mission. "I, for example, affected to regard myself as the Master Spy," Fielding reflected, "the sinister figure behind the scenes controlling a vast network of minor agents who did all the dirty work. Paddy, obviously, scorned such an unobtrusive and unattractive part. He was the Man of Action, the gallant swashbuckler and giant-slayer, a figure who would be immortalized in marble busts and photogravure plates."

At Gerakari the festive mood gave the impression that caution was unnecessary. "Though it was now too cold to sing and dance out of doors," Fielding recalled, "the revelry was still of a peripatetic nature and we reeled happily from house to house eating and drinking with hosts who seemed as carefree as though no German had ever been heard of in Crete." When the party was over, he and Leigh Fermor set out for a village in the Rethymnon district, where they were to spend New Year's Eve. Drunk and ebullient, they felt little concern for the enemy.

Then, a few miles short of their destination, they encountered two German soldiers. Or Fielding did; Leigh Fermor had stepped behind a rock near the road to relieve himself. "Since I was in full view of them there was no question of avoiding an encounter," Fielding saw at once, "so I slowly continued on my way, hoping to get past them with a conventional Christmas greeting and a cheerful nod of the head."

But the two Germans, who had also been celebrating the holiday, were in the mood for sport. They prodded Fielding with questions. Where was he coming from and where was he headed? As he responded, Fielding was conscious of the weight of the Colt pistol he carried under his cloak. The Germans were not satisfied with his answers.

"You come with us—*schnell, schnell,*" one replied. "You no come, you kaput."

Despite what the man said, Fielding could see by their grins that the threat was not entirely serious. He thought he could defuse the crisis with humor. "It was easy for me to return their grin," he recalled, "for I was genuinely amused by their harmless behaviour, and my merriment increased at the thought of Paddy listening to this conversation as he squatted behind his rock, and at the sight of an old woman outside the nearest house repeatedly crossing herself as she witnessed the scene." Smiling all the while, he began sidling farther along the road. Finally the two men heaved a few rocks at him and turned aside. "With a final unconvincing cry of 'You kaput!' they proceeded on their way chortling with satisfaction, leaving me, also chortling, to continue on mine."

When Fielding and Leigh Fermor reached their host's house, they found it filled with German officers and NCOs from the garrison based nearby. After their encounter with the two bumbling soldiers on the road, they were feeling unassailable. They greeted their host, who was "sitting back contentedly puffing at a narghile." The man introduced Leigh Fermor and Fielding to his German guests as "my young friends from Sphakia" and encouraged the two disguised British agents to mingle with the gray-uniformed crowd. "They seemed so gullible and incapable of doing any harm," Fielding thought, "that we were almost tempted to drop our inhibitous disguise and enjoy the party openly under our own proper identity."

The next day, sad-eyed Yianni Tzangarakis, who was now Leigh Fermor's runner, showed up with a message from the nearby village where Paddy's radio station was set up. A German patrol of two or three hundred men had surrounded the village. Yianni, who was there at the time, had crept through the enemy cordon and made his way up to the SOE station to warn Leigh Fermor's radio operators. Together they managed to conceal the set and its batteries. Then Yianni kept a lookout while the operators escaped into the mountains. The villagers later hid the equipment in a deep cave, along with the set's bulky charging engine. But the radio operators were still missing. Even worse, the Germans had arrested the son of the village priest, a man code-named the Vicar, who had been steadfast in his assistance to the SOE agents. In the son's pockets the Germans had discovered two letters written by Leigh Fermor. It was a terrible outcome but one the priest had foreseen. "I am a poor man," the Vicar had said to Fielding on an earlier occasion, "so I can offer you little material assistance. But I have three sons, and all three will be sacrificed, if necessary, to the cause of Cretan liberty." A German column returned to the village in search of the Vicar the next day, only to find that he had disappeared into the hills.

The raid turned out to be the beginning of a concentrated effort on the part of the Germans to eliminate the British operation on Crete. Just days later they carried out a similar operation against Asi Gonia in an attempt to capture George Psychoundakis. The young runner—whose code name at the time was "Changebug," which had evolved from "Changeling," for his elfin agility and good humor—had been given leave to spend Christmas in his home village, and an informer tipped off the Germans to his presence there. He had left soon after the new year but returned after injuring his ankle and so happened to be at home on the day of the raid. Early in the morning his mother shook him awake.

"What is it?" he asked her.

"Germans, my child," she told him.

"Never mind, mother," the unflappable Psychoundakis said. "Don't you be afraid. You mustn't *look* frightened." He dressed quickly but found that he could not force a shoe onto the injured foot. The Germans entered the houses and forced the villagers into a line. George managed to get near the front, some forty yards ahead of the soldiers, and he slipped away. Two days later a party of twenty Gestapo arrived at the village asking for him.

Another German patrol swept through the villages in Lotus Land, including Gerakari, on the fifteenth. At each village they asked for members of Tom Dunbabin's crew by name. They managed to arrest his assistant, George Tyrakis, "who escaped," Dunbabin reported, "but was foolish enough to go straight home, where a German detachment was waiting for him. He is now under arrest in hospital." Tyrakis was quick to learn from his mistake. In the coming months he would transform himself into one of the most important members of the SOE force on Crete.

On January 25 Leigh Fermor was at the hideout called the Beehive near the village of Kyriakosellia, southeast of Chania, when three German columns totaling more than a hundred men swept up the valley toward his position. One of Paddy's men caught two bullets in the leg while fighting his way through the cordon. The man's cousin shot his way out with a pistol. The distraction gave Leigh Fermor and another SOE officer named Arthur Reade time to dash up the mountainside, but the radio set remained exposed if the Germans found the hut. As the patrol drew closer, Leigh Fermor and Reade were forced to climb into a cypress tree, from where they observed the proceedings. The Germans had compelled a Cretan to guide them to the hideout, but Leigh Fermor recognized the man as a friend and was relieved to see that he was leading the search party in the wrong direction. Finally the soldiers gave up, and Leigh Fermor watched as they "came streaming down again, all their disappointed comments, and grumbling at the rock climbing being music to us." Recounting the incident to headquarters in Cairo, he was reminded of the day in 1660 when the future Charles II of England had been forced to hide in an oak tree following the Battle of Worcester. In the diary of his movements for January, he gave the twenty-fifth the name by which Charles's escape had come to be known, "Oak Apple Day."

When the men regrouped after the German withdrawal, George Psychoundakis was nowhere to be found. "The Changebug did not reappear—it was snowing hard now—and after a day I took out a search party, without result," Leigh Fermor reported to headquarters. A few days later Psychoundakis turned up and Paddy learned what had happened. After slipping through the German noose, Psychoundakis had scrambled down the mountain but found the village he fled to in the foothills occupied by Germans. With night coming on, he finally fell asleep under his cloak. The next morning he awoke to find himself covered by the snow that had fallen in the hours before dawn. He stashed his submachine gun and binoculars in a crevice, pocketed his false identity card, and walked toward Suda and Chania with the idea of warning Xan Fielding of the German operations. After spending the next night in a cave, he reached the lowland village where Fielding had holed up with an injured foot earlier in the week.

Meanwhile, on February 4, Leigh Fermor and the others transferred the wireless set to a more secure location, because all the tramping they had done in the snow had made a visible path to their hideout. With a boat due to arrive soon, Paddy hurried to the Heraklion district to prepare for the landing. He told Fielding and Reade good-bye on February 6 and headed east with Yianni, Psychoundakis, and the priest whose son had been captured. Paddy had decided it was time to evacuate the Vicar and Changebug. The next day they were in Psychoundakis's village of Asi Gonia, which the agents called Stubborn Corner. On the ninth they rested in Gerakari. By February 10, a mild day that felt like spring, they had taken refuge in a cave above the sea, where they made contact with Tom Dunbabin, who was due to return to Cairo. "I am now in an elfin grotto in the Messara, Tom sleeping beside me," Leigh Fermor wrote sometime after midnight. "We were all soaked through last night in the hellish march through the dark. Odds and ends of Bo-Peep's and Self-ridge's gangs are fondling their guns as useful. It is very much the same atmosphere as when I arrived." Then, realizing it was now the eleventh, he added, "It is my twenty-eighth birthday."

BEFORE THE BOAT arrived on the fifteenth, Leigh Fermor added a note of commendation for the stalwart allies now departing for the Middle East. "Sancho," he wrote, referring to Yianni Tzangarakis, "and Changebug"—Psychoundakis—"have been the most indefatigable and loyal collaborators in their different spheres, all the months I have been on Crete. They have been on the jobs all the time without rest and deserve all the reward or consideration that can be shown them." The priest whose son had been captured by the Germans was also going home. "The Vicar has been loyal beyond praise," Leigh Fermor's message continued. "Housing, feeding and hiding the set, and backing us in every way he can for months. His son is in prison with a possibility of being shot on account of this, and half the village is in jail or on suspicion. The Huns beat up his wife and he has been living in the hills. He wanted to remain and see the thing out, but I got him out as he is too old for life in the hills. He is full of guts and as undaunted now as ever."

There was one more thing to mention before he closed his report, though Leigh Fermor did not yet know what to make of it. From the eastern end of the island he had heard rumblings to the effect that the commander of the Italian Siena Division based in the Lasithi district, General Angelo Carta, might be willing to surrender to the British. Lasithi, which lay over the mountains east of Heraklion and stretched to the eastern tip of the island, had seen relatively little action during the Battle of Crete. The occupation of the region by Italian troops had also been milder than that of the Germans elsewhere on the island. As a result the Lasithiots had thus far taken relatively little part in the Resistance. It was hard to know whether this information about General Carta, which had come through the Communist guerrilla organization the SOE agents called the Lollards, was credible. For now, Paddy labeled this information "Snappy Bit" and signed off.

CHAPTER 4

The Fishpond

WHEN THE BOAT sailing for North Africa with Tom Dunbabin, the Vicar, and the Changebug aboard chuffed out of earshot before dawn on February 16, Leigh Fermor and his remaining men scurried up from the beach with their rifles held at the ready. Between the thrumming of the vessel's engine, the flashing signal lights, and the boisterous voices of the Cretans, he felt certain the landing had been detected by the German coastal patrol. Reaching a cave in the hills above the coast just before dawn, the men settled in to wait out the daylight hours. They passed the time smoking Player's cigarettes and watching an oblivious pair of German soldiers—"squareheads"—hunting hares on a nearby hillside with the help of a yapping terrier.

Once the moon had risen that night, they struck out again. There was no one to be seen in the whole countryside other than one lone shepherd. Moving by night and holing up by day, the men made their way across the Messara plain and into the mountains beyond. Equipped as they were—"heavily armed as pirates," Leigh Fermor remarked—it was feared their movements would provoke a flurry of rumors about a guerrilla band traveling through the territory. So Leigh Fermor devised a ruse. When they approached a village, the men, speaking in turn, were to shout German phrases (learned by rote) in order to mimic a careless enemy column on the march. Each player was assigned a set part, to be repeated at every village. "The result was perfect," Leigh Fermor reflected. "Doors were closed, windows hastily shuttered, and lingerers in the street dashed for their houses, terrified of being caught out after curfew, then we clanked through unobserved."

It took several days, but the party finally reached Dunbabin's former headquarters, where Leigh Fermor settled in and began exploring the area he had now inherited from Dunbabin. With his former runner Yianni Tzangarakis on his way to Cairo, he had also taken on a new assistant, a wiry thirty-year-old from the rugged southwestern corner of the island named Manoli Paterakis. He had been a corporal in the Royal Greek Gendarmerie before the war but had resigned once the police force fell under German command. The whole Paterakis family—Manoli had five brothers—soon started taking in British stragglers, giving them food and shelter and helping them escape from the German-held island. Manoli's older brother Vasili had become the leader of a band of armed *andartes* who served as guards and sentries for Xan Fielding's operations. And in the fall of 1942 Manoli had lent such vital help to Dunbabin during a submarine landing that he had been recruited into the SOE ranks on the spot. Since the middle of December he had been a member of Dunbabin's staff, and he had proved himself quickly, working, as Dunbabin reported, "loyally and unwearyingly." He was admired for his discretion and sense of responsibility. Just as important under the circumstances, he was utterly fearless.

Leigh Fermor christened his new henchman "Manoli the Cop" or "Copper," and the two quickly grew to like each other. "He is a grand chap and ready for anything," Paddy decided. Before long he would come to think of Manoli as his "Man Friday."

Together they spent nearly a month exploring the new region. This Leigh Fermor found to his liking too. "Working in this area, after my former haunts," he concluded, "is like settling down to a Jane Austen novel." But to his mind the relaxed surroundings meant a greater scope for activity, not leisure. "Work in my present area is spying *de luxe*; and an atmosphere in which one can spread one's wings and really get something done."

Sabotage was now at the top of his to-do list. Throughout the spring, he scrambled to come up with a workable plan for disrupting German shipping traffic. This time he focused

Manoli Paterakis.
© *Imperial War Museum (HU 66057)*

his attention on Heraklion—"Babylon" in SOE code—but he knew the port there would be a tough nut to crack. Earlier in the year Dunbabin had investigated the options and turned up a list of obstacles. First, there was no practical spot from which to launch a boat along the rocky coast to the east and west of Heraklion, and if a band of Greek and British saboteurs did somehow reach the mouth of the harbor by sea, they would find their entry blocked by a boom. It was clear that a mission against the harbor would be forced to approach by land, but this posed its own difficulties.

Dunbabin found that the harbor was accessible on foot at only one point, and even here the route down from the nearby town hall was nearly impassable. The first obstruction was a double-apron fence the Germans had thrown up to block the way. This tangle of razor wire and pickets was patrolled by sentries whose movements were coordinated to leave no part of the wire unobserved at any time. Dunbabin's agent in the area had observed the guards closely enough to recognize that, while German morale had fallen to a low point and discipline was generally lax among the ten thousand enemy soldiers stationed in the Heraklion zone, security at the harbor itself was no slapdash operation. As Dunbabin told headquarters in February, "they do not meet and stop for a cigarette."

If a sabotage party managed to make its way past the sentries and through the German wire, there was still a four-hundred-yard swim to reach the main shipping facilities. All in all, there was not much to recommend such a mission, and the Resistance leader whom Dunbabin consulted flat-out refused to help for fear of German retaliation.

"I think the chance of success is less than 50%," Dunbabin concluded, "and if it were discovered that the job was being done from inside the enemy reprisals would be on a scale to discourage any further activity."

Still, the Heraklion mission was tempting. Leigh Fermor had learned that loaded ships remained in the harbor at night. "The larger vessels withdraw to the northern edge of the harbour, and the smaller ones and the armoured ships remain alongside the jetty. A searchlight plays all round the harbour, jetties and warehouses at fairly regular intervals," he noted.

In early March, he and Manoli ventured into the city to have a good look around. Paddy got himself up as a shepherd, with his eyebrows and mustache blackened with burned cork. He put on tall boots and a splendid cloak. It was a warm day, however, and he was disappointed when the rising temperature forced him to remove the cloak.

Slipping in through a gate in the Venetian-era wall that surrounded the city, they found Heraklion thronged with visitors who had come in from the surrounding countryside for the Orthodox carnival, which was just ending. It occurred to Leigh

Fermor that with the celebration under way he might have wandered through the city just as freely wearing a funny hat and a false nose.

A Greek agent, code-named Tweedledee, led the two disguised spies through the labyrinth of streets, then turned down a lane that led to his house. "Once inside, we all heaved a sigh, shook hands and burst out laughing. It was a great moment," Leigh Fermor later reported to headquarters. Exhausted, they slept until nightfall and then spent the evening eating and drinking with other members of SOE's Heraklion network—"a huge spread was waiting, with gallons of wine." Leigh Fermor stayed in Heraklion for eight days, often meeting with Resistance leaders during the day and sometimes long into the evening. He kept his ears open even in the relative safety of Tweedledee's house. "There were Huns billeted in the houses on either side, drunk all the time, and you could hear nearly everything they said." In the evenings he corked his mustache and strolled through the city, investigated German defenses, and walked down to look around the harbor.

"When the time came to go," he reported to Cairo, "I borrowed a raincoat and a wonderful velvet trilby and bicycled out of town with Tweedledum." This was Tweedledee's cousin, also an SOE collaborator. "I looked the image of a spy—just like the ones in the Careless Talk poster, I thought—but then, so do all Babylonians." Peddling a bike festooned with a tin swastika, Leigh Fermor sped out through the Venetian gate. Another SOE agent posted near the gate to see that everything went smoothly shot him an exaggerated wink as he cycled past.

Now that he had properly scouted the area, he decided that it might after all be feasible to enter the harbor undetected and attach limpet mines to the vessels anchored there. In April he wrote to Cairo describing his plan as if he were mounting a fishing excursion. "I do not want to discuss this in too much detail for obvious reasons," he began. "But after a personal recce of the fish pond there seems to be a sporting chance of landing a couple of fish. Access can be gained by a rope ladder tied to a telegraph pole on a bastion above the pond. There is a difficult open stretch after this, with two Nasties on piquet to be dodged, till the water is reached, and for this reason, a moonless night is essential." The "Nasties" were the two sentries Dunbabin had noted. "The operation is made more difficult because the fish we are after have recently adopted the habit of swimming to the northern end of the pool at night, which means a swim of two kilometres for us, half of it with the limpets," he continued. "But it seems worth trying, and I intend to try it."

Meanwhile there were endless negotiations to be carried out between the various guerrilla factions. One result was that Manoli Bandouvas had to be placated with an official title. Leigh Fermor, privately enjoying the aptness of the literal meaning of the military term for guerrilla fighters, bestowed on him the rank of "Chief of Francs-Tireurs" in the Heraklion region— "commander of the free shooters." Bo-Peep, not entirely satisfied, expanded his new position to cover the whole of Crete.

For all his courage and patriotism, Bandouvas—who was equally unpredictable and power hungry—had become a liability, in Tom Dunbabin's view. Before he departed, Dunbabin had tried to lure the *kapetan* to Cairo, saying that his advice was sorely needed at headquarters. But Bandouvas, surrounded by his men and other *andarte* leaders, had refused to take the bait. "Crete must be set free from inside not only from outside," he argued. "The battlefield is here. My place is here. Don't you agree, gentlemen?"

Unlike Dunbabin, Leigh Fermor viewed Bandouvas as an asset. "He is the most admired man in Crete, and the only name that is universally known," he wrote to Cairo. "He is worth ten of Selfridge. He wants arms, and deserves them. I told him I would use my weight to obtain them, by drop." Grenades, Sten guns, and pistols were on Bo-Peep's wish list. Leigh Fermor urged Cairo to give the matter real consideration. Selfridge, meanwhile, had transferred his loyalty to the United States and had been putting it about that the Americans had promised him four tons of supplies.

At the beginning of May, while he was still in the Heraklion area, a German patrol raided Leigh Fermor's headquarters, which was now situated at the head of a ravine above Agios Ioannes, some forty-five miles south of Heraklion. They captured some radio parts and a battery, along with a jumble of domestic utensils. More compromising, they found two exercise books filled with writing. One contained figures for German troop distributions in the Heraklion district. In the other Paddy had been writing poetry, both his own, in English, and other pieces from memory, in Romanian, Greek, and German. There were also sketches—one "of an imaginary Cretan mountaineer, bristling with weapons"—and "comic drawings of British military life."

The raid presented a setback, but preparations for the harbor mission continued. Leigh Fermor bicycled back into Heraklion to make the final arrangements. While staying with friends of Manoli's in an apartment above a café, he drew on various contacts to acquire the necessary fuses and he arranged for the limpet mines—awkward bowler-hat-shaped explosive devices he and Manoli would eventually have to swim across the harbor—to be smuggled into the city by donkey. To serve as a storage and staging area, he leased a house near the harbor. It appeared that everything was set for the mission.

It was unclear, however, just when headquarters in Cairo wished to launch the operation. The signal Leigh Fermor received called for the fifth of July, but since such missions generally took place at night, it was customary to specify which night.

"The fifth" might mean the night of either the fourth/fifth or the fifth/sixth. And since he had just learned that other operations were timed to coordinate with his, he knew the scheduling was crucial. At the last minute he got word to go on the night of the fourth, and he struck out toward the harbor with Manoli and Micky Akoumianakis, a Heraklion-based agent who was called Minoan Mike, a code name that pointed back to his childhood. Mike's father had been Arthur Evans's overseer at the Knossos excavations, where the ancient Minoan civilization had first come to light, and had become John Pendlebury's right-hand man prior to the invasion. Mike had grown up literally next door to the palace of Minos. His father had been killed during the Battle of Crete, while Mike was himself fighting in Albania with the Cretan Division. Mike still remembered Pendlebury as a larger-than-life figure, who "could drink everyone under the table and then stride across three mountain ranges without turning a hair." Leigh Fermor knew the older Akoumianakis's reputation as Pendlebury's most loyal ally, and Minoan Mike was already proving himself "a splendid chap."

The three men reached the harbor and penetrated the outer ring of German defenses. From here it was necessary to crawl the remaining distance to the quay. They had not made it far when they ran into an unexpected barrier formed by the rubble of destroyed aircraft. This proved to be a bigger problem than the razor wire; "over under or through there was no crawling without raising a terrific clatter of tin that set the sentries on the move." At this point Minoan Mike was forced to withdraw, leaving Leigh Fermor and Manoli to carry out the mission on their own.

"The cop and I spent the rest of the night trying to find a way through, creeping at a snail's pace behind the sentries using what cover we could. But there was no way through from there without killing the two of them, which would have made our retreat impossible," Leigh Fermor recalled. As the night wore on, the sentries passed closer and closer to their position. At one point there was a guard three yards to one side, while the other crossed ten yards to the other side. Both were playing their flashlights around. For two hours Leigh Fermor and Manoli remained frozen where they lay, waiting for an opportunity to dash into the sea. But it never came. With dawn coming, they were forced to pull back. "I'm sorry about this," he wrote to Cairo, "but we had a damn good try."

The next morning the frustrated saboteurs found the household above the café in a panic, along with the rest of the town. The other operations scheduled for that night, which had been planned by Cairo without input from the officers on Crete, had already elicited German reprisals. Leigh Fermor and Manoli escaped from Heraklion just as the enemy began making arrests. In all, some fifty civilians were taken. "Shooting," Leigh Fermor reported to Cairo, "started next day."

IN FACT, REPRISALS were under way all along the northern coast. Leigh Fermor's sabotage mission had been timed to coincide with three raids carried out by a special-forces arm of the Royal Navy known as the Special Boat Section. The SBS commandos came ashore by motor launch on June 23 and fanned out in three parties, two making their way toward Heraklion and the airfield at nearby Kastelli, while a third sped toward the Tymbaki airfield, some forty miles away on the south coast. On the night of Leigh Fermor's Heraklion harbor escapade, the commandos also struck their targets. At Kastelli an SBS lieutenant, posing as a German officer, had penetrated the security perimeter of the airfield and killed four German sentries while his men destroyed several of the aircraft based there.

The most spectacular of these raids was led by a twenty-three-year-old lieutenant named Kenneth Lamonby. A good-humored, pipe-smoking Suffolk lad, Lamonby had been directed to sabotage the Heraklion airfield. But when he discussed his plan with the Cretan guide provided by SOE, he learned that the Germans no longer made much use of that facility, due mostly to damage inflicted by Allied raids the previous year. Lamonby then set his sights on the fuel depot at Peza, a village south of the city along the Archanes road.

When Lamonby and his men reached Peza around eleven o'clock that night, they found a stockpile of around fifty sixty-gallon barrels. Lamonby sent one of his men into the dump along with a Greek guide. There they placed bombs under two of the barrels and set time pencils to detonate shortly after 1:00 a.m. When the two men climbed back up from the dump, Lamonby attempted to breach the wire protecting a nearby bomb depot but found there was no practicable way through the barrier in the time they had remaining. Meanwhile, their guide had placed a Union Jack at the fuel dump to forestall reprisals against Cretan civilians.

By one o'clock the unit had withdrawn from the area, and at 1:10 they heard the bombs explode, starting a fire that, it was later learned, destroyed several thousand gallons of aviation fuel. Lamonby and his unit spent that night in a bat-filled cave in the mountains above the dump and the next morning struck out on the thirty-mile march back to the beach where they were to be picked up by motor launch. Several days later Lamonby signaled the other SBS raiders, warning of enemy patrols along the coast. Then nothing from him. Finally, on the night before their withdrawal from Crete, he and his unit surfaced and rejoined the other raiding parties at a cave near the appointed beach.

While waiting out the daylight hours the following day, Lamonby and the others drank sweet, milky tea and ate porridge and crackers with cheese. The talk was all about the mission they had nearly completed. Conversation gradually subsided and the men dozed through the afternoon. Around eight o'clock that evening a lookout spotted two Germans approaching up an adjacent gully. While Lamonby and his men held back their Cretan allies, who were all too eager for a fight, the other commandos quickly surrounded the two Germans and took them prisoner. Just then, someone spotted a second pair of enemy soldiers. This time the Cretans opened fire, and the Germans fled toward the beach with a dozen or so Cretans in hot pursuit. For more than half an hour small-arms fire echoed up the gully.

At a quarter to nine, Lamonby was sent down the gully with a handful of men to put a stop to the racket, which was likely to draw the attention of other German patrols in the area. He quickly brought the Cretan fighters under control and sent the men back up the gully, apparently intending to pursue the Germans on his own. This was the last anyone saw of him. When Lamonby had not returned by the time the SBS units were scheduled to move onto the beach, a patrol went out to look for him, with no success.

Just after midnight the engines of the motor launch were heard offshore. Less than an hour later the commandos were embarked. The unit's commander asked the skipper of the motor launch to bring the vessel in close to the mouth of the gully, but still there was no sign of Lamonby, and his comrades feared the worst. "The fact that he could not make the re-embarkation beach and we could not find his body is a bad sign," remarked the lieutenant who had led the Kastelli raid. "I think he has been wounded and taken away by the Germans for interrogation."

Confirmation soon made its way through Leigh Fermor's intelligence network. Writing in haste some weeks later, Leigh Fermor passed the report along to Cairo. "I'm afraid there is no doubt about Lamonby's death," he wrote. "The description fits him perfectly." The episode was a reminder that covert work on Crete was more deadly than it sometimes appeared. For the families of the Cretans who were executed following the sabotage, it was an unwanted lesson. Leigh Fermor wondered if the results of the missions could possibly outweigh their civilian costs. "I hope the service of this activity to our general strategy has been high," he wrote to headquarters, "because here it has caused much havoc to morale and caused much anti-British feeling."

CHAPTER 5

Spaghetti and Ravioli

IN THE WEEK following the disappointing sabotage effort in Heraklion, Leigh Fermor and Manoli made their way toward a hideout code-named Holy Friday, near Agia Paraskevi, on the far side of the Lotus Land of Amari. Here in the relative safety of the rugged southwestern coast they rejoined Harry Brooke, the wireless operator, and Tom's aide-de-camp, Nikos Souris. Once they had settled in, Leigh Fermor busied himself making arrangements to meet the supply boat that was scheduled to arrive the night of July 11. But he was preoccupied with a problem that had surfaced back in the spring, when the leader of the local Communist militia had reported that the commander of the Italian Siena Division, which occupied the eastern end of the island, might be willing to surrender to the British.

When he first got wind of the rumor, Leigh Fermor had been unsure what to make of it. Then, around the same time, he had overheard an Italian soldier in Heraklion giving vent to a sentiment that seemed to be spreading among his countrymen stationed on Crete. "Don't you think because we didn't fight in Albania, that Italians can't fight," the young man said. "You wait and see how we fight the Germans!" When the disgruntled soldier had drunk a little more wine, he went so far as to shout, *"Viva Inghilterra!"*

"Italian nonsense," Leigh Fermor had thought at the time, but he had kept his ears open in case the incident signaled a change in the weather in the Axis camp. Now it was clear that conflict between the two Axis allies was on the upswing. Just a month earlier an Italian soldier had tossed a hand grenade into a group of three Germans and killed one of them. The other two were wounded. "The German authorities complained," Leigh Fermor recalled, and the Italian soldier had been run through a court-martial proceeding and thrown into prison. But it had all been a show for the Germans, he believed, and the man was soon released.

He knew that the growing tension in the Axis camp had ramifications in particular for the Lasithi district, where the occupying force was commanded by General Angelo Carta, the subject of the earlier rumor. The easternmost of the island's four provinces, Lasithi was not yet a hotbed of resistance. In fact, many of the British officers in Crete were of the opinion that the Lasithiots lacked the pugnacious spirit common elsewhere on the island. Whether this might be due to their relative wealth or to the relatively milder Italian occupation was a matter of opinion.

Nonetheless, Leigh Fermor believed that the Lasithi region itself would prove important. Its southern port city of Ierápetra was situated at the point where the island narrowed to its smallest north-south dimension, and the nearby beaches on both coasts were suitable for landings. Northwest of Ierápetra lay a stretch of dry salt flats where aircraft could be landed. From Leigh Fermor's reconnaissance it was clear that the Axis commanders in Crete believed this area to be the most vulnerable spot on the island for an Allied invasion. They had thrown their full weight into defending the area. Leigh Fermor had not heard of anti-invasion measures on a similar scale anywhere else in Crete.

For the moment, he put the question aside and hurried off

to meet the boat from North Africa. A week or two later, he struck out on a reconnaissance mission to find a suitable landing beach for Tom Dunbabin's return to the island, which was planned for the next moonless night. He had made it as far as Gerakari, above the Amari Valley, when a runner intercepted him with a message from Minoan Mike, his right-hand man in Heraklion. According to Mike, the unrest among the Italians had surged to new levels in the wake of Mussolini's fall on July 25. Italian soldiers had been seen stripping off their black uniform shirts and tearing down portraits of the Duce.

General Carta's intelligence officer, Lieutenant Franco Tavana, had begun making overtures to the Cretans and their British allies. Leigh Fermor reported this initial contact to Cairo using typically irreverent code names for the Italian commander and his staff officer. "Ravioli," he wrote, "sent out Lieut. Spaghetti to approach leading Cretans in the provinces." What Carta was desperate to learn was how the British would respond if the Germans turned their weapons on the Italians in Lasithi, and how the Italians would be handled in the event of a British invasion of the island.

Leigh Fermor learned that Lieutenant Tavana had first approached a priest in Neapolis, the town where the Italians had their headquarters, asking to be put in touch with a British officer. But the priest, who in fact *was* an SOE agent, merely threw up his hands, professing to be interested only in "spiritual matters." Eventually Tavana made contact with a prominent figure in Heraklion, a surgeon who had recently begun working with the British, and through this man he was put in touch with Minoan Mike. Neither Mike nor the surgeon—who was called Leonidas, after the Spartan king who died in a daring last stand against Xerxes at Thermopylae—admitted to having any connection with British agents on the island, but they suggested that Tavana put anything he had to say in writing.

The letter, written in halting French, the one language the two men had in common, laid out the situation as the Italians saw it. With Italy's government in flux and the prospect of an Italian withdrawal from the war on the horizon, the Germans on Crete appeared to be preparing to attack their former allies. "We are ready to defend ourselves with great force," Tavana wrote. But he admitted that the Italian garrison had little chance of defeating the German forces in a protracted fight. "We could defend ourselves for two or three weeks."

Tavana implied that he had already secured some promise of help from the Cretans. But he feared the reprisals such a move would almost certainly bring. He sought assurance from Leigh Fermor that the British would step in if the Germans launched an attack against Lasithi, "because the Greeks can give us but a few men, in which case it would be bad for all the Cretans, because the Germans are stronger and they will defeat us and then they will do evil things against the Greeks." In return for British assistance, Tavana promised that, "*in the name of my general commanding the Italian troops*," the Italians would defend the island until the end of the war. This was to be an agreement between soldiers, he made clear, and in no way did his letter bind the Italian government in Rome. "If the Germans don't attack us quickly," he concluded, "we can make other agreements."

"Spaghetti was in a very nervous and distressed state," Leigh Fermor learned from the runner, "and said that the Italian troops would undergo any sacrifice rather than surrender their arms to the Huns, whom he cursed by every name under the sun." Tavana's demeanor had quickly convinced Minoan Mike and the others that the man was sincere.

In a second meeting at Neapolis they agreed to put him in touch with a British officer. Tavana was elated to have finally made contact. He wished to arrange a tête-à-tête right away, he told Mike. He would send a staff car for his British counterpart whenever he wished and would have him driven directly to Neapolis to meet with General Carta. Tavana would even provide an Italian uniform as a disguise.

MUCH OF THE INTELLIGENCE Leigh Fermor had been able to dig up on Franco Tavana appeared to support Mike's intuition. "He is a very Latin and nervy Italian; well educated and polished, and hates the Germans with a deadly hate." He was by profession a lawyer, the son of a respectable family from Syracuse. He had served in Albania and had been General Carta's intelligence officer since the Italians arrived on Crete. "He is also one for the girls," Leigh Fermor learned, "like all the Italians in Lasithi, without exception." These details Paddy sent to Cairo under the heading "Social Snippets."

He also suspected there was more to the story. Among the Cretans in Lasithi, opinions regarding Tavana were "mixed." It was widely held, on the one hand, that the Italian officer had protected a good many Cretans. When the German command handed down death sentences against Lasithi residents, Tavana staged "dummy executions and filled in empty graves." At the same time there were darker rumors, none of them entirely substantiated. "There is a tale of three men found dead under a pile of stones in Seteia," Leigh Fermor wrote to Cairo, "but no public blemish."

Despite these "one or two dark patches" in the Italian's résumé, Leigh Fermor shared Minoan Mike's inclination to trust Tavana. At the very least it was worth taking some risk to speak with him. He sent a runner back to his wireless station with a message telling Harry Brooke, the wireless operator, to move the set to Bandouvas's hideout in the Lasithi mountains. This was the one spot he could think of that would put the radio station close to the events unfolding in the Italian-held province.

The following day Minoan Mike, having wisely decided that an Italian staff car would attract undue attention in the remote Amari Valley, showed up in a taxi, with the surgeon he had met with in Heraklion, to pick Paddy up. Accompanied by Manoli and Mike's sister—a fellow SOE supporter known, predictably, as Minoan Minnie—they left immediately for Heraklion. The party had not driven far when they spotted a pair of German soldiers standing alongside the road. As the car drew closer, they waved for it to halt. All four passengers stiffened as the driver brought the vehicle to a stop. The German soldiers motioned to have the door opened. Leigh Fermor held his breath a moment, waiting to see which way this would go. Then, one after the other, the two men climbed in. It seemed they simply wanted a lift back to their base near Heraklion. "We took them to their barracks, exchanged cigarettes and bright chat, and drove on," Leigh Fermor told Cairo.

From Heraklion they drove south again to Knossos, where they spent the night in the house where Mike had grown up. This had once been John Pendlebury's home too, Leigh Fermor recalled. Now the German commander of Heraklion province, General Friedrich-Wilhelm Müller, had moved into the Villa Ariadne, the house Arthur Evans had built for himself adjacent to the famous archaeological site. Paddy and Mike bedded down for the night literally next door to the enemy commander's residence. The next morning Leigh Fermor received a communication from Cairo. Headquarters had decided that he should ask Carta to provide the British with bombing targets to ensure the destruction of key facilities if the Germans were to launch an offensive against Lasithi.

Leigh Fermor sent Mike out to telephone Tavana in Neapolis. He then borrowed a bicycle and pedaled the three or four miles into Heraklion, where an SOE collaborator known as Dr. Cross, a dentist from George Psychoundakis's town of Asi Gonia, was to put him up until Tavana's arrival.

When he reached Dr. Cross's house, Leigh Fermor settled in to wait for Tavana. Feeling ragged and dirty after a month in the mountains, he took advantage of the rare opportunity to have his clothes cleaned and ironed. An hour before the lieutenant was due to arrive, Paddy was lying on the sofa reading in a pair of crimson silk pajamas and crocodile slippers, when he heard a knock at the door.

Moments later Minoan Mike, who had apparently mistaken the time, escorted a slender, dark-haired man into the sitting room. As Leigh Fermor rose to greet Tavana, whatever embarrassment he felt about his unusual attire quickly evaporated. The lieutenant was a pleasant-looking man and his demeanor was amiable. But he was himself dressed very oddly, Paddy saw. He wore "the strangest of plain clothes—no stockings, sandals, green corduroy shorts and a sort of polo vest." For an awkward moment no one spoke; then, as the rival intelligence officers stood looking at each other—one in flamboyant short pants and the other in silk pajamas—both began to laugh.

It was a propitious start, and the two men were soon on friendly terms. But the meeting did not progress as Leigh Fermor had hoped. Once the preliminaries were out of the way, he explained to Tavana that he needed to meet with Carta himself as soon as possible. His headquarters, Leigh Fermor explained, wished him to deliver a message to the general. Such a meeting, Tavana avowed, was now unlikely. Much had changed since he had written his initial list of proposals.

Tavana handed over a note from General Carta that alluded to the recent developments. It was written in Italian, and Tavana explained what it said. A German attack had become much less likely, Carta now believed. If a German attack did come, then the Italian troops would think only of saving themselves . . . and of course their honor.

Tavana explained that Mussolini's fall had thrown Carta into a panic. At the end of July he had believed that the Germans would attack at any minute. In the intervening days, however, he had been reassured by a visit from the German commander, General Bräuer, who had flown to Neapolis to meet with Carta, "kissed him on both cheeks," and convinced him that there was nothing to worry about at the moment. What would happen if the Italian government surrendered was anyone's guess. Tavana believed a German attack was sure to come eventually. Leigh Fermor offered some strategic advice. When the Germans did make their move, he said, the Italians should block the entry of vehicles and artillery into Lasithi by sealing off the Salinari pass between Malia and Neapolis, through which the only usable road ran. The only other routes into the province followed goat tracks over the mountains. "This struck him as a good idea," Leigh Fermor reported to headquarters, "and he said he would put it to Ravioli." They agreed to meet in two days. The plan was for Tavana to pick Leigh Fermor up at the surgery clinic on the main street in Heraklion and drive him to Neapolis, where both hoped Carta might agree to meet with him.

When the appointed day rolled around, Leigh Fermor arrived at the clinic early. He was already there—with Minoan Mike, Dr. Leonidas the surgeon, and Dr. Cross the dentist—when Tavana turned up as planned, dressed this time in run-of-the-mill civilian clothes. Leigh Fermor noticed right away that he looked "disappointed and apologetic." In the privacy of the clinic Tavana explained that Carta had "lost his nerve at the last minute." The general had decided not to meet with Leigh Fermor. Once again Tavana produced a note from his superior. "I am bound by military honor to remain faithful to the alliance with Germany until they make an unfriendly movement,"

Carta now wrote. "When that happens, I would gladly accept British help, though I do not, of course, ask for it." His message went on to advise the Cretans to stay out of any fighting that might erupt between the Italians and Germans. The probability of German reprisals outweighed any real assistance they could offer.

Tavana was clearly frustrated by General Carta's timidity, and Leigh Fermor made an effort to reassure him. It was understandable that Carta should waver, he said. Under the circumstances, the general's position was a "delicate" one. Despite Carta's irresolute handling of the situation, Leigh Fermor told Tavana, he had himself put the *andarte* leaders in Lasithi on notice that the Italians were not to be attacked under any circumstances. (This was easier said than done, since Bandouvas—Bo-Peep—had let it be known that he was itching to get hold of the Italians' weapons, by whatever means necessary.) For his part, Tavana intimated unofficially that Italian units would do nothing substantial to oppose a British landing on the island. He also pledged not to interfere with the British organization of resistance in Lasithi and went so far as to say that if Leigh Fermor himself was ever captured by Italian authorities, he would personally secure his immediate release.

As the meeting came to an end, Leigh Fermor produced a bottle of raki and offered a toast "to liberty and peace." The important thing, he stressed, was that the British and Italians were returning to friendly terms now that Mussolini's regime had been ousted. The others present agreed, and someone pointed out that the Italian occupation of Lasithi had been humane, particularly in comparison with the brutality of the Germans. "Spaghetti nearly wept," Paddy noted. "It was all rather touching and absurd."

When Tavana rose to leave, he took Leigh Fermor by the hand and held the handshake for an awkwardly long moment.

It was evident that he had reached some private resolution, though he spoke in a reserved manner, as if inhibited by the others present. "Oh, mon Capitaine," he said by way of farewell, "we have so very many things to tell one another, but alas! this is neither the time nor the place." He sounded like a man teetering on a precipice. Leigh Fermor believed that if he could spend some time with Tavana alone, the Italian lieutenant would open up completely. "I am planning another meeting in some sheep-fold in the mountains," he wrote to Cairo, "with a roast lamb and a couple of magnums of Bollinger from Gen. Muller's cellar, where we can talk all night and I am sure that I can learn a great many things we want to know."

THE TURBULENT SITUATION in the Aegean was making ripples at the highest levels of British command. In London, Winston Churchill made it known that British forces must "be ready to take advantage of any Italian landslide." With respect to Crete this meant providing assistance "at the earliest moment" if the Italian garrison elected to rebel against German control of the island. It was less clear precisely what form this assistance might take. On August 2 the prime minister put his chief staff officer on alert. "This is no time for conventional establishments, but rather for using whatever fighting elements there are."

At the moment it was Manoli Bandouvas—the Resistance leader known as Bo-Peep—who commanded the largest fighting element the British could possibly mobilize against the enemy forces on the island. By the estimate Tavana had made in passing, there were currently some forty-five thousand German troops on Crete, staring down thirty-two thousand Italians. Bandouvas claimed he could call up a force of several thousand men at short notice. At best, the *andartes* would be jumping into a lopsided fight if it came to that. Worse still, Bandouvas's men were poorly armed in comparison with the Germans. Nonetheless, Bo-Peep had more will to fight than anyone else on the island, and his extravagant patriotism had captured the imagination of his countrymen. Cretans were unfailingly loyal to him, and to Leigh Fermor's mind he had also earned whatever support the British could give him.

By the middle of August he was making ready for an operation that would significantly boost the firepower of Bandouvas's band. In the days following their last meeting with Tavana, Leigh Fermor and Minoan Mike had been busy. Operating out of Mike's house near the Villa Ariadne, they had held a secret meeting with the driver assigned to the German commander, General Müller. Applying a judicious mix of cajolery and out-and-out bribery, they had persuaded the man to drive Leigh Fermor, who was posing as a wealthy sheep merchant, to the area of Bandouvas's mountain camp, where two of Leigh Fermor's men were already waiting. The driver had agreed, and all seemed to be settled. On the morning of the twelfth, however, just as the party was preparing to depart, Müller himself arrived at the villa, and the erstwhile sheep merchant was relegated to travel by taxi.

That afternoon the taxi let Leigh Fermor and Manoli Paterakis out at a point below Bo-Peep's camp where the terrain became impassible to vehicles. For two hours that evening they trudged up into the mountains. When nightfall came, they took shelter in a sheepfold. At first light they climbed on. Three hours later they were nearing the highest ridgeline of the Lasithi mountains. From here the view was endless. Leigh Fermor had paused to survey the province, which looked like a map laid out far below, when a dozen armed toughs appeared. For a moment there was confusion. Then it became clear that these were Bandouvas's sentries.

Under the protection of this band of guerrillas, the men pushed on and soon reached a stony rise dotted with huts woven from branches and straw, much like the wigwams of the nomadic Sarakatsani shepherds Leigh Fermor had encountered on his trek across Europe in the 1930s. There was a great deal of activity, and as they drew closer, they saw what amounted to an entire makeshift village huddled around an outsized ilex tree. Bandouvas himself was ensconced beneath the tree like an old-time patriarch, sharing a meal with a band of men who numbered somewhere over a hundred. Leigh Fermor was struck by how many types were represented. He recognized a priest and a number of monks. By their uniforms he identified scores of policemen and soldiers. There were also boys still in student caps. Most were Cretan, but there were a handful of other nationalities: mainland Greek, Australian, New Zealander, even one enormous Russian who had escaped from a nearby prison camp. The weapons on display were equally varied, among them a few ancient shotguns and a muzzle loader that belonged in a museum.

A hut had been prepared specially for Leigh Fermor, and he quickly made himself at home. Over the next week he had a chance to observe the day-to-day operation of the encampment. Although Bandouvas was forced to rely on donations from his neighbors in the valley below to keep his men supplied with various staples, his improvised village was nonetheless remarkably self-sufficient. A baker turned out bread every morning. There was a tinker and a tailor. A cobbler and a carpenter were kept busy. The most striking thing was that life, even under these rough-and-ready conditions, simply went on. One day a pair of proud parents carried their baby to Bandouvas to be baptized. The *kapetan* and Leigh Fermor performed the rite together, making them, as Paddy put it, "godmothers." The name the parents chose for the child was as unlikely as Bo-Peep's makeshift village. "The poor thing was christened Anglia Epanastasis," Paddy recalled. It meant "England Revolution."

AS THE SUMMER wore on, Bandouvas grew preoccupied with eradicating traitors. Two men accused of collaborating with the enemy were put through summary trials and executed while Paddy was staying at the camp. Bandouvas had lost count of how many turncoats his men had put to death, but Paddy estimated that fifteen or so had been "liquidated" in Heraklion province that month. And that was not the last of it. "Three 'rubbings out' were pending in Babylon," he reported to headquarters, using the code word for Heraklion. It was a brutal enterprise involving ambushes, stranglings, bodies dumped in ditches. Leigh Fermor's radioman, Harry Brooke, had been forced to intervene on one occasion, when the sound of screaming led him to a macabre scene in which a group of Bandouvas's men were torturing a man hanging by his legs from a tree. The accused traitor was taken down and later tried and executed in a more conventional manner.

While Bandouvas went about this gory war on collaborators, Leigh Fermor made ready for a parachute drop scheduled for August. Among other supplies it would contain equipment that would help give the *andarte* band a fighting chance against the Germans. An ideal location for a drop lay just a three-hour march away on a level stretch of the Lasithi plateau that had been given the unlikely code name "Sodom." It was near enough to Bandouvas's lair to permit his men to assist with the mission.

In the past Bandouvas had not always minded his manners under similar circumstances. Tom Dunbabin still had a bad taste in his mouth from an incident that had occurred after a supply drop he supervised in October 1942. The operation had been planned for the twenty-fourth, but, as often happened, it had been repeatedly delayed. After three disappointing nights waiting for a plane that never showed, everything had finally clicked on the twenty-seventh. Bandouvas and a number of his men had been present that night, ostensibly to provide security.

But it soon became clear that he had another purpose in mind. Once the parachutes had settled to the ground, he became agitated, claiming that the entire stock of weapons was meant for his band. Dunbabin's men, he alleged, were planning to steal the arms and sell them on the black market.

Words flew back and forth, and soon Bandouvas and Dunbabin were embroiled in a heated argument. For a while Dunbabin, whose flair for Greek invective never failed to impress his Cretan friends, held his own. But the disagreement escalated until finally Bandouvas brandished his rifle, leveled it on Dunbabin, and barked an order to his men to "take up positions." The two groups remained locked in a standoff when Leigh Fermor arrived at the drop zone some time later. Fortunately he was able to defuse the situation with no shots fired. In the end, however, sixteen revolvers and a handful of other items were found to be missing from the stores included in the drop. These later turned up in a nearby village, where they had been sold. A number of local shepherds helped Dunbabin recover several of the missing items. It was clear that they were also growing wary of the unbridled sway Bandouvas had accrued. They offered Dunbabin a hundred rifles if he elected to march into the mountains and "clean up" Bo-Peep's rebel band.

Leigh Fermor felt that Dunbabin's trouble with Bandouvas had been brought about by the meddling of other Resistance leaders. During his stay at the village, he had talked with the old *andarte* at length about the responsibilities that came with leadership. Bandouvas, for all his independent spirit, was eager to have his band viewed as a unit of the British army, and he seemed receptive to what this British officer had to say.

When the night of the scheduled drop rolled around on August 20, Leigh Fermor and Bandouvas set out from camp with Manoli Paterakis at the head of a large party of Bandouvas's *andartes*. The patrol made its way toward the plateau on the south flank of Mount Dikti, above Kato Symi, some three hours away. The sun set around a quarter to nine that evening, and it was under cover of darkness that the men slipped onto the plateau.

Bandouvas had marshaled a force of some four hundred men for the occasion. And he now directed his troops to form a perimeter around the drop zone. Soon the scrubby terrain of the plateau bristled with rifles. Any German patrol stumbling into the area on this night would undoubtedly get more than it had bargained for. Inside the ring of sentries, Leigh Fermor and Manoli prepared brush for signal fires and settled in to wait for the arrival of the RAF. As usual on missions of this kind, the hours seemed to creep by. When an aircraft engine was at last heard overhead, a number of Bandouvas's men squeezed off rounds of rifle fire in celebration, lending a carnival atmosphere to the proceedings.

From the coded transmission Harry Brooke had picked up earlier in the week, Leigh Fermor knew that the supply mission was being flown by Cyril Fortune, from the 148th Squadron operating out of the base at Tocra on the Libyan coast. Now he watched with admiration as the skilled pilot brought his modified Halifax bomber in as low as possible over the triangle of signal fires. Paddy motioned to Manoli, then watched as he "joyfully" launched a clutch of flares into the night sky. All of a sudden the Halifax banked over the plateau and the pilot rocked the plane's wings in reply. Sergeant Fortune had seen them.

Soon the party on the ground could discern the outlines of parachutes drifting downward through the dome of light cast by the signal fires. Fortune was right on target. All of the containers settled to the ground within a circle not more than three hundred yards across. One chute failed to open, sending a container smashing to earth with enough force to demolish the rifles inside. But everything else was in perfect condition. Leigh

Fermor first ordered the heavier crates unpacked on the spot. The contents of these he cataloged and had packed onto mules. Back at Bandouvas's camp he unpacked the smaller containers and oversaw the distribution of the supplies they contained. Bandouvas's ragtag gang was suddenly outfitted like an army. "Large numbers are now in bush shirts, with cap-comforters on their heads, belts and bayonets, and look very well," Leigh Fermor noted. More was needed—in particular, cold-weather gear for the coming winter—but the drop marked a triumphant step forward. Everyone was elated. Harry Brooke heard someone call out, "Long live Paddy!" Shouts of "Long live England!" also rose from the rough-looking crowd surrounding Bandouvas. "It was like Bo-Peep's birthday," Leigh Fermor reported to headquarters; "the whole affair was the best bit of propaganda in Crete so far."

Since his arrival on Crete, Leigh Fermor had watched supply drops go wrong time after time. More often than not, containers were damaged or lost, or they were pilfered long before the ground team could reach them. This time the combination of skilled pilot and well-chosen location had made for a tactical bonanza. "The memorial silver dagger with Sgt. Fortune's name on has already been ordered," he told Cairo.

The flawless parachute drop also planted an idea in his head that would soon prove momentous. "Sodom is an ideal dropping point for personnel," he concluded. "I warmly recommend it in preference to any other area."

IN THE LAST WEEK of August, Leigh Fermor sent Minoan Mike back to Neapolis with two letters, one addressed to Tavana, the other to General Carta himself. His message to Carta went over much the same ground he and Tavana had covered in their meeting at the surgery clinic in Heraklion, but this one was cast in language gauged to appeal to the general in particular.

His conversations with Tavana had left Leigh Fermor with

a clear sense of Carta as a man. The general was the product
of an older Europe, the fading world of monarchy and aristocratic privilege that Paddy had come to know firsthand in the
course of his travels before the war. Carta was a "palace man" on
friendly terms with the royal family. He had never been seduced
by the Fascist movement in Italy, and his view of Hitler's Germany was a matter of dread and loathing. There was reason to
think him vain. Plump and short, with grizzled hair, he was
nonetheless something of a ladies' man. He sported a monocle
and had developed a reputation in Lasithi as a smooth operator. Lately he had taken up with a married woman from Corfu,
and he frequently spent nights away from his billet in Neapolis.

He was no doubt vulnerable to flattery, which Leigh Fermor,
a natural charmer, knew how to dole out when the circumstances called for it. His letter to Carta laid it on thick. "Mon
general," it began. "What an honor it is to communicate with
your Excellence." The letter went on to say that Leigh Fermor's
superiors in Cairo were grateful for the civility and restraint
the general had shown in his command of the occupation force
in Lasithi.

Minoan Mike carried the two letters to Neapolis, where
Tavana put him up for the night in his own house. That eve-
ning the lieutenant went to dinner with Carta and delivered
Leigh Fermor's fawning letter to the general. When he returned
home, he tuned the radio to a news broadcast from London.
Then he and Mike listened to the radio and talked until morn-
ing. The next day Mike returned to Leigh Fermor's lair with
Tavana's reply.

"My dear friend," his letter began, in French. "Permit me to
call you 'friend.' I very much wish to see and speak with you.
Wherever you would like, and whenever you want. It's preferable in the mountains." He proposed Tzermiado, high on the Lasithi plateau, as a likely spot. Tavana then went on to warn that

a bundle of Leigh Fermor's letters to one of his agents had fallen into German hands.

Paddy knew the ones he meant. They must have been discovered among the effects of a man who had been shot in a recent skirmish near Psilorítis. It was a potential security breach. But the Germans already knew his name and the look of his handwriting. He had heard that they even possessed a photo of him, but since it had been taken in Cairo, he thought, it "is very unlike my present appearance, whiskered and lined from fourteen months of Crete." He felt confident that the intercepted letters would reveal nothing useful.

More important, at the moment, was the letter he had sent to Carta. Tavana set his mind at ease about this. "He has acknowledged receipt of your letter," he wrote. "He thanks you very much." Leigh Fermor felt this marked the first solid step toward a meeting with Carta himself. Meanwhile, Tavana indicated that other developments were afoot. "I have many things to tell you personally," he wrote.

In closing, the lieutenant offered to send cigars and anything else his British friend might need. He would be happy to be of use, he said. Leigh Fermor imagined that Tavana would eventually provide something more useful than cigars, but he took him up on the offer anyway. ("The cigars were excellent—Flor Fina," he would later report to headquarters, asking in the same message that a box of Coronas be sent by way of the next boat. "It's bad for any morale to rely entirely on the enemy for these comforts.")

"Please excuse my scrawl," Tavana's letter concluded. "See you soon, without goodbye."

IN THE FIRST WEEK of September someone took potshots at a German staff car as it motored along the Viannos road. Soon after the incident, a fine of one million drachmas was levied against the five villages that lay nearby. Even in the drastically inflated currency this was a great deal of money. Two of the villages were unable to raise the sum. In each case a donkey was accepted as payment in kind.

Leigh Fermor, meanwhile, was laid up in a mountain sheepfold in a state of utter distress. His legs were covered with painful boils and other assorted lesions that made it difficult to walk at all and, for all practical purposes, impossible to travel in the mountains. If the boils were not enough to plague him, Bo-Peep was also back in his usual humor and making demands. Following the euphoria that had accompanied the successful supply drop in August, Bandouvas had taken a critical look at the state of his equipment as a whole. Now he had come to the conclusion that his band needed better access to news broadcasts. He sent Leigh Fermor a letter pressing him to inform Cairo that the Resistance urgently required a dynamo to charge their wireless batteries. Bandouvas helpfully proposed that the device might be sent with Tom Dunbabin on the next boat. This suggestion introduced a new problem for Leigh Fermor to contend with, since Bandouvas should have had no knowledge of Dunbabin's planned arrival.

Information about the comings and goings of SOE officers was generally kept from the *andartes* until the moment when they were called upon to assist with the actual landing. Bo-Peep's remark was an unsettling sign of lax security somewhere along the line. Nonetheless, Leigh Fermor passed the request on to Cairo, along with a few appeals of his own. He asked for cash and arms. He was also running low on other vital war matériel: whiskey, cigarettes, cigars, and books.

By the end of the week he rallied himself sufficiently to join his radioman, Harry Brooke, at their newly established wireless station located above the Kastelli airfield, outside Heraklion, where a deluge was added to the ongoing plague of boils.

In order to put the transmitter close to the unfolding action in Lasithi, as well as the boat landings on the south coast, Leigh Fermor had been forced to direct Brooke to a spot that offered almost no protection and little in the way of succor from the locals. It was a barren outcrop on the western slopes of the Lasithi mountains. No sooner had Leigh Fermor arrived there than the skies opened up and released a veritable torrent of rain. For thirty-six hours straight it beat down on them. Again and again Brooke powered up the transmitter and tried to make contact with Cairo. But there was nothing doing. It was hard enough just keeping the set from being destroyed by the rainwater that quickly penetrated everything in sight.

Finally, on September 7, Brooke picked up a signal from Cairo warning that a major development was pending in the Italian situation. The next morning a follow-up message crackled across the sodden airwaves. The Italian government had officially declared an armistice. Shortly after the arrival of the message, a shepherd appeared at the shelter with local news. The man, who looked agitated, said the Germans had stormed a nearby Italian post at dawn and stripped the Italians of their weapons. Leigh Fermor could only assume that the same thing was taking place throughout Lasithi. That or the Italians had begun fighting back. He knew that any chance of the Italians handing over their arms to the *andartes* was fading quickly. There was no time to waste.

Leigh Fermor immediately dispatched a runner to Tavana's house and another to Bandouvas's mountaintop headquarters. He would have to speak with Tavana right away. Meanwhile, it was crucial to put a damper on any aggressive plans Bandouvas might be hatching . . . at least for now.

That night Minoan Mike turned up at the hideout accompanied by an exhausted Italian soldier. At Tavana's request, the two of them had lugged a consignment of weapons up the mountainside. Mike also brought word that Tavana had arranged for a car to be left for Leigh Fermor on the plain below. The next day, while Harry Brooke combed the radio dial for instructions from headquarters, Tom Dunbabin arrived at the hideout with one of his men, following a strenuous march up from Tsoutsouros, on the south coast, where Dunbabin's boat had landed. Close on their heels came a letter from Bandouvas that had obviously been scrawled in haste. Unable to decipher Bandouvas's handwriting, Leigh Fermor handed the message to Mike to see if he could make it out. At this point, Dunbabin, worried that the matter might be sensitive, asked quietly whether the young man could be trusted. He was delighted to learn that Mike was the son of Arthur Evans's former overseer, Pendlebury's own right-hand man.

As Minoan Mike read the message aloud, it became clear to everyone present that Bandouvas believed the British were preparing an all-out invasion of the island. Dunbabin's face fell when he heard this. Fresh from Cairo, he understood more clearly than anyone else present what trouble might be in store. In the months leading up to the armistice, headquarters had led Paddy to believe that an Allied invasion of the island was a possibility, particularly in the event of an Italian uprising. But now, with the invasion of Sicily under way, Crete was a low-priority front. If Bandouvas and his men set off a new Battle of Crete, there would be no proverbial cavalry riding to the rescue.

Leigh Fermor and Minoan Mike hurriedly scrambled down the mountain and located the car Tavana had sent. As they motored toward Neapolis, they met Tavana coming the other direction in Carta's staff car. He was frantic with worry that something had gone wrong. Leigh Fermor, accustomed as he was to seeing the lieutenant in civilian clothes, noted the striking uniform his friend had donned in the wake of the armistice announcement—"He was dressed in a most dashing Alpine uniform with spurs and plumes and a phenomenal number of medal ribbons." Tavana wheeled his car around and Paddy jumped in. They reached Neapolis in time for dinner.

NEWS OF THE Italian surrender affected Tavana like a shot of adrenaline. Over a dinner of excellent food and free-flowing Chianti, the Italian rattled off plans for resisting the German attack he now believed to be imminent. He had already burned his security files, so there would be no records on hand that might assist a German takeover of the region. When this was done, he had made contact with a number of his fellow officers and urged them to resist any attempt on the part of the Germans to disarm the Italian garrison. One friend, a colonel who commanded the artillery installation at Kritsa, in the hills above the Bay of Mirabello on the north coast, was especially receptive and planned to sabotage his battery's guns, rather than relinquish them to the Germans. Like Bandouvas, Tavana assumed that British help was on the way, and this was the selling point of his persuasive campaign. Listening to the Italian's excited scheming, Leigh Fermor felt a wave of guilt wash over him. "This was the result of my former line of talk," he believed, "and I felt like several different kinds of swine for having led them up the garden path."

The situation, he tried to explain, had changed. With Allied forces now committed in Sicily, an invasion of Crete was not on the immediate horizon. Tavana was savvy enough to recognize what this meant. There was no way the Italians could hold out indefinitely against the larger German force. Leigh Fermor now suggested that the best course was a measured transfer of small arms from the Italian garrison to the *andartes*. Tavana slowly absorbed the news before speaking. An out-and-out handover of weapons would be impossible, he said at last, but he remained determined to do what he could to help his British friend, in secret if necessary.

Later that evening, Tavana slipped out and made his way past the Gestapo patrols that now roamed the town. He went to General Carta's house and there persuaded his commander to meet with Leigh Fermor in person. Back at Tavana's house, Paddy was finally introduced to Ravioli, who looked exactly as his conversations with Tavana had led him to expect. "He is plump, rosy, urbane and very agreeable," he thought.

That evening Leigh Fermor gathered a clearer sense of how the Germans were reacting to the armistice. Carta revealed that General Müller had visited him again the previous day and demanded the handover of all Italian arms. When Carta refused, Müller had continued to badger him, first insisting on complete disarmament, then proposing to break up Carta's Siena Division and disperse his soldiers across the island's other three regional districts. These negotiations went on for eight tense hours but reached no conclusion. In the wake of this meeting, Müller had begun disarming key Italian units and papering the Lasithi region with leaflets urging Italian soldiers to honor "their old comradeship of arms." But the German commander had so far stopped short of using force.

This might well change, Leigh Fermor believed, if the Italians were found to be transferring their arms to the Cretans, especially after Carta had insisted so adamantly on retaining them. They would have to play for time. It was agreed that Carta should meet with Müller again, this time taking the same line as the German's own leaflet campaign. The Italians would pledge to stand by their former allies, provided Müller allowed them to retain their arms, including artillery and other heavy weapons, as a show of his good faith.

After the general left, Leigh Fermor and Tavana continued to mull the situation over. By daybreak they had come up with a plan to smuggle surplus arms out of the Italian munitions dumps by car. Since German soldiers now guarded the majority of the depots, this would be a delicate operation.

GENERAL CARTA met with his German counterpart the next day. His new proposal, however, hit a stone wall. Over the intervening days, Müller had hardened his stance, and he now demanded disarmament. Carta attempted to negotiate, asking on what authority Müller had recently disarmed Italian units at Ierápetra and elsewhere. An excuse was offered, but there was no question that the German was now running short of patience, and he cared little to justify his actions. This time Müller departed without a handshake.

On September 12 Müller issued an order that made it clear he had no intention of allowing Carta to maintain control of the artillery batteries in Lasithi. It offered Italian soldiers three choices—they could pledge loyalty to the displaced Fascist regime and retain only their personal weapons, they could be assigned to work camps, or they could be imprisoned. It soon became evident that the order was merely a formality, in any case. Müller's soldiers had already begun seizing Italian arms throughout Lasithi. At Sitia on the eastern tip of the island, they ran into resistance, and the garrison there had disappeared into the mountains. The colonel in command of the battery at Kritsa, Tavana's friend, had gone through with his threat and spiked the battery's guns before the Germans could reach them. He had already been imprisoned and could expect still worse treatment. In the end it was only the last point of Müller's order that mattered: Anyone caught destroying or trafficking in Italian weapons would be shot. The same went for Italians who chose to desert their units.

Although Müller's reaction was disappointing, Carta's second round of negotiation had bought a few crucial days. Working at night, with the help of one trusted orderly, Tavana had managed in this time to smuggle some two hundred rifles from the munitions dumps. He had also trucked out a good deal of ammunition and grenades, as well as a number of machine guns and two mortars.

Neapolis was now crawling with German soldiers and units of the secret police. Leigh Fermor was more or less confined to Tavana's house, where he had taken up residence. He had Manoli Paterakis making regular trips to the hardscrabble wireless station in the mountains above the Kastelli airfield, where a forlorn Harry Brooke was kept constantly busy signaling the latest developments back and forth between Crete and Cairo.

In the second week of September, Leigh Fermor was alone at Tavana's house when a German detachment came looking for the lieutenant. He slipped under the bed without being seen but spent "an uncomfortable half hour" in hiding, "clutching my revolver, and swallowing pounds of fluff and cobwebs."

By the fourteenth, Neapolis had become too hot for him to stay put there. He hitched a ride out of town and holed up at a safe house on the road to the Lasithi plain. There he met up with Tom Dunbabin, and together they decided that there was little to be done beyond arranging an evacuation plan for General Carta and key members of his staff. Leigh Fermor sent yet another urgent letter to Tavana explaining the situation and imploring him to gather whatever intelligence he could find about defenses in the Lasithi area.

The next morning Minoan Mike woke him with the news that Tavana was waiting just outside the village. Rising quickly, Leigh Fermor hurried out to meet him. "I found him beaming under a plane tree with a whole satchelful of documents," he told Cairo. Tavana, it seemed, had gotten his hands on documents that laid out the entire defensive organization of the province. There was even a map pinpointing the areas most vulnerable to Allied attack.

Among the most fascinating items was a German account of the Battle of Crete and the early days of the occupation. This revealed that the enemy had formed only a haphazard, almost comical, picture of SOE activities on the island. It mentioned that on one occasion "arms had been landed by parachute" and that four British agents who came ashore the previous winter "have not yet been captured." The document also included a string of reports on "punitive" operations conducted by the German occupation force. These might well amount to a confession of war crimes, Leigh Fermor had reason to suspect. In their defense, the Germans leveled allegations against the populace, claiming that wounded German soldiers had been systematically "assassinated," that bodies had been mutilated, and that in one horrific case in Heraklion a German soldier had been left crucified to a door. Altogether the leather satchel Tavana handed over contained so much critical information that Leigh Fermor was almost wary of handling it. "I took it back to the village feeling it might go off bang on the way."

The days following the armistice had been full of "fuss and anxiety," he felt, but the trove of documents would prove well worth the effort. This aspect of the affair had gone so well that he felt entitled to claim a souvenir of the occasion. "I wish to make it formally known that the satchel itself is my particular bit of Cretan plunder," he wrote at the end of his report to Cairo; "please hang on to it for me." He also cautioned headquarters against opening the satchel in General Carta's presence. Lieutenant Tavana had been much freer with the Italian garrison's secrets than his commander realized.

WHILE LEIGH FERMOR and Tavana nervously watched the developments in Neapolis, the feared clash with the Germans was already getting under way in the mountains to the southwest. Bo-Peep, it seemed, had started his own little war. Before Leigh Fermor was summoned to Neapolis, he had instructed Bandouvas to be prepared to take charge of Italian arms on short notice. The *kapetan* had then mobilized a force of two hundred men and put another hundred on alert, all the while scheming to draw a much larger force when the shooting started. Not long after word of the armistice reached him, he decided that his hour had come.

Charging down from his mountaintop hideout, he first pounced on a small detachment of German soldiers who were out gathering potatoes. Two of these were killed and their bodies dumped in a ravine. Bandouvas then rampaged though the Viannos district, attacking the German garrison at Ano Viannos, the county seat, and wiping it out before doing the same at a nearby installation on the south coast. His men next swept through villages to the east, eventually making their way to Males, a dozen miles from Ierápetra, where they disarmed the Italian outpost.

At this point Tom Dunbabin got wind of what was happening and issued immediate orders to stand down and await further instructions. Before the message reached him, however, Bandouvas struck again.

Two German companies had been sent out to look for him. At Ano Viannos the patrol split into three columns. One of these was in nearby Kato Symi on the twelfth, when Bandouvas passed back that way. His men engaged the German column and drove it into a gully, where, as Dunbabin heard it, they killed or captured every last man.

When word of the clash reached Leigh Fermor, he knew there would be trouble. And he was right. On the thirteenth General Müller issued retaliation orders, and his threats came thundering home on September 15, when a force of two thousand German soldiers swept from various directions into the counties of Viannos and Ierápetra, destroying everything in their path. More than a dozen villages were raided and at least seven were burned, including Kato Symi, which had been abandoned by residents who knew Bandouvas's ambush there would draw reprisals. Taken all together, it looked as if somewhere in the neighborhood of five hundred villagers had been murdered. The dead, it was reported, included men, women, and children, ranging in age from two to eighty. In one village all but seven inhabitants had been killed. On top of the casualties, another 850 civilians had been taken hostage. That would not be the end of it, either. The Germans had driven off the villagers' livestock and burned their fodder, which meant there would be more devastation from hunger as winter came on.

WITH DETAILS FROM VIANNOS still trickling in, Leigh Fermor saw that time had run out for Carta and Tavana. He now presented the general with just two remaining options. The Italians could elect to fight, or Carta and a handful of his officers could flee with him into the mountains, and from there to the south coast and, eventually, Cairo. The general, it turned out, was ready to go.

On the afternoon of the sixteenth, Carta and Tavana left Neapolis by car, bound, they put it about, for Sitia, on the far eastern tip of the island. They were accompanied by Carta's operations officer, one Captain Grossi, and his aide-de-camp, a captain named Ludovici. Tavana had also arranged for a final truckload of arms to follow. At Leigh Fermor's suggestion, he had recruited a number of friends who were remaining behind to serve as a spy network. Once clear of Neapolis, Carta's party got out of the car and turned on foot across the Lasithi plain toward the mountains. The driver then took the car on to Sitia, where, with the general's identification pennant clearly visible, it was abandoned, a red herring for Germans who might be in pursuit. Leigh Fermor and Manoli Paterakis met the general and his party at a village in the foothills just west of the Lasithi border.

From there they made for Mount Dikti. Near the village of Magoulas, some twenty-five miles southwest of Neapolis, they entered a pass that would carry them farther southwest across the mountain range toward Tsoutsouros, on the south coast. Although the going was hard, morale remained high. Whenever the party stopped, Carta produced a water bottle filled with triple sec and handed it around. The general was in an ebullient mood. While the men rested, he "regaled" his British guide "with lively anecdotes about the high life in Rome and Paris." Carta also possessed a rich repertoire of gossip about the German generals who had been his allies. Leigh Fermor was impressed by the little man's verve and swagger. "He went with a great swing everywhere," he thought.

They spent the next day ducking German reconnaissance aircraft. The unwieldy Fieseler Storch planes circled low over the mountains searching for signs of the general's party. On one pass a plane dropped a bundle of leaflets. "They landed right at our feet," Leigh Fermor recalled. The freshly printed flyers bore a message reproduced in German, Greek, and Italian: "The Italian General Carta, together with some of his officers, has fled to the mountains, probably with the intention of escaping from the island. For his capture, dead or alive, is offered a reward of THIRTY MILLION DRACHMA. Those who take part in his capture or give any assistance thereto will further receive a full pardon for any crime they may have committed." Even in the wildly inflated Greek currency it was a staggering sum. "Carta," Paddy noticed, "was very amused."

On the twenty-first, German detachments entered a string of villages lying between Magoulas and nearby Agios Georgios. Somehow they had picked up the right trail and were closing in on the area where the fugitives had disappeared into the Dikti range. But they were too late. By the twenty-third, General Carta's group had reached the cave above Tsoutsouros, where they would await the arrival of the motor launch. There they were joined by Tom Dunbabin and, to Leigh Fermor's astonishment, Bandouvas, with twenty-one of his men in tow.

A week earlier Dunbabin had visited Bandouvas's upland camp, hoping, in the wake of the Viannos massacres, to impress on the *kapetan* the understanding that his actions must henceforth be strictly defensive in nature. He found the usually audacious leader now "lean and chastened." Bo-Peep seemed to have lost authority, not only in the villages that had suffered reprisals but also in his own camp, where orders were now being issued by committee. "The behaviour of this force," Dunbabin felt, "was like that of a child which has been teasing a dog and is amazed to find that it bites." They had no idea what to do next and, having lost the support of the villages, they were already running short on food. By the twentieth, Dunbabin had arranged for a supply drop. He then asked for a guide and struck out for Tsoutsouros to meet the boat.

Along the way he had been intercepted by Bandouvas and his now much-diminished gang. Tipped off by the guide to the fact that a boat was due, the entire remaining band now wished to be evacuated to Cairo. Dunbabin knew that this would create no end of difficulties for headquarters. He pictured Bandouvas and his associates sitting in the Cairo cafés holding forth about their exploits in the Resistance. For the sake of security it would be necessary, he believed, to corral them in some out-of-the-way location. But in his view it would be worth the trouble to have the unpredictable *kapetan* out of the way. And the remnant of his gang was, though "picturesque," of little real utility on the island, Dunbabin concluded. At least the *andartes* could provide security until the boat arrived that night.

In the afternoon, while the cave resounded with the snores of sleeping men, one of Bandouvas's sentries spotted a pair of German soldiers moving about near the beach. One was leading a riderless mule, which the sentry recognized as an animal the party had employed in crossing the mountains. Fearing that the abandoned mule would raise the patrol's suspicions, the *andartes* quickly began organizing themselves for a fight. Just then a gendarme appeared at the cave entrance.

Leigh Fermor and the other men were wary. Unlike Manoli Paterakis, who resigned from the gendarmerie when the Germans took control of the force, this man had apparently stayed on to work as a guide for the enemy. But he quickly reassured them. He had already learned of their approach, he claimed, and he intended to help steer the Germans off their trail. Leigh Fermor now made an effort to calm Bandouvas and his band, who were in favor of attacking the outnumbered German patrol. He then sent the gendarme back with a story to placate the two soldiers. The fiction he devised—that the mule must have wandered away from a peasant collecting salt on the nearby flats—might avert a potential disaster. When, not much later, the patrol withdrew, the group breathed a sigh of relief. Nonetheless, the Germans had, as Dunbabin noted, "arrested our mule."

After nightfall the men slipped out of the cave and crept out onto the heights above the beach. There they waited, listening for the sound of the motor launch and straining to catch sight of a signal light out on the windswept sea.

OFFSHORE, SEVERAL MILES to the southeast, a motor launch skippered by a bearded Canadian lieutenant named Bob Young wallowed through increasingly choppy waters toward a hidden inlet near Tsoutsouros. The little ship had made a rough crossing from the Libyan port town of Derna, which served as a base for an unorthodox fleet of armed caïques and launches that ran covert operations throughout the Aegean. Now Young found the northerly breeze stiffening as the night wore on. He worried that the vessel would not make landfall in time to pick up what he had been warned might be a large evacuation party.

Among the men on board was a new SOE officer named Sandy Rendel, who was going ashore with a radio operator to establish an outpost near the newly expanded German installation at Ierápetra, in the powder-keg Lasithi province. A fit, athletic man of thirty-three, Rendel was an old friend of Tom Dunbabin's from Oxford, where both had studied classics. Rendel had gone on to become a solicitor while Dunbabin was busy building his career as an archaeologist.

Since the war had broken out, they had been in touch only intermittently. After joining the army, Rendel had been sent to Northern Ireland for training. Then, leaving a wife and young son at home, he bounced through a series of what he called "soft jobs," eventually winding up in a wing of the artillery command responsible for Persia and Iraq. By the spring of 1943, the unit had begun to feel like a backwater. That was when he ran into Dunbabin in North Africa.

Rendel was surprised to see that his old friend cut such an intriguing figure even against the exotic backdrop of wartime Cairo. When they met for dinner at what was reputed to be the city's finest French restaurant, Dunbabin turned up sporting a long black mustache that "wound itself with sickly bravado almost into a complete ring." Watching him twist and tug at the peculiar mustache through the course of the evening, Rendel began to suspect that his old friend had seen more of war than he previously thought.

Dunbabin had gone to work in the War Office, Rendel remembered, "in some intelligence job connected with the Albanian campaign." That much made sense, given Tom's fluency in modern Greek. It was what had happened next that puzzled

Rendel. Dunbabin had taken up a staff job in Cairo, but when Rendel had received a letter from him recently, it was the sort of hastily scrawled note, "written in pencil in a spidery hand," that seemed to come from the field. Even that was not unusual, Rendel knew; Dunbabin might well have been in transit.

"There were plenty of letters being written just then on a man's knee in the back of a lorry," he told himself, "and I knew Tom's handwriting was atrocious anyway." The strange thing was that Dunbabin had recently been awarded a DSO—the Distinguished Service Order, Britain's award for valor during active operations against the enemy. And you didn't get those for filing papers in staff headquarters.

By the time the entrée arrived that evening, Rendel could no longer contain his curiosity. He asked Dunbabin outright what kind of work he had been assigned in Cairo, but he got nowhere. Dunbabin revealed only that "at the moment" he found himself "doing nothing at all."

"You don't mean to say they gave you a DSO for that?" Rendel prodded.

Dunbabin remained reticent, twiddling the flamboyant mustache in a way that stoked Rendel's already smoldering curiosity. He sensed that his friend was involved in something so secret he was in fact forbidden to discuss it, and he imagined that Dunbabin had been serving behind the lines, perhaps at El Alamein, as a commando of some kind.

As his dissatisfaction with his own assignment mounted, Rendel had sometimes considered joining a parachute regiment or perhaps the commandos. He pictured himself "scrambling about at night" behind enemy lines. Now, having conjured up the idea that Tom had been doing something similar, he let his aspiration slip out.

"Well I'd better tell you something more about it," Dunbabin said when he heard this. He went on to explain that his was not precisely a commando unit. The commandos were by and large a raiding party. They made quick strikes behind enemy lines. In contrast, SOE officers disappeared into an occupied territory for months at a time. "We go with parties of Greeks in and out of Greece dressed as civilians."

This revelation shocked Rendel. "But Tom," he said, "if you go in plain clothes, you're a spy."

Dunbabin shrugged off his friend's alarm. "Spy," he said, "is an ugly word."

By this time, however, the tables were beginning to turn. It had dawned on Dunbabin that his old schoolmate could be of use in Crete, and his earlier reticence edged now toward recruitment. Before dinner was over, he had given Rendel what amounted to a crash course in SOE operations. And it was an earful.

Gathering intelligence was part of the job, he said. In fact, he had himself climbed into a tree to make a sketch that was later used to plan a bombing raid on one of the island's airfields. This at a time when Crete played a significant role in the war, because German aircraft based there were involved in the struggle for North Africa. But just as important, the SOE officers in Crete were there to help organize a fifth column. In the event of an Allied invasion, they would mobilize Resistance units to fight the Germans. There were hardships involved in the work, of course. Food was sometimes hard to come by, especially while shuttling from one hideout to another. Isolation was a problem, since communication with headquarters in Cairo tended to be unreliable. So far the Germans had not offered much opposition. But the threat was real. If the enemy caught you, you'd be shot, at best. Rendel had already heard rumors about the brutal treatment spies received from the Germans. In one story captured intelligence agents had their hands slowly hacked off with a wooden ax.

The Greeks themselves made the work worthwhile, it appeared to Rendel. It was wrong—"sentimental and unreal"—to make too much of the link between ancient Greece and the modern Greeks. But there was no denying the Greek people's longing for independence and the fierce tradition of resistance they kept alive from the Turkish occupation.

Perhaps the most significant result of SOE work, Rendel gathered, was the boost it gave to the morale of the Greeks, who felt less abandoned to their fate at the hands of the Germans when they saw British officers working covertly on the island. The Greeks' passion for the Resistance was infectious. Tom mentioned that at that moment an SOE officer named Paddy Leigh Fermor had been undercover on Crete for more than a year and was enjoying himself so much he had refused to come out on leave. This man, Rendel thought to himself, "must be a person entirely different in make-up from myself."

To Rendel it all sounded "exhilarating," but he also had concerns that were more practical in nature. "Didn't you get covered in lice?" he asked. This, Dunbabin admitted, was indeed a problem. And his brusque reply—a clipped "I don't like lice"—was underscored by the scowl that suddenly warped his face, "as if," Rendel thought, "he had been contemplating lice objectively at some distance."

Lice or no lice, Rendel felt drawn to the romantic escapades his friend had described. Before the week was out, he had decided to get himself transferred to Dunbabin's unit, "by hook or by crook." By the middle of May, his request had gone through.

NOW, BARELY FOUR MONTHS later, Rendel was fresh from training. In Haifa, where he had gone through the SOE school in what was termed "resistance warfare," he had experienced a schoolboy thrill in learning demolitions, though like Xan Fielding he wondered how useful the training, with its focus

ABOVE: Sandy Rendel in uniform.
Rendel Family Archive

LEFT: Sandy Rendel in
civilian disguise on Crete.
Rendel Family Archive

on railway sabotage, would be on Crete, where there were no rail lines to be found. At the Haifa camp he met Sergeant Dudley Perkins, a New Zealander who had made a name for himself in the wake of the German invasion by escaping from the infamous prison camp at Galatas and guiding British stragglers to safety. Rendel was drawn by the Kiwi's enthusiasm for the mission. "On the march," he thought, "he looked just like a fox terrier quivering with eagerness." But he seemed equally "reliable and imperturbable."

It was Perkins who schooled Rendel in the more practical affairs of undercover life on Crete: "How good the Cretans were to you. How one old man, whom he meant to see again, could always be relied on to give you a meal of potatoes even though he was desperately poor himself. How you could usually find potatoes to dig up." This last point struck a chord in Rendel. "He was such a virtuous young man," he thought of Perkins, "and it gave me a sudden odd glimpse of the makeshift life to think of him stealing potatoes from his allies in the dark."

After Haifa, Rendel had made one run to Crete as what SOE called a "conducting officer," ferrying supplies to one of the missions already established on the island. "The supplies were usually clothes, arms, ammunition and food." As the new man, Rendel had gone out of his way to put together "a really good consignment of stores." He had sweated through several days in Cairo, buying or otherwise scrounging a bounty of canned food. When the shipment eventually reached Xan Fielding on Crete, the delicacies—asparagus in particular—had elicited more derision than delight. Fielding had fired back a snarky telegram asking, "What about the salad dressing?"

Despite the catering fiasco, Rendel's experience as a conducting officer on that occasion had at least left him with a good deal of confidence in the motor-launch skipper Bob Young's abilities. On that earlier trip, Young had made a perfect landfall on Crete, and supplies and men had been ferried ashore smoothly. On the return to Derna, though, a flight of German floatplanes—three ungainly Arado 196s, probably based in Chania—had spotted the vessel and turned to attack. For ten or fifteen minutes the planes had circled the ship, dropping into strafing dives on each pass.

On their second run, Rendel recalled, one of the Arados cut across the bow and the fire from the plane's rear gun took aim on him. "It shot low and I saw the line of splashes scudding over the water towards us. That part of the burst, which was going to hit the ship, seemed on a line that would pass between myself and the forward gun. It showed that there were plenty of enemy bullets flying about somewhere in the air around us, and the thought that someone on that ugly enemy plane was trying to kill us—and might—made me feel anger and a personal urge to strike down the gunner, fiercer than any emotion which I had ever felt before."

When the German airplanes, no doubt running short on fuel, finally broke off the attack, Rendel looked around and began to take stock of what had happened. The motor launch was strewn with casualties. One gunner had taken a bullet in the thigh. Another crewman lay by the wheelhouse with a dangerous-looking stomach wound. One man had been hit in the chest, but the bullet seemed to have missed any vital organs.

"Bob Young himself, looking as quiet as before, but older and grimmer, had been struck by a splinter above the left eye." Rendel watched as blood trickled down the skipper's face.

Young asked Rendel to take a look at one of the most serious casualties, a gun loader whose foot had been ripped apart by an exploding cannon shell. He located the young man—"a tall, fair-haired boy of nineteen"—on the floor of the narrow companionway leading to the officers' cabin. His foot was nearly torn free at the heel, and Rendel tried to shield the boy's view as he carried him to a berth inside, "but he cried out hysterically, 'I've seen it, I've seen it.'"

Rendel quieted the boy and gave him a tablet of morphine. Then he lifted the dangling foot back into position and wrapped it with a field dressing. When the bleeding slowed, he went back on deck. He saw that the ship itself was riddled with bullet holes. In places cannon shells had torn sizable holes through the wooden decking. But the engine remained functional. As he made his way past one of the gun positions where a crewman had been wounded, Rendel lost his footing and surprised himself with a low inward laugh. "The old cliché about the deck slippery with blood was suddenly, and even for a moment amusingly, and then grimly, true."

Bob Young remained at the helm, piloting the vessel homeward. Less than half an hour after the attack ended, he had the steward serving mugs of sweet tea and bully beef sandwiches to the men. Later in the day the skipper discovered a fire in the transmission compartment, which he quickly extinguished. Eventually the ship reached the mouth of Derna harbor, where a second motor launch—alerted by radio of the casualties on board Young's ship—awaited their return and now offered to board officers to relieve the wounded men. "Bob Young signaled that we could manage," Rendel recalled, "and they left him to bring the ship in himself.

NOW, APPROACHING CRETE for a second time, Rendel was outfitted to go ashore himself. He wore Greek secondhand clothes he had bought in Cairo, and he carried a fake identity card bearing a photograph intended to make him look "suitably down-at-heel."

Bob Young throttled down when the launch was a mile or so off the beach. Despite his concern about the weather, they had reached the inlet more or less on schedule. As the vessel glided shoreward, all eyes strained to catch sight of the signal from Leigh Fermor's party, two prearranged letters of Morse code flashed at intervals. The only sounds on board were the muffled grumbling of the engine and Bob Young's voice quietly relaying orders to the engine room. This tranquil prelude to a landing would always remind Rendel of a Joseph Conrad story. The moonless night was pitch black, and he could make out little of the coastline, but the mountains did not appear to rise as steeply from the shore here as he had seen to the west on his first trip. Those heights had "looked cold and distant," he recalled, "and I wondered silently and lugubriously to myself, if before the war ended, my bones would be lying up there for good."

Such thoughts were soon cut short by the signal from shore, which could now be seen flickering repeatedly from the hillside ahead.

ON THE BEACH, Leigh Fermor and Manoli had heard the diesel rumble of the motor launch in the distance and quickly flashed the appointed Morse signal. It was apparent that the crew of the launch had located them, but close to an hour passed without sign of the landing party. At last, a man struggled up onto the beach, dragging a rope. The choppy water had made it impossible to paddle the dinghy ashore. Now Leigh Fermor directed men onto the beach to tow it in. Soon Rendel, who was aboard the rubber dinghy, heard his English voice calling out instructions, which the Greeks responded to with shouts of *"Trava, trava!"*—Pull, pull!

Onshore the two parties greeted each other. Dunbabin welcomed his old friend to Crete while a party of Cretans going ashore traded effusive bursts of news with members of Bo-Peep's gang. Then, suddenly, Tom's voice drowned out all the rest, letting loose a blistering string of curses in Greek. Rendel understood only snatches; "he called many times on 'My all-Holy mother'—presumably urging her to rise up and smite." Dunbabin had watched a young Greek officer, who happened to be the nephew of the prime minister, drop an empty sardine tin on the beach. The discarded container would provide a sure sign, should the Germans come across it, that a British landing had taken place. The tin was quickly reclaimed.

Meanwhile, Leigh Fermor and Manoli helped Carta and his party into the dinghy, launched it, and then scrambled in themselves. The men held tightly to the rigging as they were pulled across thirty yards of choppy water. At last, with the dinghy thumping against the side of the motor launch, they managed to clamber aboard the ship. Leigh Fermor had intended only to escort the general aboard, hand off the satchel of documents Tavana had given him, and then return to the beach. But the wind, already fierce, suddenly grew stronger. With the mission now running more than an hour behind schedule due to the weather, Bob Young feared that his ship would be once again caught in range of enemy aircraft when the sun rose. He decided he could wait no longer. Leigh Fermor and Manoli were still aboard when the skipper turned the launch to sea. After fifteen months on the island, Paddy was on his way to an unexpected leave in Cairo. Loose ends remained on Crete that he regretted not tying up. But he could now escort his general all the way to North Africa and see to it that the satchel of documents made it to headquarters.

Along with the commandeered documents, he was carrying a report written in haste by Tom Dunbabin that afternoon, while the shore party waited for the arrival of Bob Young's motor launch. In it Dunbabin proposed a string of more aggressive plans for future operations. He knew from his interrogation of the prisoners Bandouvas had taken at Kato Symi that German morale was at a low point. Soldiers felt betrayed by the Italians and beleaguered by an occupation that had gone on far too long. They were also running short on stores. One of the prisoners reported that since July he had been detailed to a "Potato detachment" that moved about the island gathering produce, which was then doled out to various units to supplement their dwindling rations.

As Dunbabin saw it, this was the time to strike a blow. One idea was to capture a coastal outpost. He pointed to Tsoutsouros, now disappearing in the darkness behind the launch, as a likely candidate. This possibility had been considered before. In May 1942, Dunbabin had recommended an attack on a coast-watching station—involving a submarine if possible—that would be made to look like an outside job. This time around, he imagined a similar operation could take place without help from outside the island. The attack, he recommended, "would be carried out from the land on receipt of a signal."

Now, however, Dunbabin was also hatching an even bolder

plot. He proposed a mission to capture the general who commanded the German garrison in Heraklion district, the man responsible for the recent massacre of villagers in the Viannos region. "It should be easy to kidnap Müller," he believed. "One of our agents is on good terms with his chauffeur, and he might be abducted on the road. Alternatively, it sounds easy to break into the Villa Ariadne with a strength of about 20. This operation, if carried out, should be synchronized with operation Bräuer." Putting this new plan into action at the same time as the Bräuer operation—Xan Fielding's long-standing plot to capture the German commander in Chania—would deliver a humiliating one-two punch to German morale and organization. Dunbabin was not the only one beginning to think this way.

PART TWO

IN THE MINOTAUR'S LAIR

CHAPTER 6

Fleshpots

THE MOTOR LAUNCH carrying Leigh Fermor and Manoli Paterakis, along with General Carta and members of his staff, chuffed into the port of Mersa Matruh, west of Alexandria, the following evening. There the entourage boarded a plane that carried them on to Cairo. Lieutenant Tavana was not with them. Eager to fight the Germans and hoping to convince other Italians to defect to the British, he had volunteered to stay behind on Crete. "I am sure I can be useful," he had written in a letter Leigh Fermor was now carrying to headquarters. The letter included a request to be put under Paddy's command, but the unexpected departure of the motor launch made that impossible for the moment. By now Tavana would be making his way toward Tom Dunbabin's old wireless station with Sandy Rendel and his men. Leigh Fermor could picture the outpost, which occupied an oleander-fringed gully above the Heraklion plain. From there they would strike out to the east through the village of Demati and finally up the rocky path into the Lasithi mountains, where Paddy had left a wireless transmitter, which they would use to set up a new outpost in the heart of the Lasithi province.

When the plane reached Cairo, a detachment from the office of the commander in chief was waiting to take charge of Carta. The general was joined in Cairo by another Italian commander, one General Negroni, who had recently been extracted from

Athens. Over the following days, Carta cooperated willingly with a string of British interrogators, who were particularly anxious to learn whether the German and Italian commanders had exchanged information about their intelligence networks. If they had—if Carta was aware of the identities of German agents in Crete or if the two armies had secret agents in common—that information could prove vital to the ongoing operations on the island. Meanwhile, Carta had one request of his own. Recognizing that his family in Italy might be put in jeopardy if word got out, he asked that his cooperation not be publicized. Once the interviews had concluded, it was agreed that he would be sent to Brindisi, in southeastern Italy, closer to home than he had been in some time.

Before Carta left Cairo, however, Leigh Fermor helped him deliver a stinging message to the German commander of Fortress Crete. General Bräuer had by now raised the reward for Carta's abduction severalfold. Dead or alive, the Italian was worth one hundred million drachmas, and Carta understandably felt that Bräuer's unsavory tactic warranted a response. The reply he drafted gave him a final chance to put his former ally in his place. "I am in Egypt," Carta wrote to Bräuer. "I assure you, however, that no one, and especially no Cretan, would be found to betray me and take your 30 pieces of silver. But be sure that there are a great many Cretans who would be only too happy to kill you for no reward at all."

While General Carta vented his anger at Bräuer, discussions were under way in the Crete section at SOE headquarters about Bräuer's counterpart in Heraklion, General Müller. No one knew quite how to respond to the brazen massacre the German divisional commander had ordered in the villages of Viannos. The problem was that any form of retaliation SOE might undertake against Müller would only call down more reprisals against Cretan civilians. It looked as if there was nothing to be done. Again and again, the daily meetings ended in little more than hand-wringing. Keeping his recent experience with General Carta in mind, however, Leigh Fermor was beginning to formulate a plan. Although he had not intended to leave Crete just yet, perhaps taking a leave after some fifteen months would be for the best. He would now have time to think.

And he was certainly not the only one fretting about the situation in Crete that fall. By the end of September, anxiety about the destabilizing effect of Italy's surrender had reached the highest levels in Germany. Fearing Allied air attacks as the Italian withdrawal weakened their grasp on the Aegean, German commanders considered pulling out of the region. During a high-level meeting at Hitler's headquarters, officers of the army and navy called for the evacuation of Crete "while there was still time." But Hitler said no. He knew that the loyalty of Germany's remaining allies required shoring up their faith in the Nazi war machine. Abandoning the Aegean islands— Crete in particular—"would create a most unfavorable impression." Instead, German forces began mobilizing for attacks in the Dodecanese, and Crete was becoming an important staging ground.

Near the end of the month Sandy Rendel reported sighting some sixty Stuka dive-bombers winging their way toward the Dodecanese. After that his radio fell silent and would not be heard from for weeks. The RAF was now bombing German-held facilities in Heraklion on a nightly basis. In Cairo, however, Leigh Fermor found that life went on as usual.

RETURNING TO CAIRO after months in the field always entailed a jolt to the system. Partly it was the sheer number of people. Egyptians from rural areas had been flocking to the city since the late 1930s, nearly doubling its size in a decade. And they were not alone. Although Egypt had been granted indepen-

dence in 1922, the British retained the right to protect the Suez
Canal, as well as the power, in time of war, to establish bases in
Egypt and occupy ports and airfields. Now Cairo had become
headquarters not just for SOE but for all British forces in the
Middle East. As a result, the city was bursting at the seams with
British and Commonwealth soldiers. And sometimes it seemed
there were nearly as many French nationals and Greeks and
Poles. The city swarmed with people. It was a far cry from the
mountains of Crete.

More than just the bustle, though, Cairo was a world apart
in other ways. "There was death and tragedy in Europe," one
wartime resident wrote, "but here all was affluence and spar-
kle—or so it seemed." Despite the uniforms in evidence, the war
felt far away. In fact, Cairo could seem to a British officer more
like home, as it had existed before the war, than London itself.
Wherever you went you were likely to run into someone you
had known back then. "Dickens would have had no need to tie
up his stories with the fantastical granny knots of coincidence,
if he could have set them in war-time Cairo," Evelyn Waugh's
friend Christopher Sykes believed. "The amount of meeting and
re-meeting and unlikely hearing about friends was worthy of
the craziest melodrama."

Although it was Crete that Leigh Fermor and his SOE colleagues called "Never-Never Land," life in Cairo often felt even
more like a game of make-believe that had been lifted out of
time. The effect was strongest on the Gezira island, a lush oasis
in the middle of the Nile that was home to the majority of the
British in Cairo. "What was so remarkable about Gezira was
that, unlike the rest of Cairo, it was so *green*," recalled an SOE
coder named Margaret Pawley, who lived aboard a houseboat
docked at the island. Relatively cool breezes filtered through the
lush tropical gardens of the island, creating what one wartime
resident described as "an atmosphere of permanent holiday."

Leigh Fermor's friend Annette Crean, an attractive and athletic young woman who worked in Sykes's office at SOE headquarters, started her days before dawn with an hourlong pleasure ride on one of the polo ponies kept at the Gezira Sporting Club, which was called by one historian "the most magnificent sports grounds ever seen in the heart of a capital city." Later Crean lunched by the club's pool. After work she rounded out the day with tea at Groppi's, the popular café off Soliman Pasha Square, then dinner and dancing.

In many ways the city was a hybrid—both ancient and modern, glamorous and primitive. At times the streets were clogged with vehicles. But in the predawn hours before motor traffic took over the roadways, you might still see a leisurely cow ambling across the Bulaq Bridge, which linked Gezira to the rest of the city lying east of the Nile. In the posh urban neighborhoods grand villas were protected by Sudanese guards whose faces were scarred by ritual markings.

A traveler marveling at Cairo's grandeur in the fourteenth century had called her "mother of cities," but to many of the Europeans now living there it seemed that a few basic matters of urban sanitation were yet to be worked out. Margaret Pawley, who had come at the end of 1942, fell ill almost immediately, and it did not take long for her to fix the blame on her new surroundings. "The air we breathed was heavily polluted and what we ate and drank loaded with a deposit of bacteria," she noted, "and then there were the omnipresent armies of flies." At the same time, Cairo had an atmosphere of elegance and style that was unmatched anywhere else. A message Xan Fielding had dispatched from Crete earlier in the year hinted at the mixed feelings Leigh Fermor and his friends had toward the city. "Hope you're enjoying the fleshpots and cesspools of Egypt," he wrote.

It was hard to say whether the past or the future had the upper hand in Cairo. An American journalist who fled to the city from Crete in the wake of the invasion thought the Egyptians were working overtime to "keep alive the tradition of Oriental splendor and mysticism while Ford automobiles zip around the streets and movie houses show the latest Hollywood films and you can buy Granger tobacco for sixty cents per ten-cent package." Altogether the mixture of people and the whirl of vehicles—heavy trucks and sleek limousines vying with donkey carts—created a hurly-burly atmosphere. "The hot dusty streets were crammed with humanity which seemed to represent the culture of several centuries," one SOE officer concluded.

Julian Amery, a Cairo friend of Leigh Fermor's who had been a war correspondent in Spain and was now an SOE captain awaiting infiltration into Albania, liked to tell a story about a popular Arab restaurant near Shepheard's Hotel called Hatih, where diners who lingered over evening meals in the rooftop garden often wound up tangling with the city's less glamorous nightlife.

"The food was good," Amery claimed, "but late in the evening, as the guests began to leave, rats used to come out to eat up bits of food from the floor. They were the biggest rats I have ever seen and quite tame." One night, when he found himself alone at the restaurant with a beautiful but demure Englishwoman, Amery took advantage of the situation by discreetly scattering food around her chair. "Presently three very large rats crept to within a few inches of her feet," he said. "When I pointed out that we had company, she literally fell into my arms."

NOT LONG AFTER his return to Cairo from Crete with General Carta, Leigh Fermor met a young lieutenant in the Coldstream Guards named William Stanley Moss. Billy Moss was a tall, languorous twenty-two-year-old with striking good looks. Not only did he have the chiseled face of a movie star, but his manner somehow suggested he had just stepped out of an actual movie. He had fought with his regiment at Tobruk and El Alamein. Now he was awaiting his next assignment.

When they met, Moss and Leigh Fermor were both living in an officers' flophouse known as Hangover Hall. It was a cramped and cheerless accommodation that felt even less desirable than usual that fall, which was particularly hot, with afternoon temperatures edging past 110 degrees even as late as October. Neither of the young men was happy with the arrangement, but in the dismal surroundings they quickly became friends. To Paddy, Moss was a "charming figure, with his fondness for books, his humour, spirit and knack of enjoying things."

His parents' only child, Moss was born in Yokohama, Japan, where his family had deep roots, one branch having served as missionaries there, as well as in China. His grandfather was a onetime manager of the *Japan Gazette* who went on to become head registrar for the court formed in 1879 to try cases involving British subjects in Japan. Moss's grandmother served on the committee of the Yokohama literary society. The grandfather's family crest—on which a shield that bore a griffin's head between two sprigs of moss rose over a motto reading *Pro patria semper*—had passed down to Moss's father and uncle. His father, and namesake, was a merchant with business in Tokyo. His mother, Natalie, was the youngest daughter of a Russian landowner from Nikolsk-Ussuriysky, a trading outpost sixty-odd miles north of Vladivostok. Moss had picked up his mother's language, but there was not much call for Russian in North Africa. (It would turn out, much to his surprise, to be useful later on, in Crete.) Even before he could walk, Moss began to see the world, traveling with his father to Shanghai when he was only a few months old. It was the first of many family trips. Before his first day of school, he had been around the world more than once.

He was just two years old in 1923 when a powerful earthquake struck the Yokohama area, destroying thousands of buildings and killing more than a hundred thousand people. The quake triggered a towering tsunami and ignited fires that raged all around Tokyo Bay.

Later that same fall, Moss left Japan with his family and returned to England. As he grew into a tall, athletic schoolboy, he began to develop a wide range of interests. He boxed and played soccer, tennis, and cricket. He had a knack for drawing and was soon filling pages with beautifully detailed sketches, often of the plants and animals he enjoyed spotting in the English countryside. He loved to sing and liked going to movies and plays. And he read a great deal. In particular, he admired Rudyard Kipling and Robert Louis Stevenson. *Treasure Island* was his favorite book, and when, at the age of fifteen, he wrote a book of his own—and published it in a handwritten eighty-page "presentation copy"—the debt to Stevenson could be seen even in the title: *Island Adventure.*

In 1938 Moss was at Charterhouse, the prestigious boarding school in Surrey thirty miles southwest of London, when he received word that his father had died. He remembered how the bespectacled housemaster had called him to his office in the middle of the night to tell him that his father was ill and he should prepare himself for bad news. The news came first thing the next morning. Moss later learned that his father had in fact died the day before. The midnight ruse was the housemaster's personal touch. "He always did it like that," Moss had heard, "so as to soften the shock."

This was not the first death Moss had been aware of. He knew vaguely that his uncle Edward had been killed in action with the Gloucester Regiment on the first day of the Battle of Loos in 1915. Then when he was a boy in Japan, he had watched a man pulling a rickshaw collapse and die on the street. "Most of the rickshaw coolies died young from heart strain," he recalled, "and this one just flopped down between the handle-bars and lay in the middle of the road, quite still." Some years later an Austrian housemaid who worked for his family had slit her own throat in the room she occupied in the attic of the family house. But none of these deaths had hurt him as his father's did. It was a wound he carried with him all his life, and the pain of it seemed to grow stronger, not weaker, with time.

Not that it showed. On the outside Moss remained energetic and charming. With the help of a classmate he launched a new school magazine and invited illustrious "old boys" to send him articles. Many did, including Robert Baden-Powell, the founder of the scouting movement, who submitted a story of the Boer war. Moss produced a stunning series of posters to publicize the new magazine.

When he finished his last year at Charterhouse, the following August, he traveled with his mother, aunt, and uncle to Gottenberg and from there on to Riga, finally settling in a picturesque village near the Latvian coast outside the capital. It was there, while swimming and taking walks among the pines that grew by the sea, that Moss listened to the increasingly distressing news of German troop movements along the Polish border. On August 20 he spent the day swimming and reading in the sun and noted in his diary that it was a relief to tune out politics for a while.

The book he had with him—a fantasy novel called *Kai Lung's Golden Hours*—provided a welcome escape, but the respite did not last long. Throughout the following week, Moss heard reports of skirmishes along the Polish border. He was scheduled to begin a job in England on September 4, and it was beginning to look unlikely that he would be there on time.

By the end of August he was in Stockholm. On September 1 he went to see *The Four Feathers*, a popular recent movie about a

British officer caught up in the Sudanese war at the end of the nineteenth century. The next day Moss heard that fierce fighting had broken out in Poland, as Germany launched the invasion that would plunge Europe into war. Reaching home would be even more challenging than he had thought. He and his family traveled to Gottenberg, where they boarded the Swedish Lloyd liner *Suecia*. They were about to sit down to dinner when it was announced that the ship would not sail. "We are in the soup now," Moss recorded in his diary.

In the following week he made his way by train to Bergen, Norway, where he was able to book passage to Newcastle on a yacht that had once belonged to Kaiser Wilhelm and had been taken by Norway in what was now coming to look like the *first* World War. The ship sailed on the twelfth with some two hundred passengers on board.

By the fourteenth Moss had reached England, and soon after the new year he joined the Coldstream Guards. Like Leigh Fermor, he found the routine at the Guards' Depot in Caterham, where both of their units conducted training, vaguely ludicrous. But military discipline was less inimical to Moss than it was to Paddy, and he waded through the flurry of regimental charades in reasonably good humor. After training he had even put in a stint in the King's Guard at St James's Palace. And for a while he was assigned to the guard at Chequers, the prime minister's house in Buckinghamshire. "It had been wonderful staying at Chequers at a time when every word spoken by Churchill was gospel, and thrilling to see him 'off duty' and to speak with him and eat and drink with him and to understand him and his ways," he recalled. On the whole, though, he thought the life of a regular army officer was not what he was looking for.

When he eventually joined his regiment for active duty, Moss found that brawling with Rommel's forces in North Africa came still more naturally to him. During the two or three months he spent on campaign in the desert, he relished the "lovely feeling of advancing and beating the Germans." Not that he liked everything that came with war. He would never forget the loneliness that washed over him while burying a sniper who had been killed on a rainy, mosquito-infested night in Tunisia. Nor how useless he had felt as he listened to one of his fellow guardsmen crying out for help as the man lay dying in the middle of a minefield after a blast had torn off both of his legs.

Moss had a theory about the way everyone around him managed to get through the war. He believed none of them really felt the impact of dreadful events as they whizzed past. You watch a man die on the battlefield, as he had, or a woman giving birth in the middle of an air raid, and your mind cannot absorb what you have seen. The same was true of any kind of bad news. "The floods of tears may be instantaneous, so too the feeling that the end of your world has come," he believed, "but, in fact, the real horror, the ultimate implication of what you have learned, is reserved for later—and by then you find yourself strangely the better equipped to accept it." It was only in retrospect, he thought, that anyone could see things clearly.

SOON AFTER he arrived in Cairo to await reassignment to SOE, Moss began to hear horrifying news from the desert where the Coldstream Guards were still engaged in heavy fighting. One day an old acquaintance turned up with his left arm blown off and told him that three other comrades of theirs had been killed in action, including the closest friend Moss had ever had. A few days later he met another friend, whose right arm had been blown off, who reported still more casualties. It was utterly devastating news, and by his own theory it would be a long time before he could see it all clearly.

At the time, Moss was engaged to a young woman named Patsy, who was supposed to come out to meet him. He took a room above the cinema at Shepheard's Hotel, bought a ring he could not afford, and waited, but she never arrived. His assignment to SOE came through on September 24, and there was still no sign of Patsy. Soon, however, a letter arrived from her breaking off the engagement. Moss sold the ring and used the money to finance two more weeks at Shepheard's, before moving to his SOE quarters. But it was not long before he began plotting to move out of Hangover Hall. By chance he found an airy villa in a leafy neighborhood north of the Gezira Sporting Club, which was practically a second home to the British officers stationed in Cairo.

At first he moved in alone, then began recruiting a handful of SOE officers to join him and pitch in on the rent. Paddy Leigh Fermor signed on right away. But he and Moss worried that the house would fall into shambles when they were sent into the field. If they could convince a few women to share the place, they reasoned, it would remain occupied as the men came and went on various missions. They had asked two of the young English women who worked with SOE, but they were still making up their minds when Moss decided to ask a young Polish countess, in Cairo working with the Red Cross, whom he had met earlier that summer.

Sophie Tarnowska was a striking, slender woman with shoulder-length fair hair swept back from her face. She had remarkable green eyes and a smooth high forehead. Even her hands were beautiful. She spoke English with a charming accent. Her manner was graceful and self-assured but also light-hearted. Moss had to admit that she was as captivating a woman as he had ever met, but she also managed to seem like one of the boys.

Moss and Leigh Fermor were happy when Sophie accepted the invitation to join the new household that was forming in Gezira. But then, when the time came to move in, the other

William Stanley Moss.
© Imperial War Museum (HU 66053)
Sophie Tarnowska.
Photograph © The Estate of William Stanley Moss—
reproduced by permission

two women backed out, and it looked as if the plan would fall through. Sophie worried about the impression that might arise if she was the only woman living in a villa full of men. "No, I can't possibly come," she told Moss. He and Leigh Fermor tried everything to convince her. They took her to see the splendid house; they pointed to the benefits of pooling their money; they unashamedly begged. But she still wavered. Finally they came up with a scheme that would keep up appearances.

When Sophie moved out of the National Hotel, where she had been staying, she took up residence at the Gezira villa with Moss, Leigh Fermor, the other SOE officers, and one Mrs. Khayatt—a respectable, somewhat sickly, and, though no one was to know this, entirely fictional chaperone. Whenever a guest dropped by, the residents of the house made elaborate apologies for her. "Mrs. Khayatt is so sorry that she can't join us," someone would announce, "but she has a terrible headache."

The ruse proved so amusing that before long everyone in the house had taken on a fictitious identity. Sophie became "Princess Dnieper-Petrovsk," Moss was "Mr. Jack Jargon"—after the gigantic guardsman in Byron's *Don Juan*—and Paddy was "Lord Rakehell." The others assumed equally colorful personas. Soon a brass plaque appeared at the entryway bearing the outlandish names of the new tenants.

AS AUTUMN FADED into winter, Leigh Fermor, Moss, and the others came to know Sophie better, and it was fair to say that all the men became a little infatuated with her. Everything about the countess bore a tint of adventure. Sophie had grown up on her father's estate along the River San in southern Poland, in an atmosphere of country aristocracy that might have come from a Tolstoy novel. Indeed, the resemblance was more than coincidental. Sophie's father admired Tolstoy and had modeled his management of the estate, called Rudnik, on the Russian novelist's benevolent principles, providing housing, schools, and medical care for the peasants who lived and worked there. Rudnik was a vast realm in which Sophie and her younger brother enjoyed the run of some ten thousand acres. Its well-managed forests—forestry was one of her father's passions—extended for miles in every direction, and the grounds held greenhouses and orchards, vegetable gardens, beehives, and a vodka distillery. There was even a hydroelectric power plant.

Sophie's grandparents had been fixtures in Kraków society. Her grandfather, Count Tarnowski, was a respected academic whose ancestors, five hundred years before his time, signed their names to the charter of the nation's oldest university. Sophie took great pride in all he had achieved, though he died the year she was born. Her grandmother was a countess from a still wealthier family, whose forebears had been favorites in the court of Catherine II.

Sophie's parents were married in the anxious summer of 1914, little more than a week after the assassination of Archduke Franz Ferdinand in Sarajevo. By the time Sophie was born, in 1917, the family estate had been devastated by the war. More than three thousand bodies were hastily buried on the grounds after one particularly fierce battle. And there was more turmoil to come. Sophie's earliest memory recalled her parents' defiance and resolve as the Red Army advanced toward the estate, when she was three years old.

As a young girl, Sophie seemed to put on a mantle of precocious ruggedness. She flung herself into outdoor pursuits, soon becoming the "Lion" to her younger brother's "Hare." The two spent their time shooting and hunting, eagerly flirting with whatever dangers they could find in country life.

But their rugged childhood idyll came to an end in 1930, when their parents separated and Sophie was sent to a convent school some eighty miles from home, where she was often in trouble with the nuns. On one occasion she was discovered taking a bath naked, something the administration frowned upon. (Convent rules required the employment of a "modesty garment.") To make matters worse, the nuns later intercepted a letter to her parents in which Sophie had made "rude comments about the Mother Superior's body odor." (She called it the "odeur de sainteté," the odor of sanctity.) Finally, early in 1931, when she was thirteen, she scrawled "Goodbye—Sophie" on a blackboard and caught the train for Kraków to rejoin her family.

Four years later she had fallen in love with Andrew Tarnowski, a tall, gregarious young man from the main line of the Tarnowski family. By 1937 Sophie and Andrew were married. The couple's first son, born that fall, died just two years later, on the very day their second child was born. It was while bringing the new baby home from Kraków in the summer of 1939 that Sophie, already sick with grief, had a vision of the terrible future that would eventually tear her family apart, along with the fabric of Europe itself. She and Andrew were waiting at the railway station when the train they were to take pulled into view. As it came even with the platform, they were horrified to see blood streaming down the sides of one carriage. It turned out that a number of army conscripts who were riding on the roof of the car had been killed as the train passed under a low bridge. For Sophie it was not just a horrific sight but also an omen. She felt that some powerful force was about to destroy everything she had ever known.

That August the couple, in the company of Sophie's brother Stas and his new fiancée, a beautiful nineteen-year-old girl from Warsaw, basked in the pleasures of an aristocratic way of life that was about to be shattered forever. They spent their days riding through the forests of a remote estate that Sophie's family owned in the Carpathian Mountains, hunting deer in the evenings, and coming together for meals served outside under the willows.

Then, on the morning of September 1, Sophie was awakened by the sound of airplanes roaring over their house. "They were going so low," she recalled, "that I saw the curtains moving and dust lifting off the road. I looked out the window and I saw quite a lot of farm hands waving at the planes." At first she imagined, as the farmers did, that these were British aircraft, part of a force moving in to help repel any German advance. But the news reports coming over the radio soon dispelled that hope. "And this," she recalled, "is how we learned that the war had started." While Sophie was upset by the news, Stas was electrified. "Hurrah," he called out, "we'll show the buggers. We'll be in Berlin in a couple of months."

Over the following days, radio news reports tracked German tanks and troops as they rolled across Poland. Meanwhile, Sophie and Andrew heard rumors of a coming British counterattack. But all around them the signs were ominous. German planes were often visible overhead, apparently circling the house in regularly timed patrols.

Sophie had her hands full caring for the refugees who began to converge on the estate from the surrounding countryside. When one young woman lay dying of typhus, Sophie stayed in the house to tend to her, even as the others took shelter from the German bombers in a nearby icehouse. Stas and Andrew drove to a nearby village to buy medical supplies, but they found the stores and pharmacies shuttered. As they pressed on toward a larger neighboring town, a German plane forced them to turn back to the estate.

By the end of the week, Andrew had decided to move the family to a hunting lodge that lay secluded in the forest not far from the main house. It was a practical measure, but to Sophie's mind the move loomed like the first act of a tragedy in which she wanted no part. Whatever happened next, she refused to leave Poland and was willing to take extreme measures to ensure that she would stay. Before she left the house, she burned her passport.

That night, just hours after the family had settled in at the hunting lodge, word came that a German column was approaching. Sophie and Andrew piled into a hulking blue Ford with their baby, accompanied by Stas and his fiancée, and they drove north into the night, toward Sophie's childhood home. Traveling on bomb-rutted roads with the headlights turned off, for fear of attracting German planes, they made slow progress, but they managed to reach Rudnik a little before dawn. What they found there was nothing like the pastoral paradise Sophie and Stas had known as children. The estate was already crowded with refugees from the nearby town, where the railway station and surrounding buildings had been targeted by German bombers. And the German front was still only a day's drive away.

It was clear that they would have to keep moving. That evening, as Sophie said good-bye to her father for what would be the last time, he handed her one of the treasures of the estate, the royal standard of the Swedish king Charles X Gustav, which had been captured by the Polish cavalry at Rudnik nearly three hundred years earlier. With this relic of Poland's earlier struggle packed among their belongings, Sophie and the others drove east toward the River San. Once across the river, they turned north, but they soon found themselves swept up in a tide of refugees moving southeast through rolling, forested terrain toward the Romanian border. On September 17, as German bombers pounded the Polish town behind them, they were forced across the River Dniester, which marked the border between the two countries, leaving their homeland behind.

In the coming months Sophie's party was driven by advancing Axis forces from Poland to Bucharest to Belgrade and then to Tel Aviv. Her brother married his young fiancée, her remaining child died, and her husband fell in love with her new sister-in-law. By summer she was on the move again—this time boarding a train that carried her south toward Cairo through the stifling heat of the Sinai desert.

WHEN SHE REACHED CAIRO, Sophie moved into a villa owned by a well-traveled nephew of King Farouk who had gotten to know Andrew at hunting parties in Poland. There was a cook who served up delightful meals, and the staff included a night watchman and a servant who impressed Sophie with his pristine manners. Her host filled the house with flowers, provided his guests with champagne and French perfume, and even made daily deliveries of wine and cigarettes. After months living a hand-to-mouth existence, this new life felt like stepping into a dream. "Altogether it is a bit of a fairy tale," Sophie felt.

But for all the excitement of life in Cairo, she never stopped worrying about her husband and brother—who were now fighting in the desert with the Carpathian Lancers—and the rest of her family, many of whom had remained in Poland. She soon went to work for the Red Cross and before long had founded a Polish branch of the organization. Unlike Red Cross volunteers elsewhere, who wore dark woolen uniforms, Sophie's unit wore khaki, which was more suited to Egypt's desert climate. She also specified that there would be no system of military rank in the new branch, a radical idea in a time of war. It may have been that the young woman who had kicked against the authority of the mother superior at school in Poland had a hard time, at the still-youthful age of twenty-five, imagining herself in command.

She set up an office outfitted with a typewriter and a sewing machine. The director of the British Red Cross supplied a heavy truck, which Sophie drove around the city and countryside, collecting clothing for Polish refugees.

But Sophie's life in Cairo was far from all work. She was on friendly terms with the wife of the British ambassador and got along well with the commander of the British forces in Egypt and most of his officers. A flashier set also sought out her company. Not long after her arrival in Cairo, Sophie was befriended by Aly Khan, the Ismaili prince whose father was a former president of the League of Nations. The thirty-year-old prince was passionate about horse racing and thrill sports of all kinds. He loved skiing and motor racing and had set records for risky long-distance flights. He would later marry the actress Rita Hayworth and had already established a reputation as an international playboy. When the war broke out, he had joined the

French Foreign Legion, but he was now attached to the British army. Sophie enjoyed his company, especially when he took her up for a joyride in his private plane.

Another admirer was King Farouk himself. On one occasion, when Sophie encountered Farouk at a nightclub, he called her over to join him at his table. Realizing too late that there was no chair for his new guest, the king called out, "A throne, a throne for Countess Tarnowska!"

Sophie was particularly fond of Farouk's wife, Queen Farida, who invited her for tea at the Abdin Palace, the royal family's sumptuous house in Old Cairo. Since the queen was forbidden by Islamic custom from appearing in public, she and Sophie often met surreptitiously. At parties, the queen would call Sophie away from the ballroom to join her in an out-of-the-way room or a hidden spot on a balcony so they could spy on the social swirl below. Other times Farida sent Sophie tickets to a movie theater, where, after the lights went down, the queen would join her, her identity disguised by a strategically draped veil.

For all that she had lost since the war began, Sophie recognized that she was now living a kind of charmed life. "This is like being in heaven," she wrote to her now estranged husband. "My life is seven hours of work (just like the seven lean cows in the Bible) and then, whoopee. After that I sleep very little."

Sophie's Cairo fairy tale lasted until the summer of 1942, when a crisis in the desert sent a wave of panic through the city. All year Erwin Rommel's Afrika Korps had been on the offensive, taking Benghazi, on the Libyan coast, at the end of January, then pushing east throughout the spring. By June, Rommel was on the march toward the crucial harbor city of Tobruk, just five hundred miles westward along the coast from Cairo. When Tobruk fell near the end of the month, the residents of Cairo were left wondering whether Rommel could be stopped before his tanks rolled into the city itself. Two days later he crossed the border into Egypt.

July was a time of year when few would have chosen to be in Cairo under the best of circumstances. The air hung still and hot beneath a sun so bright it seemed to bleach the color from everything in sight. Now the threat of siege, or worse, had the British and their allies streaming out of the city. A letter arrived from Andrew asking Sophie to come to Palestine. But it was her sister-in-law who went. Finally, the head of the Polish legation ordered Sophie to evacuate. She refused. But on the following day she drove her car out to the main road to see what was happening. The roads were choked with vehicles. One long line stretched eastward, carrying evacuees toward safety in Palestine. In the other direction, along the road to Alexandria, trucks loaded with soldiers rattled slowly toward the front lines.

It was obvious that she ought to join the convoy headed for Palestine. But recalling her earlier departure from Poland, Sophie refused to let herself be forced, once again, to give up her home. "I'll be damned," she said to herself. She would not run away. In fact, she would do the opposite. "I'll take the train and go to Alexandria, to be closer to the front."

That evening she made her way to the railway station and boarded an eerily empty train. A little more than three hours later—an air raid had caused a short delay—she stepped down in Alexandria and walked ten minutes north to the waterfront esplanade known as the Corniche, where she took a room at the Beau Rivage Hotel. Though it cost more than she could comfortably spend, she was drawn to the hotel for its garden terrace by the sea. Alexandria was smaller and quieter than Cairo, and she felt that she had left the chaos of the city's evacuation behind her, though in fact she had put herself closer to the action. Except for the blackout restrictions that were still in place following a recent attack by the Luftwaffe, it was hard to believe a battle was raging only seventy-odd miles away. That evening, when Sophie went down to the restaurant on the terrace, she found that she was the only guest. She had the entire staff of waiters to herself, and the manager of the hotel—grateful to have such an agreeable patron in a difficult time—treated her to a bottle of his best wine. As she enjoyed the meal there by the sea, she was convinced she could hear the faint rumble of the guns at El Alamein.

Over the following days, while Sophie read books on the beach near the hotel, British troops fighting in the desert to the west at last managed to stop Rommel's advance. She returned to Cairo. By the end of the month, the evacuees flooded back. The crisis, which the British began to call "the flap," was over. But for Sophie the near disaster, weathered entirely on her own, marked a turning point that allowed her to put the past behind her. It was the following summer that she met Moss. A friend who saw them together called them "the best looking couple he had ever seen."

CHAPTER 7

Tara

THE HOUSE Moss had found sat on the northern end of the Gezira island, near a point where the river flowed past a colonnade of mature sycamore figs. Cultivated lawns bordered the villas that dotted the area, and not far to the south began the outlying stretches of the golf course, cricket pitch, and polo fields maintained by the nearby Gezira Sporting Club. Jasmine and honeysuckle flourished on villa gates and railings, sending out scents that, once picked up by the river breezes, "made the air of summer nights intoxicating."

The villa itself offered everything a field-weary SOE officer could want. A wide balustraded stairway swept up from the garden to the front door, which opened onto an airy and inviting first floor. The half dozen bedrooms scattered throughout the house were a comfortable step up from the lodgings at Hangover Hall. From one or two of the upstairs windows you could scramble out onto the roof to gaze at the night sky or bask in the sun. There was an ample dining room and a drawing room dominated by a cozy hearth. Moss thought one room would make a good study. Most important, as it turned out, was the parquet-floored ballroom, a grand, open space that seemed to demand lavish parties. The new residents put this to good use before they had hardly moved in.

They soon gave the new house a name, christening it Tara. Although SOE had spirited him away from the Irish Guards, Leigh Fermor still felt the pull of his Irish ancestry. To him the name pointed to the legendary seat of the high kings of Ireland, a great hall situated on the River Boyne. It was there that "thronged assemblies of all the notables were held," one historian wrote of ancient Tara, "rude Parliaments of the kings and their free-born kinsmen, and of bards, historians, and druids." It was easy to see why this romantic idea appealed to Paddy's imagination. But "Tara" was also the name of the once-stately plantation house in *Gone with the Wind*. And that was an even more apt model for the house that had brought this group of wartime friends together. Sophie Tarnowska even dressed as Scarlett O'Hara for one of their house parties and was caught in a photograph that might have been of the fictional heroine herself, if not for the cigarette held delicately between her first two fingers, its lit end angled upward.

AMONG THE FRIENDS who took up residence at Tara was a twenty-five-year-old Sandhurst graduate named Billy McLean. Moss had been the conducting officer when McLean was extracted from his most recent mission, and he had liked the young man's disarming smile and romantic outlook on the war. Born in London, McLean came from a family with Highland roots, and he could trace his lineage back through seven centuries' worth of Gaelic chieftains. He was stronger than his tall, thin build made him appear, but he had an easygoing way about him. It was tempting to say he was lazy, until you had seen him stirred into action.

He had served in Palestine in 1938, at the time of the Arab revolt, and had picked up some Arabic there. Later on he organized irregulars to fight the Italians along the Gojjam heights in Abyssinia. Waiting in Addis Ababa before going into action, he had tried to learn Amharic, without much success. But he still took pleasure in mimicking the kind of syntax he had tangled with, thickets like "the mule who-riding-man-is-having-gone is now going."

When Xan Fielding, Leigh Fermor's friend from Crete, moved into the house later in the winter, he at first took McLean for some kind of fop. It was true his name appeared at the top of the party lists maintained by Cairo hostesses. And he wore his fair, straight hair so long that he was continually brushing it away from his eyes. "He struck me as a human epitome of cavalry dash and swagger, even though he had long ago exchanged his steed for a parachute," Fielding later wrote. "But, as I soon discovered, this charming and lackadaisical façade concealed a toughness of steel, great powers of physical endurance, and a needle-sharp intelligence."

In Albania the previous July, McLean had ambushed a German staff car, ostensibly to capture documents that might disclose something of the enemy's plans in the Balkans but more for the fun of it. His mission, which had been under way since April, had been drawing to a close, and there had been no engagements with the Germans. "I'm damned if I'm leaving here without having a crack at something," he had told a fellow officer. When the story reached his friends, they thought it sounded like characteristic McLean behavior.

Also becoming a fixture at the house, though he lived elsewhere, was the former war correspondent turned SOE officer Julian Amery, a trim young man with a narrow, delicate face, penetrating dark eyes, and hair swept back from a high forehead.

David Smiley was a friend of McLean's who had been living elsewhere too. But he decided to move in when he found he was spending all his time at Tara *and* too much money on Moss's *suffraghi*, Abdul, who tapped guests for contributions to the household fund as they came and went. Smiley had met McLean three years earlier aboard a troopship in the Red Sea. Both were then in mounted cavalry regiments and were returning to their units in the Middle East after an aborted volunteer mission intended to help the Somaliland Camel Corps fend off an Italian advance into British Somaliland. As they became acquainted, trading stories about their experiences in Palestine, they convinced each other that horse units were unlikely to see real action in the fighting that lay ahead. Rather than rejoin their cavalry regiments, both men made a detour to Cairo and wangled their way into other units.

Smiley wound up in a commando detachment leading long-range raids against enemy supply lines behind the Italian front in Abyssinia. When he learned that his former cavalry unit had traded its horses for tanks and was on its way to Iraq, he asked for a transfer back. The regiment fought its way to Baghdad, and Smiley stayed on for campaigns through Syria and Persia. Later on, reequipped with fast-moving armored cars, they were sent to the Western Desert. "After the breakthrough at Alamein," he recalled, "we pushed ahead collecting thousands of Italian prisoners, having occasional shoot-outs with pockets of German or Italian resistance, and passing vast quantities of abandoned enemy guns, tanks, vehicles and equipment."

On leave in Cairo before heading out into the desert, he had bumped into McLean again and heard tales of his exploits in SOE. Although intrigued, Smiley was looking forward to his own unit's upcoming tussle with Rommel's forces in the desert and thought no more about it. However, when his unit was later pulled back from the fighting due to dwindling fuel supplies, SOE suddenly looked like the best route back into the thick of things. McLean helped him secure an interview, during which he laid out his qualifications.

"In Palestine I had done a course on mines and explosives," he explained. "I had trained with explosives again in the commandos, served in guerilla-type operations in Abyssinia, operated against guerillas in Palestine, and gained battle experience from fighting in Iraq, Syria, Persia and the Western Desert." On top of all that, he had also completed a secret course in guerrilla warfare and demolitions that was conducted at a monastery on the site of the biblical Emmaus, outside Jerusalem.

It came as no surprise when SOE accepted his application. Just after the first of the year Smiley traveled to the SOE camp near Haifa for the standard training course. "We studied German and Italian weapons, uniforms, insignia, badges and organization, map reading, explosives and demolitions, as well as such unorthodox subjects as sabotage of all types, the use of secret inks, tapping telephone lines, lock picking and safe blowing." One lesson on the use of a timed incendiary device reduced the classroom itself to cinders. Smiley called the program "my dirty tricks course."

When it was over, he went to Kabrit, on the Suez Canal, for parachute training. By the middle of April, a week after his twenty-seventh birthday, he was lounging in the cargo hold of a Halifax bomber, reading *Horse & Hound* while he waited to drop into Greece as McLean's second in command. They touched down in the mountains on Greece's northwestern frontier and set out toward the north. Several days later they slipped into Albania.

Smiley's arrival at Tara had an immediate impact on the atmosphere of the house, at the olfactory level. For an outdoorsman, he had an unusual weakness for what he called "smells," by which he meant various exotic scents and perfumes. Whenever he came home, the aroma of the sandalwood oil he wore wafted in with him. And he took great pleasure in burning incense, first in his room and later in the drawing room or Moss's study, wherever he happened to be. Sophie, for one, did not mind this quirk, and when Christmas rolled around, her present to him was a sizable flagon of sandalwood oil. Unfortunately the gift led to some unexpected difficulty when Smiley applied the scent a little too freely as he was leaving for a meeting with a delegate from the Yugoslav partisans. He arrived smelling like the proverbial French whore, and the delegate apparently got the wrong impression about his sexual interests, causing an awkward exchange. Smiley preferred not to talk about it.

A fondness for scents was not the only peculiarity Smiley brought with him to Tara. Unlike many of his housemates—Leigh Fermor and Moss, in particular—who shared literary interests, Smiley found even the workaday writing that went into mission reports pure drudgery. When his housemates discovered him hunched over a half-written report in obvious misery, they wondered aloud whether, as Paddy put it, "perhaps he was happier with the sword than the pen." Julian Amery agreed: "Smiley lived for action alone and was happiest on a dangerous reconnaissance or when 'blowing things up.'"

Smiley and McLean labored for over a month on the summary of their recent Albanian mission. The two of them could often be found encamped in Moss's study, surrounded by the loot they had brought back with them, staring at the typewriter. Moss sometimes overheard them sniping at each other out of frustration. Smiley would shout, "You bloody communist!" And McLean would snap back, "You bloody fascist!"

The two remaining inhabitants were Arnold Breene—he worked behind the scenes at the SOE headquarters—and Rowland Winn. Winn, the son of an eccentric baron from Yorkshire, had been a reporter for Reuters during the Spanish civil war. He was captured by the republicans and had turned twenty-one in a Barcelona jail, where he would have been executed if the British consul had not managed to spring him. Now twenty-seven, he was in an armored cavalry regiment but had applied for transfer to SOE. His friends were trying to push his application through.

Much as they liked Winn, however, it was sometimes hard to imagine his faring well in the field. Around three o'clock one night, driving home from a party with him, Julian Amery suddenly realized his friend was not in the car. He wheeled around and drove back to find Winn sitting by the side of the road cursing. It seemed he had not managed to secure the door when he got in, and he had tumbled out as Amery rounded a curve.

His misfortunes seemed part and parcel of his persona. Winn used a monocle, had an awkward manner of walking, and wore an extravagant waxed mustache, all of which seemed to invite mockery. Sophie quickly made a game of hiding his cap, just to watch him bang the table and demand to know where it had gone. On one occasion her teasing went too far. She found him asleep on a sofa in the drawing room, stole back to her room to retrieve a pair of scissors, tiptoed back in, and snipped off one waxy wing of his mustache. When it came free in her hand, she was mortified to see that he had worn it to conceal a scar on his lip. Winn nevertheless remained devoted to Sophie, bringing her a little gift of chocolates or some household luxury whenever he had been out. He had a volatile personality and could be incensed or sociable by turns. But there were women who found him chivalrous. Paddy thought him "quixotic."

Leigh Fermor was on less friendly terms with another member of the household. While Moss was still living at the house alone, he had acquired a German shepherd puppy, at first no bigger than a teapot, that came with an unusual pedigree. Its parents had been captured at Tobruk, where they were trained as police dogs by the Gestapo. Moss called the dog Pixie, a name that put a cheerful spin on the mischief he was constantly stirring up. For some reason it was Leigh Fermor who wound up cast in the role of long-suffering victim. As Pixie grew by leaps and bounds over the course of the fall, so did the ongoing feud between the two. The dog had a particular knack for adding insult to injury whenever anyone was involved in some sort of mishap.

One morning Paddy lurched awake just before dawn to find the couch he was lying on in flames. He realized later that he had come in after a night out and fallen asleep with a cigarette in his hand, a practice he was engaging in more and more often these days. The drawing room was filling with smoke as he dashed down the hall to wake Moss, and when the two of them returned, flames were already sweeping up the wall as high as the ceiling. They grabbed a bowl and a wastepaper basket and dashed for the kitchen sink. What ensued was a scene out of a slapstick comedy. At one point the bottom fell out of the waste-basket, which was made of parchment. When they finally had the fire doused, Pixie arrived, sniffed the couch, raised his leg, and urinated on it. In fact, at the height of the emergency, Moss and Leigh Fermor had resorted to the same tactic, so Moss felt the dog was simply pitching in, but this opinion was under-mined by the fact that Pixie had once performed the same act on the leg of King Farouk, who was not on fire at the time of his visit to Tara. Two days later Paddy set the sofa in the hall-way ablaze under similar circumstances. This time, Pixie did not respond.

Leigh Fermor was not the dog's only victim. One evening, at the tail end of a particularly boisterous drinking session, Sophie was awakened by a patrol sent out from the drawing room to locate aspirin for Rowland Winn, who had somehow broken his ankle. Sophie could not make out exactly what had happened, but it seemed that Winn, perhaps upset at being passed over for assignment to SOE, had decided to demonstrate his parachut-ing form. He had clambered onto some artificial precipice—a window ledge or the balustrade outside, it was unclear which—and leaped. When Sophie went to Winn's room to deliver the aspirin, Pixie trailed along behind her, and as soon as the door opened, the dog flopped onto Winn's bed, eliciting a howl of distress from the injured man.

It was not Pixie, however, who won the title of Tara's most exotic resident. That distinction was shared by a pair of mongooses Sophie had rescued one day from a street performer. No one could tell them apart, so they had just one name between them. Sophie called them Kurka.

Unusual pets were nothing new to the countess. When she was a girl, she had had a pet fox, and she had kept a rifle in her room for shooting crows to feed it. Her family had also kept a pet boar.

At Tara the two Kurkas slept in Sophie's bed, and if they found their way under the covers they would sometimes nip at her back to prevent her from rolling over on them. Now whenever she wore a party dress that revealed her shoulders, she found herself compelled to explain the tiny bruises that dotted her pale skin. "Oh, it's nothing," she said. "It's mongooses."

It was harder to explain away the Kurkas' activities some time later when the animals killed a parrot kept by the well-connected Englishman who lived in the villa next door. Word of the incident soon reached the director of SOE in Cairo. He called Smiley and McLean to his office, issued a harsh reprimand, and ordered the mongooses destroyed. "It so happened that I had rather a good .22 silencer so I was nominated executioner," Smiley recalled. "I got up behind the brutes and blew their brains out."

"LIFE AT TARA was luxurious rather than comfortable," Julian Amery thought. "Sometimes there were lavish dinners. Sometimes there was only bread and cheese. In principle, there were hot baths for all. But sometimes there were no baths at all because Vodka was being made in them. There were two kinds of Tara Vodka; Vodka and Old Vodka. Vodka took only twenty-four hours to make; Old Vodka, three days."

The household had gone into vodka production once the frequent Tara parties had exhausted all other sources of alcohol. Earlier in the war it had been relatively easy to buy whiskey and French wine in Cairo, but these were now next to impossible to obtain. There was a variety of brandy imported from Cyprus and a locally distilled gin, but even these were in short supply. Sophie explained the method used to produce drinkable vodka on her father's estate in Poland, but the six weeks of aging she recommended was out of the question at Tara. At least one guest stumbled home from a party at the house with a case of alcohol poisoning that left him temporarily blinded.

Dodgy vodka or not, the revelers kept arriving. Guests included the usual assortment of British officers, plus officials from the embassy and their wives, Greek friends and Polish soldiers, as well as more adventurous members of Cairene society. Even King Farouk made the occasional appearance. Casual dinners at the house frequently progressed to riotous merrymaking as the night wore on, and the revels might not die down until the muezzin's call drifted in from neighboring mosques at dawn.

Moss's former fiancée came to the Tara housewarming party, and the two of them had an awkward talk together on the stairs, after which she left Cairo for good. Sophie's estranged husband, Andrew, also turned up, on a night when things got wildly out of hand. Guests started smashing windows—nineteen of them shattered before it was finished—and Andrew snatched up a bowl of flowers and hurled it through the biggest window in the house. Meanwhile, Arnold Breene had climbed onto the roof and begun chucking makeshift missiles at the neighbors. On a calmer evening one of the revelers had broken a finger while performing a belly dance. When they ran out of money, the inmates, as they liked to call themselves, rented out the house for someone else's party and locked themselves in their rooms while all hell broke loose downstairs.

One of the highlights of the social season came when the Tara residents staged a mock bullfight in the drawing room, with Paddy as the toreador, flashing a great scarlet cape borrowed from Gertie Wissa, one of three Coptic sisters who were belles of the Cairo social scene. Sophie, McLean, and two of the guests were picadors, and Moss took the role of the bull. They all played their parts so enthusiastically that McLean wound up injured—a cornada, Moss dubbed it—and the bull's death throes sent Sophie sprawling to the floor.

Tara parties were thrown to welcome friends home from the field or to see them off on a secret mission. Parties marked arrivals, departures, promotions, new assignments, and race day at the track. Lunch presented another occasion for carousing. As did breakfast. Julian Amery turned up at the house one morning to find the men of the house holding a breakfast party in their dressing gowns. This would not have surprised him, except that they were all perched on the edges of Sophie's bed at the time. "She reclined on the pillows armed with a cavalry sword and used it to make sure they kept their distance," Amery noted.

IN THE MIDST of the boisterous life at Tara, Leigh Fermor remained preoccupied with the Müller question. He could not get the massacres in Viannos out of his thoughts. At headquarters the effort to formulate a tactical response to General Müller's brutal assault on the civilian population had made little headway. Any confrontation with German forces would only redound on the Cretans once again. Still, there must be some way of striking back.

"Were such a thing possible," Leigh Fermor told himself, "it would have to be some kind of symbolic gesture involving no bloodshed, not even a plane sabotaged or a petrol dump blown up; something that would hit the enemy hard on a different level, and one which would offer no presentable pretext for reprisals."

Killing Müller outright had been rejected as a possibility; the ramifications were unacceptable. There might, however, be another way to target the general. More and more, Leigh Fermor was coming to think that his recent flight over the mountains with Carta offered an answer. If he could find a way to get to Müller, perhaps he could bring him out alive. An unexpected blow of that kind, if obviously mounted from outside Crete, might forestall reprisals, and it could well cause even more consternation in the German ranks than a more bloodthirsty attack. Not to say that it would be easy. Carta had come willingly, of course, but Müller could be . . . convinced.

At first Leigh Fermor struggled with the problem of how to get to Crete, strike quickly, and get out. Then he remembered how smoothly the airdrop of arms for Bandouvas had been carried off back in August. A raiding party could drop in by the same route, parachuting onto a high plateau in the Dikti range. From there, at the western edge of Lasithi, they could slip into Heraklion district and mount an ambush to catch Müller in the course of his daily travels, most likely somewhere between his headquarters in Ano Archanes, south of Heraklion, and his residence, the Villa Ariadne at nearby Knossos, where John Pendlebury himself had once lived.

Soon parts of the plan were welling up in his imagination. Carta's staff car had been abandoned near Sitia on the eastern tip of the island, where the proximity to deep water presented a red herring, inviting the Germans to assume he had escaped by submarine. Meanwhile, the general had been hightailing it over the mountains to the southwest. Capturing Müller as he traveled in his car would make the same ruse possible again. And with Müller's car pointing to a deepwater extraction, Leigh Fermor and his party would again disappear into the mountains and make for the south coast.

When he thought about it like this, smuggling the Italian General Carta off the island looked like a successful dry run for a much bolder strike against German morale.

AS THE DAYS began to grow cooler with the deepening of autumn, the idea of kidnapping General Müller took on clearer outlines in Leigh Fermor's mind. When he could no longer keep it to himself, he floated the idea to a few of his housemates. True to character, he took an opportunity to broach the subject that gave the whole enterprise a whimsical air. It came up one day in the bathroom.

"We were all pretty well stark naked," recalled David Smiley. The walls of the bathroom were fogged with steam and as the men talked they used wet fingers to sketch diagrams on the wall. Maps and arrows took shape in the mist. "A sort of road was here," Smiley remembered someone saying, "we'd be able to stop the General's car there, we'd have a covering party there—all that sort of stuff. But it was all in the bathroom."

The kidnapping scheme passed the bath test. But whether it would fly at headquarters was another question. Around the beginning of November, Leigh Fermor went to see Jack Smith-Hughes, now head of the Crete branch, at his office at the SOE headquarters. There he laid out the plan that had taken shape in the bath. He explained the ambush, the false trails, and the escape through the mountains to the south coast, where a motor launch would pick up the party. As he talked, he scanned Smith-Hughes's jovial, round face for some signal of his reaction. There was no way of predicting what he would say. A proposal for a similar undertaking had been squelched earlier in the year. But Paddy knew that spiriting General Carta out of Crete, right under the noses of the German garrison, had been a coup. And it had gained him an undeniable measure of clout.

As it turned out, there was no need to worry. Smith-Hughes endorsed the plan wholeheartedly. Later he accompanied Leigh Fermor to the office of their commander, Brigadier Barker-Benfield, where he went through the details once more. When Leigh Fermor finished talking, the brigadier, who had overall responsibility for SOE in the Middle East, voiced his support for the plan. Like that, the mission was approved, and Leigh Fermor was assured he would receive the resources he needed to mount the operation. The one open question was whom to tap as second in command. When the brigadier asked if he had anyone in mind, Paddy had to admit that his thinking had not progressed that far. "Not yet," he replied.

Of course, he *had* given a good deal of consideration to the makeup of the team that would carry out this plan. Manoli Paterakis would play an essential role, it went without saying. He was staying nearby at a villa in Heliopolis. And Paddy would like to have George Tyrakis—Tom Dunbabin's former guide from the Amari, who had come out of Crete on a boat earlier in the year—provided he could find him. But only now did it occur to him that he might ask Billy Moss to sign on as his lieutenant. Moss was aware of the plan, but it was not in his character to put himself forward as one of its leaders, though the idea must have crossed his mind.

Back at Tara, Leigh Fermor offered Moss the job outright, and he jumped at the opportunity. Some time later, when Paddy told his friend Annette Crean about his decision, she blanched for a moment. It was not that Moss was untrustworthy or lacking in the kind of courage required to pull off such a mission, she finally explained. He was simply too debonair. She was afraid his good looks would be a dead giveaway.

NOW THAT HEADQUARTERS had given the mission a stamp of approval, it was time for the real work to begin. Fortunately, Manoli Paterakis turned up at just the right moment, with his compatriot George Tyrakis in tow. It turned out that Tyrakis had been away at the RAF base at Ramat David, in the Jezreel Valley south of Haifa, where he had taken the parachute training course many SOE operatives received. It was good to find him all in one piece at the end of the course.

There was a story going around at the time that illustrated the greater risks these fierce Cretan *andartes* ran in such an undertaking. "During a parachute course in the Middle East the instructor, jump-training a group of commandos from various islands, saw one of them fumble with his harness and hesitate to advance into the bay for the jump," as the writer Lawrence Durrell told it. "Incautiously, he made a pleasantry—asking if the novice was scared. The response was unexpected. 'Scared?' cried the young man. 'You dare to tell a Cretan he is scared? I'll show you who is scared.' He unhooked his safety harness altogether and jumped to his certain death." Nobody believed the story, but there was no arguing with its spirit.

Tyrakis's safe return was a good omen for Manoli. Since the mission plan had the team parachuting onto Mount Dikti, he and Leigh Fermor would both soon depart for Ramat David to take the same course. Moss, it turned out, was judged too tall for parachute training. It was feared that an injury received during a practice jump could jeopardize the mission itself. When the time came to drop into Crete, he would have to wing it. Although he enjoyed being told how brave it was to make an operational jump without any training, he was in fact happy not to have to risk getting hurt before it mattered. And he was having too much fun at Tara to go traipsing off to Ramat David for a few weeks.

Once Leigh Fermor and Manoli completed the course, they would have the core unit they needed in order to launch the mission. As always, Manoli would serve as Leigh Fermor's guide and right-hand man, his "man Friday," as Paddy liked to say. George would take up the same role for Moss. He quickly became "Man Thursday." Once on the ground in Crete, they would gather the rest of the team.

THE PARACHUTE COURSE started with basic instruction in how to land. At first, students tumbled from stationary platforms of various heights, learning to absorb the energy of the fall by rolling when they hit the ground. From there they progressed to flinging themselves off the back of a moving truck. This went on for three days, until finally the students could hit the ground and roll safely at forty miles an hour. Then, on the fourth morning, they boarded a modified bomber to make their first real jump.

Statistically it could be shown that parachuting was not particularly risky, but as Julian Amery learned when he made his first jump in a similar course, hurling yourself from a plane for the first time "is undeniably contrary to every human instinct." Even worse than the actual jump was the anticipation. Each man was assigned a number designating the order in which they would jump, and they waited nervously in the cargo bay as the bomber spiraled its way up to altitude. "As the roar of the engines drowned our talk each of us was left to his own thoughts and fears all too clearly mirrored in the tense features of his fellows," Amery recalled.

Once the aircraft leveled out over the drop zone, the instructor removed a trapdoor from the floor and the first two jumpers edged into position and sat on the rim of the hole with their legs dangling below. When it was your turn, you took your place, and at this point the only dignified thing to do was muffle the inevitable doubts and fix your eyes on the instructor, who stood watching a signal light that flashed red above the doorway. Soon the light turned green and the instructor brought his hand down. You eased over the edge and immediately felt the impact of the wind ripping past the plane. Tumbling through this slip-stream was like being rattled by a giant hand, but as you passed through the plane's turbulence, the shaking gave way to what Amery called "the full horror of falling through space." For several seconds the acceleration continued. Then, finally, the chute opened and falling turned to floating. Since there was no spare, an open chute came as a tremendous relief, and it was accompanied by a sense of elation that you could enjoy for a few minutes before you had to wrestle yourself into position for landing. In the last few seconds the ground seemed to rush at you faster and faster, and the wallop of the first landing often took students by surprise. The instructors compared the impact to jumping from a twenty-foot wall.

The training jumps continued for another week. Students were dropped from various heights—ending as low as five hundred feet—and under differing conditions. The final jumps took place at night, when darkness made the whole enterprise much more challenging. At the end of the course, both Manoli and Leigh Fermor had made it through successfully. As qualified parachutists, they were now eligible for a bump in salary, an extra two shillings per day in Paddy's case. But for now there was to be no outward sign of their accomplishment. In order to avoid telegraphing the nature of their mission, SOE officers did not wear the parachute-wing insignia on their uniforms until they were in the field. The compensation was that, after making an operational jump, they could wear them proudly on their chests, rather than on the sleeve as ordinary paratroopers did.

THE DROP onto Mount Dikti was planned for the beginning of December, and there was much to do before departing. Leigh Fermor and Moss devoted their time to gathering the equipment they would need. Before long, Tara began to look like a munitions dump, its cabinets and cupboards larded with weapons and explosives. As the departure date neared, the stockpile grew to include rifles, machine guns, revolvers, a large cache of ammunition, and a strange assortment of bombs made of a moldable explosive called gelignite, some of them disguised as ordinary objects, including cow manure and, more useful on Crete, goat droppings. If the mission went as planned, none of this would be needed. If something went wrong, all the munitions they could possibly carry would be a drop in the bucket compared to what the Germans would throw at them.

Still more outlandish equipment waited to be picked up at Jasper Maskelyne's office. Maskelyne had shown up in Cairo in 1941 with a task force of a dozen-odd camouflage officers and a very peculiar history. Both his father and grandfather were well-known stage magicians, and before the war he had made a name for himself in the family business. He was just ten years old when he first appeared onstage at the Palace Theatre in London, as a magician's assistant in a show performed before George V and Queen Mary at the 1912 Royal Command Performance. The act involved an illusion in which eggs were retrieved one after another from an apparently empty hat. Not long after he turned twenty-one, Maskelyne was performing on his own. He soon became famous, as much for his dapper good looks as for his illusions. As a boy Paddy had seen his show at the Regent Theatre in London. "He used to lock ladies into boxes, then saw them in half, and they would step out blowing kisses," he recalled.

But show business turned out to be an unreliable source of income. At one point in the late 1920s, Maskelyne had been forced to take work as a motorcycle messenger. When he ran into financial trouble again in 1935, he hired a ghostwriter and cobbled together a potboiler autobiography.

Soon after the war began, he found his way into the Royal Engineers. Since then he had been busy conjuring up illusions to help mask the British army's movements in North Africa. Maskelyne still wore the thin matinee-idol mustache he had sported onstage, and he was still known to put on a show from time to time. He had even launched into a performance on the back of a truck in the middle of the desert. But his real magic was now worked behind closed doors. He had a workshop off Soliman Pasha Square where he developed ingenious devices and tactics for SOE agents and other servicemen, such as bomber crews, whose missions put them at high risk of capture by the enemy. He conducted courses on escape and evasion in which the men learned strategies that might well save their lives one day. They frequently found themselves treated to a magic trick or two in the bargain.

When Leigh Fermor and Moss dropped by the workshop to inquire about the latest advances in the spy trade, Maskelyne led them to a small, poorly illuminated room off the main office, which was crammed with what looked at first like everyday objects. As the former magician began to lay out his wares, the character of the room seemed to change. "The air of sorcery," Moss sensed, "emanated from every shelf in that dim cell."

Maskelyne's stock included clothing buttons that could be screwed apart to reveal a working compass, and boots that hid everything from hacksaws and wire cutters to minuscule silk maps. He had specially magnetized pencil clips that would swing around to point north when you balanced them on the tip of the pencil. There were pistols disguised as pens, cigars, and cigarettes, as well as brushes and braces that concealed hidden compartments. Moss was impressed by the air of routine

Maskelyne brought to his job, as if these astonishing devices were perfectly ordinary and there were nothing resembling a war going on. Nevertheless, he felt swept up in the sorcery of it all when he gathered up the gadgets Maskelyne selected for him, "as though I were a witch's bowl into which were being thrust the ingredients of some devilish brew."

Moss and Leigh Fermor picked up a few of Maskelyne's "toys," as he liked to call them. Officers in the field had found that some of these items came in handy in unexpected ways. The ether knockout drops, for example, could be popped open and used to start a fire under wet conditions. Maskelyne also furnished them with supplies from his medicine cabinet, which held the various elixirs involved in the modern alchemy of war. These included Benzedrine stimulants. Most unnerving were cachets of poison designed to be sewn into a lapel and bitten in the event of capture by the enemy. The mere sight of these suicide pills lent an ominous note to the start of any covert mission. But Moss and Leigh Fermor gathered them up with the rest of the toys and made their way back out to the street, leaving Maskelyne to potter in his cave.

JUST WHEN the operation looked set to begin, an unexpected hitch arose. Days before the scheduled departure, a wireless transmission crackled through to headquarters revealing that the weather on Crete was not cooperating. Sandy Rendel, who was now operating in the Lasithi district, had climbed up to the plateau on the southern flank of Mount Dikti several days earlier to check conditions at the "Sodom" drop zone Leigh Fermor had selected following the successful arms drop to Bandouvas in the autumn. At first it looked feasible. But when Rendel returned to prepare for the actual drop, he found that the situation was rapidly changing for the worse.

By the time he reached the hut where he and his men were

planning to wait for Leigh Fermor's arrival, it was clear that there might be problems with the location. Winter had swept in with a vengeance, and it turned out in addition that the Germans had unwittingly done their part in foiling the plan. "Most of the day it had rained, sleet or melting snow, but now it became colder and the snow set steadily in for the night," Rendel noted as he approached the hut. "Crunching up to the door we realized that what should have been a flat roof of branches, bracken, and peat sods, had been stove in, and that the hut was one of those which the Germans had demolished in the summer in the reprisals against Bandouvas."

Rendel and the young Greek who was with him spent a wet, cold night huddled under an intact section of roof. By morning Rendel could see that the deepening snow would make it impossible to wait here for Leigh Fermor's arrival. He made his way back to the wireless station, where it was agreed that the mission should be postponed until the following month.

Meanwhile he would search for an alternate location, though he knew finding a suitable spot might prove difficult, since it had to be remote, which pointed to the mountains, but also open enough for a parachute landing. And it must be within reasonable striking distance of the Villa Ariadne, where General Müller lived.

While Rendel scouted a new site, Leigh Fermor and Moss bided their time at Tara. Both felt attached to the villa—not least because Moss was growing more and more fond of Sophie—but with progress on the mission suspended, the leisurely pace of life in Cairo began to feel burdensome. Manoli and George sometimes came for dinner, and Leigh Fermor and Moss made trips out to their camp to visit them. Time crept by, and all four members of the team were chomping at the bit as the first of December came and went. At last a message arrived from Rendel. He had been forced to expand his search beyond the area around Bandouvas's camp. Skirting farther and farther northeast, he had finally settled on the Katharo plateau, a vast open plain on a northeastern shoulder of the mountain range, roughly ten miles west of the small village of Kritsa. Here the coming of winter weather was an advantage, since the area was accessible to German patrols during the summer. At this time of year it would be relatively safe. It looked like the best option for the airdrop. There was cover nearby, and it would not be difficult to reach Heraklion from here. Rendel signaled that he would soon move his radio station to a spot near Kritsa, on the eastern fringe of the plateau.

Once the details were worked out at headquarters, however, there followed further postponements. Then at last a new schedule was set for the drop. If all went as planned, Leigh Fermor, Moss, and the others would leave Cairo early in January.

WHILE THE DELAY was disappointing, it also meant that the Tara inmates could ring in the new year together. On the evening of December 31, the whole crew trooped to the palatial town house of Princess Shevekiar, an eccentric Cairo luminary, to attend her annual ball, one of the city's biggest parties of the year. To Leigh Fermor and the others the princess's story was even more enticing than the ball itself. Now in her seventies, she had married Prince Fuad in 1895, when she was nineteen and he had not yet ascended to the Egyptian throne. But the royal couple quickly found they had different ideas about marriage. When the future king tried to confine the young Shevekiar to the haremlik, she packed her bags and left, setting in motion a family struggle that within a matter of months exploded into violence. Shevekiar's elder brother cornered Fuad in the Khedival Club on al-Manakh Street and opened fire with a pistol, striking him in several places. Doctors were later able to remove bullets from his chest and legs, but one that had lodged danger-

TARA ◇ **199**

ously close to an artery in his throat would remain there for the rest of his life. He soon agreed to a divorce. Since those days, Princess Shevekiar had gone through a string of husbands, and she was now married to a considerably younger man, who was said to powder his hair in order to appear closer to her age. Fascinating as the princess's story was, however, the Tara residents did not have high hopes for the ball, which despite its splendid setting had developed a reputation as a monotonous affair.

What they found when they arrived surprised everyone. From outside they could already hear that the music was not what they had anticipated. Instead of some staid waltz, the dance band was belting out what Moss called "le Jazz Hot." And the scene inside turned out to be even more astonishing. Beneath one of the sparkling chandeliers that swung over an immense ballroom, the elderly princess herself perched next to her younger husband, looking to Moss like "a stately old hawk in a high chair, chain-smoking, surveying the scene as from afar."

All around her swirled a crowd of young revelers. Moss recognized the sons and daughters of the Egyptian aristocracy, princes and princesses, rubbing shoulders with their Western friends. King Farouk, Fuad's successor, had shaved his beard for the event, so that he too looked younger and more amiable. On the fringe of the dance floor, where a ring of chairs had been set up, a stiff contingent of conservatively dressed women had alighted with their daughters, all of them looking on at the melee in postures that reminded Moss of a Jane Austen novel. The party was clearly not going as they had expected either. But the new arrivals from Tara dove happily into the fray. There was hardly any need for the Benzedrine a few of them had borrowed from their mission stores to keep the evening going.

The scandal of the night involved Billy McLean, who disappeared with the beautiful younger daughter of a prominent Coptic family. When their absence was noticed, it stirred up an immediate reaction among the older guests. It was widely known that the young lady had vanished with McLean in a similar fashion during a party at Tara a few weeks earlier. On that occasion her elder sister had set out with a group of nervous cousins to find them, but half an hour of frantic searching had failed to turn up any sign of them. Then out of nowhere McLean and the girl had appeared, looking as if nothing had happened, both of them completely composed, except for their faces, which were smeared with lipstick. She had also lost an earring, which later turned up in the henhouse. This time, at Princess Shevekiar's ball, the two lovers slipped away from the crowd and were drifting toward a private-looking cluster of rhododendrons, Leigh Fermor told a friend later, "but before they had made a dozen paces in the garden, a group of Nubian retainers materialized from nowhere and escorted them back to the bright lights, urbanely but firmly, with flashing smiles and, no doubt, apt snippets from the Koran."

AT LUNCHTIME on January 5 word came that the departure was on for that night. In the afternoon McLean helped Leigh Fermor and Moss as they scrambled about trying to ready their gear. They were scheduled to depart at two thirty in the morning, which, once they had done the worst of the packing, left time to celebrate their last night in Cairo.

By Tara standards the farewell party was a quiet affair. A half dozen friends remained as midnight passed. Sophie was taking their departure hard. When someone mentioned that SOE officers operating behind enemy lines could be shot as spies if they were caught out of uniform, she began looking in wardrobes for army insignia to sew on their Greek clothes. All through the evening Moss noticed tears welling up in Sophie's eyes, and after a while the two of them disappeared upstairs to her room, where they lay on the bed with their clothes on, holding each other and at last falling asleep.

When Moss crept back downstairs sometime after 2:00 a.m., he found everyone in the drawing room, which was illuminated by candles. Leigh Fermor sat on the sofa drinking kümmel—a send-off like this called for something better than three-day-old vodka—and singing "Stormy Weather" in a voice that sounded a little tipsy. He was flanked by two lovely women, and he had an arm around each of them. On one side lounged a woman named Diana; on the other was a woman dressed in something that reminded Moss of a Hungarian peasant costume, except that the neckline plunged lower than any dress he had ever seen. This was Inez Walter, the fiancée of a secretary from the British embassy. Denise Menasces, whose father had been president of the Alexandria Jewish community, sat curled up in an armchair across the room. To Moss she looked as sleek and willowy as Kurka.

David Smiley had been asleep earlier in the night and now sat blinking as if he had not quite managed to wake up. He still wore pajamas and a robe emblazoned with small figures of horse guards at Whitehall. Gertie Wissa reclined nearby in a stately pose. She reminded Moss of a battleship at anchor. Alexis Ladas, a young officer in the Anglo-Hellenic Schooner Flotilla, was singing along with Paddy. Tall, handsome, and just twenty-three, Ladas had served in the Resistance and spent two years in an Italian prison, escaping on the day of the Italian capitulation. After a while, Sophie came down from her room wearing a voluminous borrowed coat with sleeves that engulfed her hands and perched on the arm of Moss's chair. "Stormy Weather" gave way to "Swing Low, Sweet Chariot." Moss sang a song in Russian, with Leigh Fermor singing along. Then Ladas and Paddy tried a song in Greek.

A little before four o'clock the doorbell rang, and someone let in a man who identified himself as the conducting officer. Moss recognized him as a second lieutenant named John something whom he did not particularly like. The obviously agitated lieutenant explained that Moss and Leigh Fermor were over an hour late for their departure. He looked awkwardly around the room, realizing he was interrupting. Just then Pixie, who had been sleeping on his back with all four paws sticking up in the air, leaped to his feet. A small mongrel dog had slipped into the house behind the lieutenant, and Pixie now tore off after it, and the two animals went careening around the room.

Leigh Fermor and Moss hauled themselves upright and headed to their room to retrieve their gear. What had not already been packed lay in a state of disarray. They filled a large cloth sack with their travel papers and four thousand pounds' worth of gold sovereigns, which had been strewn across the floor. Dragging the sack back through the drawing room, Moss noticed that the lieutenant was busy with the dogs, while the others sang "Auld Lang Syne."

He and Paddy could take a moment to say good-bye to McLean, who had gone to bed early with a toothache. They slipped upstairs and found him asleep in his room and woke him. Propped up in bed, he smiled at them as they talked. Then he pulled out two handsome leather books, explaining that he had carried them with him in Albania. One was Shakespeare, the other an Oxford poetry anthology. He wanted Moss and Leigh Fermor to have them, for luck. When he had inscribed them, they said a last good-bye and went out to the landing where Sophie waited.

When Leigh Fermor disappeared downstairs, Moss folded his arms around Sophie. "Is this the last time?" she asked him. He told her yes, it was time to go, but the mission would be over quickly and he would be back. He could tell she was crying again, and she could not seem to find the right words to say good-bye. Finally, she told him she would take good care of Pixie.

Downstairs the conducting officer was finishing a glass of beer. Leigh Fermor and Moss moved their things to the hallway and kissed everyone in turn. Moss noticed Diana standing close by, "staring wistfully at Paddy, saying 'goodbye darling.'" Denise stood pensively in the background. Smiley and Sophie accompanied the two travelers down the stairs to the gate, where a staff car was parked. They heaved their gear into the trunk and fell into another round of good-byes that went on until Smiley's teeth began to chatter from the cold. A wave of affection for his housemates and the good times they had enjoyed at Tara swept over Moss. He would miss them all, not least Pixie. At last, he and Leigh Fermor piled into the car, pulled out onto the street, and steered toward the Bulaq Bridge on their way to pick up Manoli and George.

AFTER A LONG DRIVE, which passed with Manoli and George singing hoarsely in the back of the car and Leigh Fermor occasionally indulging a spell of kümmel-fueled wistfulness, they finally arrived at the Cairo West Airport. When all the gear had been weighed in, they found their way to the canteen, where they ordered coffee and sandwiches and waited for their departure to be called. Sitting at the table surrounded by their equipment, Moss felt conspicuous, and with good reason. "Everyone in the canteen stared at us—understandably," he admitted, "for we must have looked a strange party. Two Greeks and Paddy and I, all dressed like something out of 'For Whom the Bell Tolls,' with a cargo of Marlin sub-machine guns, a sack of gold, covered in revolvers and other strange gear."

Before long they were told that the plane would be taking off soon. Gathering the rifles and other gear, they climbed aboard a trolley, which carried them out to the plane. The sun was just beginning to rise. A few minutes later, when the aircraft lifted off the runway and banked into its climb, they could see the Giza pyramids in the distance, looking "like triangles cut out of a sheet of transparent paper," Moss remarked. When the plane leveled off a little while later, there was nothing to see but the red, white, and green signal lights flickering beyond the windows. The thrum of the engines soon lulled them all asleep.

CHAPTER 8

Moonstruck

BY FEBRUARY 4 the four men were airborne again. And this time it was the real thing. Around a quarter past nine that night, Paddy sat perched on the edge of the jump hole cut into the fuselage of a Halifax bomber. They had been in the air nearly four hours. In the cockpit, Warrant Officer Cyril J. Fortune, whose flying Leigh Fermor had admired when he dropped supplies to Bo-Peep and his men the previous fall, shifted the controls and banked the bomber into a sweeping turn above the Katharo plateau.

Despite heavy cloud cover that was rapidly closing in above the plateau, Fortune had homed in on the coordinates chosen for the drop—N 35°08'30", E 25°33'56"—and managed to spot the ground crew's signal fires. He warned Leigh Fermor that the weather would force him to make the drop from a dangerously low altitude. Now he was bringing the Halifax in for a jump run. Peering down through the hole, Paddy soon caught a glimpse of a triangle formed by pinpoints of light in the darkness below. Just at that moment, the bomb aimer signaled go. He lifted his weight off the metal floor of the fuselage and, without giving himself time to think, slipped through the opening.

Moss, who had been anticipating this moment in one way or another for weeks, was surprised at the jolt of feeling that

shot through him when Leigh Fermor's jumpsuited form disappeared into the blackness. Since leaving Cairo he had been
telling himself that this was a good war. "Perhaps I have been
lucky and had the best of it," he had reflected. Now he felt the
reality of war striking home in a new way. Seeing his friend sitting there and then . . . not sitting there . . . shocked Moss. What
it reminded him of was an episode he had witnessed in Poland
before the war, when he had heard buglers blowing a call for
each hour. "And the call stopped right in the middle of a phrase,
it seemed—right in the middle of a note," he recalled.

The story he had heard about this strange practice said that
when the Tatar army was advancing on Kraków in the thirteenth century, a bugler had climbed to a turret in order to
sound a warning call. The poor fellow succeeded in alerting the
townspeople, but his call was cut short by a Tatar arrow. The
latter-day buglers kept his memory alive by halting their own
calls "abruptly, just as the call had died on his lips those long
years ago." It was this story that stirred in Moss's memory when
Paddy slipped through the drop door of the Halifax. "It was as
sudden as death," he thought.

Moss felt the Halifax banking again, and he knew it would
soon be his turn to take that same sudden leap into the darkness. But the moment never came. By the time Fortune brought
the plane around again, the ground was completely concealed
by clouds. The Halifax continued to circle for nearly half an
hour. Then, at 9:46, Fortune gave up and turned toward the
Greek mainland, where earlier in the evening he had attempted
to drop supplies for an unrelated SOE operation.

Some two hours later the Halifax reached the mountainous
area near the small village of Triklino, in northwestern Greece,
where the drop was expected. But the weather here was no better than it had been on Crete. After quickly surveying the dete-
riorating conditions, Fortune dropped one wing and turned

the plane for home. Quick as his decision had been, however, it came nearly too late.

Cruising at an altitude of thirteen thousand feet, the Halifax soon began to ice over. Fortune sacrificed altitude in an attempt to find warmer air, but rime continued to form on the wings, and soon the plane was losing altitude no matter what he did. It was not until they had descended to four thousand feet that the problem abated. But at this point a break in the clouds revealed a mountainside looming terrifyingly large in the Halifax's windscreen. There was little time to react before the bomber and its passengers became a permanent part of the local landscape.

THE DIRE SITUATION was not unfamiliar to Fortune. Piloting another Halifax the previous December, he had wound up in a similar situation, midway through a flight so full of mishaps it was almost comical. The weather on that occasion had been as bad as it was now, and Fortune's plane had "hit a colossal bump" while he was busy changing places with the second pilot. The blast of unexpected turbulence flipped the Halifax over on its back, hurling both men out of the cockpit. Fortune wound up lying on the "roof" with the rest of the crew. With the plane "turned turtle" like this, it began losing altitude at a gut-twisting rate. All of a sudden its load of incendiary bombs tumbled from the box they were held in and burst into flames, igniting the cargo and parts of the fuselage.

While other members of the crew struggled to put out the blaze, Fortune managed to get hold of the plane's control column. Still standing on the roof, he heaved back on the yoke to slow the rate of descent. But since the Halifax was upside down, the controls were reversed and his attempt to maneuver the plane sent it screaming still faster toward the ground. The aircraft lost some five thousand feet of altitude before Fortune finally wrestled the ailerons into position to roll it right side up again. As he leveled the plane off at four thousand feet, however, he discovered that it had dropped into a valley surrounded by mountains that peaked out around eight thousand feet. There was nothing to do but give the Rolls-Royce engines full throttle, sending the Halifax roaring into a steep climb that just cleared the surrounding peaks. That wasn't the end of Fortune's trouble. When the plane finally touched down on the runway of the aerodrome, its tail caught a strong crosswind and swung hard to starboard. When Fortune gunned the portside engines to arrest the slide, he found there was not enough fuel remaining to supply the power he needed. The plane careened off the runway and slammed into a Spitfire fighter plane parked nearby. The Halifax, as if intent on finishing what it had started earlier, flipped over and burned out, taking the Spitfire with it. Fortune and the crew managed to get out safely, the only casualty a cut to the wireless operator's face.

THIS TIME, as Moss and the two Greeks held their breath, Fortune wrenched the bomber into a sickening climb that just barely carried them over the lip of the ridgeline. An hour later, they were touching down at Brindisi, where the mission had begun some eight hours earlier. In that brief window of time much had changed. Paddy was now on his own, somewhere in the mountains of Crete.

As Moss climbed down from the Halifax, he was left wondering what to do next. Since leaving Cairo, it had taken nearly a month to put one member of their party on the ground in Crete. He did not see how he, Manoli, and George would ever get there.

THE EVENING of January 6, a month earlier, had found Leigh Fermor and Moss, fresh from Cairo, drinking and trading stories with an American commando in the officers' mess at Tocra, a ramshackle RAF base in northeastern Libya. The flight from

Cairo had been long and uneventful. There had been a hasty stop at an air base near Tobruk, where they had nipped off the plane and ordered coffee, only to be rushed back aboard before they had time to drink it. By lunchtime they had landed in rain at the Benina airfield outside Benghazi and were busy loading their baggage onto a truck for a slow, muddy drive forty-five miles back the way they had come to reach Tocra, which perched midway along the thumb Libya projected out into the Mediterranean, east of Benghazi. At last they stopped at a cluster of tents and temporary buildings that would be home until they dropped into Crete. And now here they were.

Outside, the mud-red sand and lowering black clouds made for dismal surroundings, and at first Moss had been equally depressed by the atmosphere at the mess bar, which felt like a parody of an English pub, with a darts match under way and a clientele inclined to tag "old boy" onto the end of every utterance. The American they talked with in the bar, however, turned out to be an interesting fellow who was waiting to be dropped into Greece. The three men talked and laughed happily until they ambled off to their tents at eleven o'clock. It was twelve hours later when Leigh Fermor and Moss finally stirred themselves awake. They passed the next evening in much the same way and fell asleep with their throats sore from singing.

Over the next several days they could occasionally hear aircraft taking off nearby, but the foul weather had suspended any operations involving passengers. With nothing to do but wait, the two men quickly established a routine. They persuaded an orderly—a one-pound inducement was all it took—to deliver their breakfasts to them in bed, where they usually stayed until lunchtime. Moss spent the time reading and writing in his diary. Leigh Fermor was knee deep in *A Farewell to Arms*, which Moss had read a few years earlier, and they laughed about Hemingway's habit of focusing obsessively on the small, often unappealing details of the scenes he described. "Sometimes he finds something a little better, such as copulation in a sleeping bag, on which to harp," Moss pointed out, "and that is more tolerable." For a while they amused themselves by composing parodies of Hemingway's style, but they soon gave it up as too easy.

One morning they went to the supply depot and drew what clothing and gear they lacked. Moss acquired a white duffle coat that made him impervious to Tocra's damp, cold evenings. Later they sorted through the luggage they had brought from home, and both were surprised when a hard rubber ball belonging to Pixie rolled out. Even Leigh Fermor, not Pixie's greatest admirer, was touched by this unexpected souvenir of life at Tara. They spent another enjoyable afternoon on the seashore, trying out the weapons they had brought. It was a pleasure to blast away at nothing. All the guns worked beautifully, and they were especially impressed with the Marlin submachine guns.

They were still in bed just before lunch on the ninth, when another conducting officer turned up at the tent and warned them that they should be ready to depart on a flight leaving that night. They hastily began packing their equipment into the cylindrical containers that had been provided for the drop. As they scrambled to fit everything in, they decided to add one item just for luck: Pixie's rubber ball. Their packing had not made much headway when the officer returned an hour later to say that the flight was canceled due to bad weather.

The friendly American they had met in the bar did manage to take off on his way to Greece that evening, but he was back by morning. On the following day he went again. Moss and Leigh Fermor heard that this time he had made it into Greece. But he had been forced to jump blind through a layer of clouds that obscured the drop zone—or the supposed drop zone, since the pilot was unable to confirm their location—when the colonel he was going in with elected to risk it.

For the most part, however, none of the men waiting to hitch rides with the RAF made it off the airfield. By January 12 there had been no improvement in the weather. "It has rained a great deal during the past few days—it's raining like hell now, and everything is muddy and horrible," Moss wrote in his diary. "The weather in Crete must be absolute hell if this is anything to go by." He was right. Cairo relayed a report from the field to the effect that conditions at the drop site were terrible. It was beginning to look as if the airdrop would be scrubbed entirely. Another message arrived two days later, but it settled nothing. The rain held day after day, and time continued to creep by. They drank in the tent most afternoons. In the evenings they drank liqueurs in the officers' mess until the bar opened, and then they drank there. As the days wore on, they drifted from making fun of Hemingway to making fun of Graham Greene.

In fact, Moss changed his mind about Hemingway after rereading *A Farewell to Arms*. The sad last half of the book touched him deeply now, and he longed to go back to Switzerland, which he felt Hemingway had described so sweetly. On January 14, still feeling nostalgic and perhaps thinking of Sophie, he inscribed in his diary the sixteenth-century poem Hemingway's hero recalls in the midst of a retreat, when he is trying to sleep under miserable conditions and suddenly pictures the woman he loves at home in her bed. "Western wind, when wilt thou blow / The small rain down can rain?" the poem went. "Christ, that my love were in my arms / And I in my bed again!" It would be a while before Moss returned to his own bed or to Sophie's arms. For now he was stuck with nothing but the rain.

Manoli and George often dropped in for a visit and sometimes whiled away a whole day in the tent talking with Leigh Fermor, who was the only other Greek speaker left in camp once the American departed for the mainland. Moss felt for them, since they had even less to keep them occupied during the interminable wait than he and Paddy did. They had no books to read and passed the time playing cards. Yet they were always cheerful, and Moss enjoyed their company, though he could not follow their conversation and relied on Leigh Fermor to pass along any interesting stories. One day Manoli arrived at the tent wearing a grin that looked to Moss "like a slice of water-melon." Unable to conceal his pride, he coaxed them outside to look at the four cows he and George had rustled from the herd of a local tribesman. Paddy had mentioned some time earlier that Manoli came from a part of Crete where stealing livestock was the rule rather than the exception. In his world letting a perfectly good animal stray back to its owner was cause for shame. Here, on the hoof, was all the evidence Moss could ask for.

Another week went by. Leigh Fermor fell asleep reading a novel set in eighteenth-century Scotland and burned a hole in the cover. Moss read *The Bridge of San Luis Rey* and thought it "flawless." By this time, the moon phase required for the drop had passed without any break in the weather, and the mission was once again postponed. They would have to wait for the right moon to come around again in February.

There were other complications too. The 148th Squadron, which flew missions to support SOE, was now moving its operations to an air base at Brindisi, in southeastern Italy. The Crete mission would depart from there when the time came. Meanwhile, a message had arrived summoning Leigh Fermor back to Cairo, and it looked as if Moss and the Greeks would have to travel to Italy by sea. But at the last minute they were able to hitch a ride with the RAF. By January 24 they were settled in Bari, a bustling port town north of the air base, where Leigh Fermor joined them a few days later.

Bari had suffered during the war years. Moss noticed that the inhabitants were almost universally tattered and unkempt.

And the decline evidently went beyond appearances. Everywhere were posted warnings about venereal disease, which had become endemic. But even in its run-down state the town felt like paradise after Tocra. Although it was not especially beautiful, Bari offered a lot in the way of amusement. The cinema was still in operation, and whenever a new movie arrived Leigh Fermor and Moss went to see it. Wandering through the side streets they came across several restaurants that turned out to serve surprisingly good food. (At Tocra the only edible meal had been breakfast.) Here there was even an opera house, where they watched a performance of *The Barber of Seville* put on by the local troupe. Leigh Fermor thought the production "looked wonderfully buoyant and professional," though he admitted his standard might have fallen after being deprived of such pleasures since the war began. It was also possible that the evening's ebullient feelings had another source. "Paddy had a strange and most satisfactory adventure with a Yugoslav girl whom he met that night—at midnight," Moss noted in his diary, "and this led to a buoyant lightness of heart on his part for the following 24 hours."

Leigh Fermor's spur-of-the-moment rendezvous with his new Yugoslav friend was not the only engagement on his and Moss's social calendar. Like Cairo on a smaller scale, Bari was turning into a busy crossroads for the British, as operations shifted from North Africa to Europe. In their first ten days in town, they ran into several old acquaintances. Sophie's estranged husband, Andrew Tarnowski, of all people, turned up for an impromptu lunch on February 1.

On February 5 word came that it was at last time to go. Leigh Fermor and Moss once again packed their gear in preparation for the drop. That afternoon they piled into a car for the seventy-odd-mile drive along the coast to Brindisi. It pleased Leigh Fermor to see that their journey back to Crete was starting out along a pathway trodden by the ancients. The road they now motored along followed a stretch of the Appian Way, by which legions once marched to and fro between Rome and the ancient port city of Brundisium, near where the airfield now lay. As the car passed through the village of Alberobello, another relic of the past leaped into view. Along the road clustered white-washed houses with beehive-shaped roofs. The locals built these *trulli*, as they were called, without mortar, wedging each small stone carefully into place until the whole structure held itself together. To the two Greeks the houses looked unexpectedly familiar. "They're exactly like our cheese huts in the White Mountains," Manoli told Paddy.

By six o'clock that evening they were airborne in Cyril Fortune's Halifax. A little more than three hours later, Leigh Fermor's parachute was floating to the ground in Crete, while Moss and the Greeks winged their way back to Italy.

THAT SAME AFTERNOON, Sandy Rendel stood waiting in a cave near Kritsa while his radio operator worked the knobs on his wireless set, trying to catch a signal from Cairo. Looking at the man hunched over the device with earphones on, Rendel was reminded of "an eastern priest bowing forward to conduct some mysterious ritual." For a time it seemed fruitless, but at last the technician's ministrations produced the desired effect. The receiver latched on to the coded signal from Cairo. When it was decoded, Rendel had the news he was waiting for. Leigh Fermor and his team were on their way. They would arrive tonight.

Rendel and his men struck out at once for the Katharo plateau. When they reached the drop zone, they fanned out and began gathering wood for the fires that would mark out the location of the drop for the pilot of the transport plane. Before they could finish this work, however, one of the men spotted two Greeks lingering in a hut nearby. Members of Rendel's party warned him that these two interlopers were known collaborators, and it took some effort on his part to keep his men from shooting them. He ordered them kept under watch in the hut for the time being. When the drop was completed, he would send them packing, once his most ferocious henchman had issued a bone-chilling warning to keep their mouths shut.

Some time later, with the firewood stacked in mounds and ready to light when the time came, Rendel settled in to wait. At twilight the sky had been clear, but now he noticed clouds rolling in. For the moment it was still only a scattering. At times a dark bank drifted across the moon, which was just beginning to rise. As the minutes ticked by, the cloud cover grew more and more dense. But there were still patches of open sky when Rendel heard the sound of an engine approaching. He checked his watch and saw that the plane was right on time. He called for the signal fires to be lit, and the flames soon illuminated the plateau. The plane could now be heard circling overhead, and suddenly it emerged from a bank of cloud that was backlit by the moon. It seemed suspended directly above the drop zone. Now Rendel felt sure the pilot would see the signal fires. But just at that moment a blinding light appeared in the sky, drifting downward. For some reason the crew on board the plane had released a Verey light, and now it was floating above the drop zone like a beacon for any German patrols in the area. The sight of it angered Rendel, since it put his men, in fact the whole mission, in danger. "How filthily artificial the little pink star looked as it flickered out in the middle of that dark wild scene," he thought.

As the flare winked out, Rendel watched the plane circle the plateau. When it crossed the moon again, he saw what he thought was a puff of smoke issue from the underbelly. "The plane flew on and was lost to view," he observed, "and then suddenly the puff of smoke had changed into a tiny marionette dancing beneath a billowing shred of fabric that blew out as we gazed at it, into the graceful circle of a parachute." His first reaction surprised him. "It looked so frail and lonely against the night sky that I felt momentarily sorry for the human being dangling beneath, who was dropping swiftly into what must look to him like an infinite blackness." But he reminded himself that Paddy Leigh Fermor, the swashbuckler about whom he had heard so much, was not the kind of man to be fazed by a simple parachute jump into the black hole of a mountain night on Crete.

Before the marionette reached the ground, Rendel's Greek helpers charged toward the descending figure. Rendel heard an English voice call down asking if everything was in order. He tried to answer back that everything was fine but doubted he could be heard over the shouting Greek voices all around him. Suddenly, the man was on the ground and the Greeks were rushing to help him to his feet and shake his hand. "It's Captain Livermore," Rendel heard one of them call out.

Rendel had set eyes on Leigh Fermor only once before, when they had brushed past each other on the beach, as Rendel was coming ashore for the first time and Paddy was ushering Carta onto the boat that would carry him to Cairo. He had given some thought to how he would handle this second meeting. In his mind he pictured himself stepping cinematically toward Paddy with his hand outstretched, like Stanley greeting Livingstone on Tanganyika: "Mr. Leigh Fermor, I presume." But in the heat of the moment formality went by the boards. All at once the two men were shaking hands like old friends, and Rendel asked Leigh Fermor if he was all right.

Overheard the roar of the airplane's engines grew louder once again as it banked and came in low for another run. Rendel was aware that there were three men still to come. As he turned his attention from Leigh Fermor back to the sky, he saw that the clouds, which had been scattered before, were now rolling together in a dense tumult overhead. Soon the moon was completely obscured. Rendel worried that aborting the mission tonight would lead to more trouble. The Verey light would not have gone unnoticed by the enemy, and any subsequent attempts to repeat the drop at this location would incur much more risk as a result. The only hope, to his way of thinking, was to get Moss and the others on the ground tonight. It seemed the pilot was equally anxious to complete the mission. For nearly forty minutes the aircraft remained audible—"still low above us," Rendel sensed, "snoring away like some lumbering blind monster." But as the minutes went by, the heavy curtain of cloud only closed tighter over the plateau. Finally, around quarter to ten, the growl of the Halifax engines faded and did not return. That was it for tonight.

Leigh Fermor was thirsty after the lengthy flight and the excitement of the jump, but Rendel and his men had emptied their water bottles in anticipation of the heavier loads they would be carrying on the return trip to their camp. So with a dry throat he set out with them on the three-hour march back in the direction of Kritsa. Some distance short of the outlying village of Tapais, they arrived at the cave where Rendel had set up the radio. When he next made contact with Cairo, he included an urgent request that on future attempts air crews refrain from lighting up the area with flares.

The following morning, patrols poured out of the German garrison in nearby Kritsa, drawn by the peculiarity of an aircraft circling over the plateau and dropping flares. One detachment entered Tapais, putting Rendel on edge. He and his men had established a rapport with the villagers, and he numbered the mayor of Tapais among his strongest supporters. Any reprisals against the village would come as a personal blow as well as a threat to the mission. Rendel would later learn that the

Germans had indeed swept through the village without doing much damage, but this proved not to be the end of the affair. Not long after the incident in Tapais, a hundred reinforcements were added to the garrison in Kritsa, tripling the enemy strength there. "As time went on our more rustic friends wildly inflated this figure till it grew in their accounts to three thousand," Rendel noted.

The next week Leigh Fermor and Rendel ventured back to the plateau on two nights to wait for the plane, but without success. By the following week the moon had waned to a point that made the drop unfeasible, so they kept to the cave to await the next opportunity. They passed the time playing a word game called Consequence and talking about books, though with Paddy's equipment cylinders still undelivered, they had nothing to actually read. Rendel was delighted with the company. "I could hardly have had a more cheerful companion than Paddy, or a better guide to all things Cretan," he felt. "For all his literary tastes and background, he was clearly wrapped up in his war job, and his touch with the locals seemed to me absolutely perfect." One minute Leigh Fermor would be embroiled with one of the Greeks "in an enthusiastic discussion about the different types of patch to put on the heel or toe or instep of a Cretan jackboot (a most technical and important subject)," and the next he and Rendel would find themselves debating the relative merits of various poets. Although he regretted putting the mission on hold, Paddy too was enjoying the camaraderie. "I have been a guest since my arrival in Sandy's area," he wrote to Cairo after he had been there awhile, "and a most patient and friendly host he has proved."

Leigh Fermor's singing was an especially welcome addition to the routine at Rendel's cave. His repertoire included a huge number of folk songs in nearly as many languages. These new additions rounded out the English pub songs—"The Farmer's

Boy," "The Lincolnshire Poacher"—that Rendel's wireless operator liked to sing. Now the cave resounded with songs in Arabic
and French. The *andartes* joined in when Paddy launched into a
tune in Greek, and it sometimes surprised them to find that he
knew more verses than they did. This was the case with a ballad he taught Rendel about a girl from Samos. "And in your boat
golden sails will I set, and silver oars, Girl of Samos, to bring
you home," ran one verse. When Rendel had mastered a handful of verses, the ballad became his trademark song. The analo-
gous tune for Leigh Fermor was a song called "Philadem" that
had been sung at the time of the Turkish occupation. Its title
soon became an informal code name for him in the mountain villages.

Their hiatus from the Katharo plateau at this time turned
out to be fortunate. The same brand of village gossip that had
puffed up the strength estimate of the garrison at Kritsa was
by now turning the activity on the plateau into a virtual invasion. Rumor had it that a force of more than fifty British commandos had been parachuted onto the plateau. Meanwhile, the
Germans began to patrol the area in earnest. After monitoring
Katharo for several nights running without encountering an
invasion force, they eventually withdrew, but they were soon
stirred up again. On the first attempt to stage a drop on the next
moon in early March, the pilot once again issued a gilded invitation to the enemy in the form of a Verey light.

Rendel was incensed. But there was little he could do beyond
calling off the attempt scheduled for the following night. Apparently, though, his message failed to reach Cairo. That night,
under perfectly clear skies, he and Leigh Fermor sat at the cave,
listening to the Halifax buzzing around the plateau in the distance. Spotting no signal fires, the pilot eventually gave up and
turned for home. Paddy and Rendel, disappointed at missing
what might have been their best opportunity yet, resolved to be

ready the following night. But the next afternoon, as they were preparing to leave for the plateau in order to set up the necessary signal fires, a return message arrived from Cairo. *Now* the signal to postpone had gone through, and there would be no attempt that night.

At least the message had arrived in time to save them the two-hour climb up to the plateau. Although winter was beginning to loosen its grip on the mountains, the evening grew cold quickly as the sun went down. The men settled into the cave for the night. Someone had brought a flagon of wine up from the village down below, and they filled mugs with this and passed them around. Before long the cave was once again echoing with Leigh Fermor's songs. Then they heard something that silenced everyone. Somewhere outside, and by the sound of it not very far away, a gun went off. They rushed to the mouth of the cave. As they stood listening, one shot turned into two, and soon bursts were being traded somewhere out in the darkness. "No Germans should have been there then," Rendel believed, "but it was clearly more than the odd sheep thief firing surreptitiously with a captured pistol."

The German presence in the area was steadily growing in response to the flights over the plateau. Kritsa by now housed three hundred soldiers, and another nearby base had grown to five hundred. With small-arms fire echoing through the night, it felt as if a net were beginning to close around the cave. There was little they could do under the circumstances. Rendel posted a sentry outside, prepared to sound an alarm if anyone was heard approaching; then he and the others went to bed.

A shepherd arrived at the cave first thing the following morning with astonishing news. The gunfire in the night had indeed come from a German patrol. Or rather two German patrols. It seemed that German command had somehow gotten wind of the route Leigh Fermor and Rendel followed from the cave to the drop zone on the Katharo plateau. Sometime after twilight, just when they would have been striking out to meet the plane had the drop not been canceled, a detachment from Kritsa made its way into the gully where the path they took from the cave met the mule track that led from Kritsa to the plateau. The detachment was all set up for an ambush when a party came trundling down the trail from the other direction. In the darkness the Kritsa unit opened fire. The other men blasted back and a chaotic gunfight erupted. In the heated exchange several men were wounded and two were killed. It was only when the dust had settled that it became clear that the men on both sides wore German uniforms. The other party, it turned out, was a column dispatched from the garrison on the far side of the plateau.

Later that day Leigh Fermor and Rendel watched from a copse of pines as the column marched back toward Kitsa carrying the men who had been killed or wounded in the night. With no effort on their part, German morale had suffered a blow. But they could hardly chalk the incident up as a victory. What it amounted to was a warning shot, very close at hand, and it did not bode well for further operations on the plateau. Paddy and Rendel had a long talk back at the cave and concluded that the drop had become impossible. As it turned out, they were not the only ones who saw the writing on the wall. Evidently it was visible as far away as Cairo. "We were contemplating a telegram that day to say that the party would have to come by sea after all," Rendel recalled, "when we received one ourselves saying that the airdrop had been cancelled and that Moss and the others would be arriving on the next boat."

WHEN THE CANCELLATION order reached Bari, Moss, Manoli, and George packed their bags and boarded a plane headed back to Cairo. The flight was broken in Malta, where Moss spent an evening with old friends in high style, drinking Möet & Chandon '19, "which was partly flat but heartwarming to discover." By the next evening he was back in his room at Tara. But he was disappointed to learn that Sophie was away. She had gone to visit Luxor with a party that included Xan Fielding. When she finally returned on the morning of March 24, it was a very happy reunion. "Unfortunately I was due to leave in 24 hours," Moss recorded in his diary, "so we had to cram a lot into a short time—but this we did most successfully, and I must have resembled some moribund animal as I crept into a taxi next morning."

With the airdrop off the table, Moss and the others were now bound for Tobruk, where a motor launch would be waiting to take them across to Crete. Reaching Alexandria late in the afternoon, Moss decided to stop for the night. Again he looked up some friends for dinner, which was followed by his second trip to the opera since the war began. He saw *The Phantom of the Opera*. The next morning they pressed on. But when they reached Tobruk at midday, they discovered that there was no boat to be had. They traveled a hundred miles farther west to Derna the following day but again found no boat. Still, this beat waiting in the rain at Bari. Derna was a pleasant town, Moss thought, and after a month of storms the weather had now turned fair. Manoli and George also helped to keep Moss's spirits high—"they 'acquired' a couple sheep on the way here, which have since been killed and cooked, and eaten with relish. I can see that as long as I stay with that pair of toughs I shall never go in want of anything!"

Anything, that is, except a boat. Next they tried Bardiyah, which meant backtracking to Tobruk and then another hundred retrograde miles east along the coast road they had traveled from Alexandria. Here Moss again failed to turn up a motor launch prepared to make a run to Crete. "Of course there wasn't a boat waiting for us," he quipped; "no one had even heard of a boat. I think I must be Jonah!" But at Bardiyah he did meet a South African lieutenant who invited the three of them to stay at the villa where he and his men were boarding. It was situated on a lovely cove and had plenty of room, so Moss decided to stay on there and wait for a boat, rather than continue the wild-goose chase up and down the Libyan coast.

LEIGH FERMOR and Sandy Rendel were experiencing difficulties of their own. They were now in the process of moving Rendel's headquarters south, both to avoid the dangerous situation that was developing in the area of the Katharo plateau and to be on hand for Moss's eventual landing on the south coast. But before they managed to leave, Leigh Fermor became entangled in a conference with three *andarte kapetans*, who sought his help in petitioning the British for more arms. Among them was a man named Bodias who had been in prison for murder at the time of the invasion. Word was that he had assaulted a village boy and when the lad's father confronted him, Bodias killed them both with a hoe. In prison he underwent a transformation, educating himself in politics and re-styling himself as a Communist. Despite the man's violent past and political leanings, Leigh Fermor thought Bodias could prove useful to the Resistance. The other two leaders—"a bitter, sneering man" who commanded a band based half an hour above the plateau and a "plucky" Athenian who inspired Leigh Fermor's confidence—were both more predictable than Bodias. With some reservation, he would recommend arming the bands the men represented. But it turned out that they did the British a still bigger service in return. When Bodias and the other two men left the cave on the morning of the twenty-fifth, they stumbled into an ambush apparently set for Rendel, who was returning from a reconnaissance trip south of Katharo.

By the time Rendel reached the cave a little later that morning, the Germans had moved into the nearby village of Tapais. The scouts he and Leigh Fermor dispatched to look the situation over soon came gasping back into camp with the warning that a column was advancing up the ridge and would soon reach the intersection of trails below the cave. If they turned one way they would spill onto the plateau; the other way would bring them to the doorstep of Rendel's cave.

With the Germans only a matter of minutes away, Rendel hurried through the list of things he had to do before evacuating the camp: "we had stowed the stores—half a dozen sacks of dehydrated food, clothes, bandages and such—under various convenient boulders with a special cranny for the wireless; and prepared for what Paddy described jauntily as 'another Oak Apple day.'" Rendel had heard the story of Leigh Fermor's earlier close call—when he had dodged a German patrol by disappearing into the crown of a cypress tree—and he did not relish the idea of climbing into one of the bristly Cretan holm oaks he had seen growing nearby.

Instead they slipped off about twenty yards above the cave and crouched among the rocks to see what would happen. When the German column reached the fork in the trail, it split ranks, one detachment continuing to the plateau while the other marched in single file up the trail leading to the cave. The enemy soldiers were so exposed at this point that Rendel worried his men might be unable to resist taking a potshot, setting off a battle that could only end badly. Almost as soon as the thought crossed his mind, he noticed that one of the Cretans "had begun to advise the party in a tremendous stage whisper how best to ambush and massacre the foe—until he began clambering about to illustrate his strategy, and was told forcefully to shut up."

To Rendel it looked as if the German soldiers were also putting on a show of their own. "When they had climbed level with the cave," he saw, "they stopped and made a tremendous noise crashing about the trees, shouting to each other, and giving us no excuse whatever to clash with them unwittingly." He and Leigh Fermor could only hold their breath and wait while the patrol settled down near the cave, where they stayed for the next hour. Finally they set off a series of smoke grenades, presumably as a signal to the other half of the column that they were now advancing in their direction. Then they withdrew and went clanging off up the trail to the plateau.

Just before dusk that evening, Rendel and his men loaded up the wireless set and their stores and set off toward the new headquarters he had scouted out to the southwest, above the village of Males. Nearing the plateau, they happened upon the returning German patrol, but they had the luck to be hidden by the same Katharo fog that had foiled the airdrop. They crossed the open area in darkness and continued on their way. The next morning Leigh Fermor and a pair of guides struck out to reconnoiter the south coast.

BY MARCH 30 Leigh Fermor had once again linked up with Rendel and the two of them were holed up at the small, rustic Monastery of the Twelve Apostles near Kastelliana, in the hills west of Ano Viannos. The abbot, "a young, spectacled, alert, courageous and amusing man, with a whispy beard, bun tucked under his stovepipe hat, and a gold pectoral cross," as Leigh Fermor described him, was a longtime friend of the Resistance.

Rendel arrived at the monastery with a horrifying new story to tell. Shortly before his rendezvous with Leigh Fermor, he had been eating raisins one night at his hideout to the east when he noticed that one of them had a peculiar rubbery texture. The other men were asleep and he was eating without any light, so rather than spit it out to look at it, he kept chewing. Or trying to chew, since the resilient morsel was resisting all his efforts. As he rolled it around his mouth, it suddenly hit him that he had somehow gotten hold of one of the chewable caches of cyanide that Jasper Maskelyne, the former stage magician turned SOE conjurer, handed out as a last resort in the event of capture. The slightest puncture in the rubber skin of this death capsule could kill him almost instantly. In a panic, he leaped up and managed to spit the thing out, but he woke up the entire camp with the frenzy of mouth rinsing and sputtering that followed.

Though he did not know it, Rendel was now on a collision course with another close call. On the morning of the thirty-first, he and Leigh Fermor and their Greek guides were lounging about in the small bedroom the abbot had given them at the monastery when a young monk, the abbot's only acolyte besides one nun, rushed in to say he had spotted a detachment of seven German soldiers approaching the front door. There was no time to escape without being noticed, and Leigh Fermor and the others were at a loss for what to do. But the abbot calmly pushed back the bed Paddy had slept on the night before, lifted a trapdoor, and motioned them into the cellar. The whole party, slowed only by Leigh Fermor, who fumbled with his boots for a nerve-racking eon, disappeared down the hole just as the Germans entered at the front door. For the next two hours they hunched in silence just beneath the floor while the abbot entertained his unexpected guests. "We could see them through the chinks in the floor boards," Leigh Fermor wrote to Cairo later that day.

The abbot handled the incident with remarkable composure. Listening in the dark down below, Rendel was struck by the urbane welcome he extended to the Germans. "If they would have the great goodness just to sit down for a few minutes, he would be honoured to have a dish of the monastery's eggs prepared. It was a simple abode, and they must excuse it, but they were good fresh eggs and he had plenty of potatoes. Meanwhile they would naturally take a glass of raki, and his boy would just run out to the cellar to fetch a flask of the monastery's own wine. It was not, perhaps, as well known as the best wine of Arkhanes, but he hoped and believed they would like it."

The savvy young abbot laid it on with a trowel, and the well-feted Germans seemed not to suspect a thing. Paddy and the others started momentarily when the boy pulled open the door and entered the cellar from outside, but he had only come to draw the wine. In a hushed voice he assured them that everything was going smoothly, then ducked back out and closed the door, plunging them again into darkness. The boy's assessment was accurate. Once the soldiers had their fill of the abbot's exaggerated hospitality, they trooped out without looking back, and the moles in the cellar soon filed back upstairs.

When the excitement was over, Leigh Fermor withdrew to a quiet corner to write up his first field report since returning to Crete in February. By now he was convinced that Moss and the others would arrive by sea any minute, and he took the opportunity to reflect on the failed airdrop on the Katharo plateau. The weather was not the only problem, he believed. And although he did not fault the aircrews, he did blame faulty scheduling that failed to take into account the time of moonrise and the security requirements of the ground team, which needed time after nightfall to move onto the plateau. "The actual pilot, W/O Fortune, did the most painstaking job of work, and my own drop was as near perfection as it could be, although the weather conditions were the worst of any night we were told to wait except one," he wrote. If subsequent sorties had been planned to reach the drop zone within the same window of opportunity, Moss might have arrived on time and Müller would be cooling his heels in a Cairo prison by now. Leigh Fermor also grumbled at headquarters for failing to pass along the message of gratitude he had sent to Fortune after his on-target drop of arms for Bandouvas the year before. Fortune had heard nothing of the engraved knife Bo-Peep and his men had promised him. These things make a difference, Paddy emphasized.

But his report quickly moved on to more pressing matters. He had some surprising news to deliver. The "original quarry has left," he reported. Word of this change had come from Minoan Mike, Leigh Fermor's agent in Heraklion. General Müller, the author of the massacres in Viannos and the target of the entire kidnapping mission, had been removed from the district. On the face of it, this changed everything. But Leigh Fermor saw no reason to give up on his objective. In fact, he felt that once Moss and the others arrived, they need not miss another beat. Müller had already been replaced, he went on to say, and he had every intention of capturing the new general.

Because so much of his time since February had been absorbed by marches to and from the drop zone on Katharo or twiddling his thumbs at Rendel's former hideout at the cave while waiting for conformation of a drop on one night or another, he had not been able to investigate the new situation "in the snatch area" as much as he would have liked. But he was confident the plan, in broad strokes, remained sound. He warned headquarters not to expect immediate results. "I am going to try and pull it off as quickly as possible, however," he concluded.

Expecting Moss's boat to arrive that night, Leigh Fermor rounded off his report quickly, so that he could send it back on the boat's return trip. Three days later, still waiting, he appended a friendly note to Jack Smith-Hughes that gave vent to his frustration. "Hope Billy and the lads arrive tonight," he wrote; "it has been a very trying wait." For good measure, when he added the report to the bundle he had prepared for the landing, he threw in a bottle of *tsikoudia*, the local grappa, for Smith-Hughes and Xan Fielding, who was now back in Cairo.

MOSS'S DECISION to await the motor launch at the villa in Bardiyah turned out to be a wise choice. He and Manoli and George feasted on three meals a day of bacon and eggs. For the most part they had the cove to themselves, and on March 30 they took the opportunity to give their weapons another round of testing. The next day Moss was contemplating a little demolition training. "Might go fishing with explosives this evening," he wrote in his diary. "Shark for dinner would be fun—and a change!"

Just as the blasting was about to begin that evening, however, the motor launch they had been waiting for, *ML-842*, came gliding into the cove. The sight of it after all this time sent Moss and the Greeks scurrying to pack their gear. At five o'clock the next morning they clambered aboard and the boat slipped out of the cove, bound for Crete. Not five hours later, they were back at the villa, in time for a late breakfast. The choppy seas had been too rough for the launch to manage. They were hardly out to sea when the roller-coaster motion of the boat had Moss thinking wistfully of Cyril Fortune's storm-tossed Halifax, which now seemed like the smoother ride. He was conveniently forgetting that one of the flights had encountered such severe turbulence that the bombardier had joined Manoli and George in vomiting through the jump door in the floor of the plane. In fact, a jump door would have come in handy for just that purpose aboard *ML-842*. By the time the launch turned back some two hours later, seasick passengers sprawled all across the deck.

The skipper of the motor launch was a blue-eyed naval reserve lieutenant from Sussex named Brian Coleman, whose full-bearded face reminded Moss of the seaman on Player's cigarette posters. Coleman had received orders to complete the mission to Crete, code-named "Moonstruck," "as soon as possible after 25/26 March," but he had run into delays in outfitting the boat and reaching the embarkation point designated in the orders. The mission had first been scheduled to depart from Tobruk, but when Coleman got there he found that because of special operations under way there, the harbor had been placed "Out of Bounds." When the order came through on the twenty-fourth, rerouting the mission through Bardiyah, it meant that Moss and the others could sit back and wait for the boat to come to them. Now Coleman regretted giving in to further weather delays, but they would try again the following day.

The motor launch put to sea once more on the morning of April 2 and wallowed for nearly four hours through churning seas before again turning back. They were anchored in the cove at Bardiyah again by midafternoon. Moss summed up the day in his diary: "the sea rougher than before, the Greeks greener, and myself a corpse on the wardroom settee. God, what torture!" April 3 proved much the same, though the aborted voyage was mercifully briefer. That evening Moss wondered in his diary how Paddy and the others on Crete were holding up against the string of delays. At least they were on dry land. He had watched the daily battle with seasickness knock the stuffing out of Manoli and George. Fortunately, once ashore they quickly returned to normal. "As I write I can smell the cooking of meat," Moss recorded, "and I think it's a safe bet that yet another Arab shepherd, when next he counts his flock, will find it down in numbers!"

The following morning, April 4, dawned clear and calm at Bardiyah. With the entire company now in a more jovial mood, Coleman angled the launch out of the cove across a long, slow-running swell that held throughout the day. The passengers felt much more comfortable than on the previous attempts, and Moss, Manoli, and George for once had stomachs fit for the bacon sandwiches and coffee Coleman's steward brought up from the galley. Around midday they caught sight of a convoy in the distance. Moss and the others dozed through the late afternoon and went below at dusk to organize their gear for the landing, which at last seemed likely. Around 10:00 p.m. a sailor came down to tell them they were drawing close to their destination.

On the bridge they found Brian Coleman trying to make out the landmarks that would steer him to Dermatos Beach, east of the village of Tsoutsouros, where the landing party should be waiting. In the background the Cretans on board mounted a chorus of geographical advice, which the skipper finally silenced.

IT WAS NEARLY midnight when Rendel and a handful of his Cretan helpers heard the first rumble of an engine offshore. As the rising sound began to echo off the cliffs that backed the cove, Rendel flashed his light into the darkness and waited anxiously. Dah-dah. Dah-di-dah-dit. It had been agreed that he would flash the Morse letters *M* and *C* every ten minutes. But to avoid alerting German observers onshore, the ship would not signal back. Intelligence reports from Cairo noted patrol boats operating in the area, and Rendel had no way of knowing whether the vessel now entering the harbor was a friendly landing craft or a German patrol boat dispatched from one of the coastal guard stations that lay just a mile east and three-quarters of a mile west of their position. Each of these outposts had a garrison of seventeen men, and the one to the east was connected by phone to the garrison at Viannos, from which a more substantial force could be summoned.

A short distance up from the beach, Leigh Fermor had his hands full dealing with a few dozen *andartes* who had turned up days earlier asking to be evacuated to Cairo. Sending them packing might lead to security risks, so he was doing his best to accommodate them. There were also four German deserters to put aboard and a few evacuees sent by Tom Dunbabin, along with an Italian and two wounded men, including a Resistance fighter whose daughter was Leigh Fermor's godchild. In all, forty-five people would be boarding the launch for the return trip. Meanwhile, Rendel was supervising preparations on the beach, where he and his men had been waiting for more than an hour.

Thus far luck had been with them. When the party had reached the appointed landing area earlier in the day, they had seen how the fierce wind that came howling across Crete from Africa every spring had thrown sand dunes over the barbed wire German soldiers had left strung along the shoreline. More important, the land mines that had once ringed the cove had also been cleared, their triggers accidentally tripped by the flocks of sheep that sometimes strayed onto the island's beaches. Bad luck for the sheep was a break for the mission, but Rendel knew that luck like this was unlikely to hold.

When the throb of the boat's engine fell silent, the unit fanned out along the edge of the surf. All eyes peered into the mist, but there was little to be seen. Rendel and the men could only wait, the passing minutes ticked off by the sound of waves lapping at the sand. Then, at last, they heard the rhythmic stroking of oars. Before long a dinghy materialized out of the fog. When the dinghy drew close enough for Rendel to see that the man being rowed ashore was a British naval officer, he could finally breathe again.

Having spotted the Morse pattern Rendel was flashing out to sea, Brian Coleman had called his wireless operator up from below to confirm that these were the expected letters, then piloted his motor launch to a spot some fifty yards offshore and dispatched a dinghy under the command of his third mate, whose job it was to ferry a tow rope across the harbor. Now this line stretched from the stern of the dinghy out into the darkness, pointing the way to comrades and desperately needed supplies. The sailor flashed an all-clear signal back to Coleman as the Greeks clustered around the towline, some of them wading into the sea. The night was suddenly filled with voices as they began to haul away. Within minutes a second dinghy, heavily laden and sitting low in the water, materialized out of the darkness.

Riding astride a pile of gear and weapons, Moss watched as the shoreline grew nearer and nearer with each heave of the towline. Soon he could make out the bustling activity on the beach. "Some of the men stood waist-deep in water, while others lent no more than verbal encouragement from the wings," he saw. "Then, in a moment, I was among them, right in the middle of them, being pulled up out of the surf, and a score of hands were grabbing at the containers and kitbags and heaving them out of the dinghy away on to the dry sand. My first impressions were of dark faces, heavy moustaches, turbaned heads, black and shabby clothes, tall boots or bare feet, a score of voices doing their utmost to find hearing, and, above all, the strange nauseating smell of unwashed bodies and dirty clothing which hung upon the scene like some oppressive blanket."

As Moss stood gaping at the strange tableau on the beach, a man with a week's growth of beard, perhaps the shabbiest of the figures scurrying around on the sand, approached him and extended his hand. He wore a frayed coat and a rag turban; his pants and black puttees were filthy. It was only when the man said hello in perfect English that Moss realized it must be Sandy Rendel. Rendel explained that Leigh Fermor was on his way, then rushed back into the surf where another dinghy was coming ashore. Moss was left standing with a more distinguished-looking Cretan in a sports jacket who lifted the Marlin gun from Moss's shoulder as he grinned with admiration and said, "You friend Paddy? Me friend Paddy too." Like a child with a new toy, he fumbled with Moss's gun for a moment, then gestured up the beach and added, "Here come Paddy now."

Moss turned to see his friend striding down the beach with the dashing style of a pirate. Unlike Rendel, Paddy looked rugged but faultlessly groomed. His skin was tanned by the sun and he appeared more fit than Moss had ever seen him. "He wore a smart moustache," Moss noticed, "and sported a fine Cretan waistcoat, a long wine-colored cummerbund into which was thrust an ivory handled revolver and a large dagger; a pair of riding breeches and tall black boots." Even more striking than his clothing was the air of authority he now had about him. Manoli and George rushed to him and kissed him on both cheeks. As other Cretans who had shared the voyage with Moss came ashore from the launch, they did the same or slapped him on the back. All the newcomers looked pleased to see him.

Leigh Fermor's first concern was whiskey, followed by cigarettes. Moss assured him he had brought along plenty of both. As the two of them talked in the darkness, they were joined by another British officer named John Houseman, a fellow passenger on the motor launch who was on his way to work with Tom Dunbabin. "We sat, chatted and smoked on the beach until the stores were loaded onto the waiting donkeys," Houseman later wrote to Cairo. Leigh Fermor seemed not to have a care in the world. All the while, Houseman felt himself growing more and more anxious. "I could imagine," he confided, "that there were Germans round the corner."

Houseman was reassured when, as the engines of the motor launch thrummed back to life in the distance, the party finally moved out toward the cave where they would spend the night, a journey of roughly an hour and a half, according to one of the Cretans. It was in "true Hemingway style" that they mounted the cliffs leading up from the beach, Houseman felt. All along the way he could hear Leigh Fermor's calls of encouragement and the muleteers urging their animals along, "and after three hours of most terrible mountaineering we slid into our first

Billy Moss on Crete.
© *Imperial War Museum*
(HU 66085)

cave for the night." Moss, feeling spoiled by the high life he had been living in Cairo, put the trip at more like four hours. Either way, it taught him that a Cretan's estimate of the duration of an impending journey must always be multiplied. The only question was by how much.

As they bedded down in the shallow cave perched at the top of a mountain gully, a light rain began to fall. Moss had brought along the down-filled jumpsuit he had never had the opportunity to use as it was originally intended. Now he found it made an excellent sleeping bag. He noticed that Paddy had made the same discovery. As he drifted off to sleep, the sixteenth-century poem he had discovered in *A Farewell to Arms* wound itself into his thoughts—*the small rain down can rain*. Back at Tara, Sophie was no doubt snug in her bed.

CHAPTER 9

The Intersection

EARLY THE NEXT MORNING the men at the cave launched into the feast they had been too exhausted to put on the night before. Moss, Manoli, and George had finally reached Crete, two months to the day after Leigh Fermor's drop, and this happy end to an interminable string of disappointments called for celebration. By eight o'clock two goats were roasting in the coals of their campfire and a water bottle filled with raki made its way from hand to hand around the cave. Before breakfast, Moss, who had come ashore in uniform, changed into black plain clothes that had seemed shabby in Cairo, before he laid eyes on Sandy Rendel in his Cretan disguise.

"I haven't washed for six months," Rendel told Moss, scratching himself proudly as he said it. "A man of the people, that's me."

Leigh Fermor hastened to explain that he himself took the opposite tack. "Xan and I like them to think of us as sort o' dukes."

Between them they staked out the extremes of Cretan fashion. Moss would have fallen somewhere in the middle, had he not been betrayed by a Swiss ski sweater that peeked out from under his black woolen shirt. The sweater, that is, and his matinee-idol looks.

Leigh Fermor and Moss spent the morning planning their first move. It seemed to Paddy that they should set up their headquarters outside Kastamonitsa, one or two nights' march to the north. A base there would give them security while putting them in striking distance of Heraklion.

Around lunchtime the drinking began in earnest. Moss broke out the whiskey and cigars he had brought from Cairo. He had even packed a bottle of kümmel, so Paddy could drink a toast in the same style as on the night they left Tara. They drank, smoked, and talked until the middle of the afternoon, when the men began drifting to shady spots and dozing off. By the time the others woke up, Rendel was bustling around the campsite, gathering his equipment. At six o'clock he set off down the trail toward his hideout near Males. A party of Cretans who had come over on the launch followed not long after.

As the camp cleared out, Leigh Fermor and Moss settled down on some nearby rocks to wait for dusk, when fresh mules were due to arrive for the journey to Kastamonitsa. The delay gave them a chance to catch up. Paddy was anxious to hear the news from Tara, and they both had stories to swap about the nights they had spent in February and March just missing each other on the Katharo plateau. The big news, of course, was Müller. Leigh Fermor explained that the general they had come to capture had been replaced as commander of the Twenty-second Sevastopol Division. The new man was named Kreipe. He was in his forties, a career soldier since the First World War. His most recent command had been on the Russian front. Rumor had it that he was looking forward to a restful time on Crete after escaping the meat grinder of Stalingrad. He might well be in for some R & R, Paddy quipped, but in Cairo.

"It was a pity," Moss admitted, "that we had lost the opportunity of catching Müller, for he was a tyrant much loathed by the islanders, but as far as the ultimate effect of our plan was concerned we supposed that one general was as good a catch as another." Leigh Fermor agreed. Nothing would have pleased the Cretans more than the capture of Müller, who had more than earned his sour reputation on the island. But whoever this Kreipe turned out to be, his removal would strike a blow at German morale.

When nightfall came, they set off with four loaded mules heading roughly northward along the ridgeline. In addition to Leigh Fermor, Moss, Manoli, and George, the band now included two new men. One was Zahari Zographakis, the well-turned-out young fellow who had taken so much interest in Moss's Marlin gun on the night of the landing. The other was a Cretan by the name of Antoni Papaleonidas, who had been on the launch from Cairo. Moss had already decided he was "a gay rogue, full of fun and storytelling." The ten years he had spent at sea were evident in a swashbuckling kind of swagger. To Leigh Fermor and Moss he looked exactly like the American actor Wallace Beery, who had played Long John Silver in *Treasure Island* ten years earlier. Before the night was out, that's what they were calling him— Wallace Beery.

George Tyrakis, Antoni Papaleonidas ("Wallace Beery"), Manoli Paterakis.
Photograph © The Estate of William Stanley Moss—reproduced by permission

The party arrived at a small village called Skoinia sometime after midnight, and since there were not enough hours of darkness left to reach Kastamonitsa, they stopped at the house of a friendly man who fed them lentils and boiled eggs. Before they left the next evening, Leigh Fermor met with a string of visitors, including a local *andarte* chieftain named Athanasios Bourdzalis, an enormous, barrel-chested ruffian with an equally oversized personality. Bourdzalis commanded a band that was part of Bo-Peep's network, and Paddy imagined that their firepower might come in handy in the ensuing days. There were other visitors too. A young mother who had heard Leigh Fermor was visiting also dropped by with her baby daughter. The child was Anglia Epanastasis—England Revolution—the baby Paddy had christened at Bandouvas's mountain camp the previous August. Leigh Fermor was able to assure the mother that her husband, who was one of the two wounded men he had helped aboard the motor launch, would by now be receiving medical care in Cairo.

Sometime after nine o'clock the band was on the trail again, marching through a light rain. Paddy's step was noticeably uncertain after entertaining visitors all day in the expected Cretan fashion. Moss was having trouble too, but less from drink than from the slippery, rain-wet rocks that lined the path. At dawn they reached Zahari's house in Kastamonitsa. Their only encounters along the way were with dogs, who announced their passing at each village, and the odd party of snail gatherers, whose lamps they saw dancing on the hillsides as they slipped past.

Zahari's parents gave the party a warm welcome. His father was an old friend of the Resistance who had helped in the raids on the Kastelli airfield in 1942 and again the previous summer, when Lieutenant Lamonby had been killed.

Minoan Mike—Leigh Fermor's chief agent in Heraklion—arrived after lunch the next day to escort Paddy into the city to have a look at the layout of the nearby German headquarters and the general's residence. On the morning of the eighth, Leigh Fermor set about transforming himself into what Moss called a Heraklion "gadabout." His aim was to look like a shepherd on a visit to the city. He put on a clean suit, stuffed his light hair under a cap, and darkened his mustache with a little burned cork, then presented himself to Moss, who thought he looked like a new man. After supper he and Mike struck out down the mountainside to catch the bus headed toward the city the following morning. They would scout the situation at the Villa Ariadne while Moss and the others set up their headquarters two or three miles above Kastamonitsa.

That night, with Zahari's father leading the way and his mother crying softly at the doorstep, Moss's party set out with the mules on the three-hour climb to the cave that would be their base of operations. Just before dawn, the Cretan "Wallace Beery" stopped them, saying they would need daylight to find their way to the entrance. After sunup they moved on and soon reached a small, completely hidden cave. For the next week, Moss was content to wait there for Leigh Fermor's return.

PADDY AND MINOAN MIKE rattled into Heraklion by bus the next day and then backtracked a few miles south toward Knossos. They soon arrived at Mike's house, which would serve as their base of operations for a few days. It sat adjacent to the Villa Ariadne, which Kreipe, like Müller before him, had commandeered as his residence. Leigh Fermor knew that he was walking in the footsteps of his forerunner on Crete. Knossos and the villa had been John Pendlebury's bailiwick before the war, and would be still, if the man he had seen brandishing his sword stick that day in a cave outside Heraklion had had his way. It was strange now to think that this symbol of his legacy had fallen into the hands of the Germans. Minoan Mike had his own ghosts here too. His father, Pendlebury's right-hand man, had also been killed during the invasion, while Mike was himself fighting the Italians in Albania.

Mike led Leigh Fermor to a window from where they could observe the layout of the compound. Leigh Fermor took it all in, "the guards, the barbed wire, the German flag . . . and the General's villa."

It was Easter Sunday by the Western calendar, and that evening Leigh Fermor and Mike made their way to a neighboring villa to attend a party put on by a Greek officer by the name of Sergiou. General Sergiou's daughter Kyveli, a trim twenty-two-year-old with a light complexion and a mass of black hair, was one of Tom Dunbabin's most important agents. In her work as a translator at the Germans' Heraklion headquarters, she had been able to intercept sensitive German military documents, which were then photographed and funneled to Dunbabin's headquarters. Cairo considered her one of the best agents in the Heraklion network, and it was known that "the risks which she took to obtain information were truly amazing." More to the point, she had helped Mike track General Kreipe's movements in order to work out his schedule.

When Leigh Fermor and Minoan Mike arrived at the Sergiou villa and were shown into the large open room where the party was under way, they were at first unsettled to see that the guests included a trio of German sergeants. But the convivial atmosphere soon put them at ease. There was dancing and bright talk. Leigh Fermor found that the three Germans made charming companions. In fact, as the wine flowed, Mike became a little too comfortable in their company. Late in the evening, hoping he might pick up a crumb of useful information, he found himself talking and laughing with the German soldiers. Without thinking, he fished a pack of cigarettes out of his pocket and was in the process of shaking one out for his new friends when he realized he was holding a pack Moss had brought from Cairo. Drunk as they were, the Germans still noticed the English brand and wanted to know where he had acquired them. Mike did not miss a beat. He had bought them on the black market, he admitted. The vendor had hinted that they had been diverted from a stock captured by the Germans in their recent victories over the British in the Dodecanese. It was just the kind of flattery that worked wonders on the enemy. Before long the tension evaporated, and when the evening came to an end, the Germans embraced Paddy and Mike as they said their farewells.

A LITTLE WORSE for wear, the two spies were back on the job first thing the next morning. From watching the comings and goings next door, Mike was convinced that a raid on the villa itself was out of the question, as Leigh Fermor already suspected. Although the Resistance had one or two friends working inside the compound, it was still simply too well defended. Paddy counted three rows of razor wire around the perimeter. And it was patrolled by a veritable army of sentries. The security measures at the villa made the defenses he and Manoli had run up against at Heraklion harbor the previous year look soft by comparison.

But that did not mean that Kreipe was never vulnerable. Mike and his second in command in the Heraklion intelligence network, Elias Athanassakis, had worked out that Kreipe left the villa in the morning shortly after eight thirty; he was at work at his headquarters in Archanes by nine o'clock, and he returned to the villa just after one o'clock for lunch. Sometime before four o'clock he traveled back to headquarters and worked as late as eight thirty, before being driven back to the villa for the night. By that time the sun was down, and it might be possible to waylay the car without drawing much attention.

Over the next several days, Mike and Leigh Fermor scouted the area. They drove out to the intersection where the Archanes road joined the main road running between Heraklion and Choudetsi. Here a car traveling from Archanes was forced to make a sharp turn to continue in the direction of the villa. The general's car would slow almost to a stop at a point where a steep bank skirted the road. It looked tailor-made for an ambush, except that heavy traffic could be expected to pass by on the main road. Still, at night it might work. When a car approached the intersection as they stood looking over the turn, it gave them a chance to see just how much a vehicle would slow. It was only as it rattled to a rolling stop and then motored off that they realized they had just waved to General Kreipe himself.

As Leigh Fermor and Mike gathered intelligence about their quarry in Heraklion and around the Villa Ariadne, Paddy began to piece together a clearer sense of the difficulties he faced. It would be trickier than his housemates had foreseen in the bath at Tara. There were a few evident obstacles to consider. Since it was necessary to conduct the operation at night, to avoid observation from the busier Heraklion road, it might prove difficult to distinguish the general's staff car from any other vehicles that happened up the Archanes road that night. And other vehicles could be a problem even once Kreipe's car had been flagged down. In the case of a truck loaded with soldiers, the threat was obvious, but even a passing driver or motorcyclist, if allowed to get away, could alert others. One difficulty in particular would remain even if the mission went off without a single hitch: reprisals.

When he left the Villa Ariadne, Leigh Fermor spent two further days meeting with contacts in Heraklion. One was Minoan Mike's man Elias Athanassakis. A student before the war—and ostensibly a student still—Elias had now made the Germans his field of study. He had memorized the markings that distinguished each unit deployed on Crete and could track their movements with the precision of a scientist. He also had some technological tricks up his sleeve that might come in handy in the coming ambush.

On his last day in Heraklion, Leigh Fermor was joined by Manoli, and together they went over the facts he had picked up at the Villa Ariadne. By the time they left, Leigh Fermor had come to think that the first two problems—identifying the general's car and subduing anyone else who might stumble into the ambush—could be overcome with some clever planning. How to avoid reprisals would require more careful deliberation.

On April 15 Leigh Fermor, Elias, and Manoli returned to Kastamonitsa, and the next morning, Easter Sunday in the Greek Orthodox calendar, they made the three-hour climb up to the cave, where, around noon, they found Moss and the others waiting. Moss was happy to have Leigh Fermor back. He had spent the intervening days reading—Mallarmé and *The Travels of Marco Polo*—and getting to know the rest of the party. But he was anxious to get on with the mission.

In his absence the band had grown in numbers, Moss told Paddy. Two days earlier, Moss and George Tyrakis had climbed down from the cave to investigate a shepherd's unlikely report that two escaped Russian prisoners had been spotted nearby. It turned out to be true. On the strength of the Russian he had learned from his mother, Moss was able to gather that they were soldiers captured in the Crimea and that they had been brought to Crete nearly a year earlier and put to work on a road gang at the Kastelli air base. A third companion had been killed as they made their escape, and these two—Ivan from the Caucasus and a Ukrainian named Vassily—were weak from exposure and hunger. Moss brought the men back to the cave. "We have given them all our spare clothing and fed them like fighting cocks," he explained. They were making a speedy recovery, and now in the evenings the cave resounded with Vassily's Ukrainian songs, the singer himself resplendent in a dress uniform jacket Moss had not worn since he left London.

Another new face belonged to an older Cretan named Grigori Chnarakis, who had joined the band just as Leigh Fermor left for Heraklion. He had arrived, fresh from Cairo, with Paddy's recommendation as an old hand at raids against the Germans. Moss had been struck by the strange mishmash of clothing he wore— riding breeches, blue serge jacket, pinstripe shirt, and an army beret poised on the very top of his head. The older man's habit of spitting indiscriminately and breaking wind under one's nose had at first rubbed Moss the wrong way. But Grigori's determination to fight the Germans had quickly won his respect.

By the time Leigh Fermor and Manoli reached the cave, Moss and the Cretans already had a lamb roasting. And the Easter celebration was soon in full swing. This was done in Cretan fashion, with colored eggs, gallons of wine, and plenty of gunplay. In a letter posted by a runner from Heraklion, Paddy had warned Moss what to expect out of the paschal celebration, in the event he did not himself make it back in time. "Christ is risen—Bang!" the letter said. "He is truly risen—Bang! again."

As the afternoon wore on, the spirited shooting soon played itself out, but the drinking went on well into the evening. It was sometime after midnight when Moss and Leigh Fermor polished off the last of the Cairo whiskey and went to bed. The next day the two of them sat down with Manoli, Elias, and George Tyrakis to discuss the facts the recent reconnaissance mission had turned up at the villa. After Leigh Fermor had laid out what he knew about the villa's defenses and Kreipe's comings and goings, Moss had no trouble anticipating the very difficulties Leigh Fermor had himself foreseen.

They went on to discuss a plan Elias had devised to deal with the problem of identifying Kreipe's car. The student from Heraklion proposed rigging up a buzzer system that would let an observer perched some distance up the road, where he would have a clear view of approaching vehicles, transmit a signal back to the ambush party waiting at the intersection. Elias himself would study Kreipe's staff car in advance of the operation. He would have no trouble committing its distinguishing features to memory—not just the make and model but also the shape of its headlights and the way the light played out of the blackout hoods, even the particular note of its exhaust rumble. If some other car happened along, the ambush team would know to sit tight and let it pass. Then, when they heard the signal designating General Kreipe's car, they would be ready to spring into action. It sounded like a workable plan, though it would require them to come up with several hundred yards of wire, a battery, and a few other electrical components.

Once the ambush was under way, the signal would be of little use. So there was still the problem of disposing of unwanted guests. Leigh Fermor had an idea for that too. He would enlist Athanasios Bourdzalis, the barrel-chested *kapetan* from Bo-Peep's network he had met with at the safe house on the march up from the coast after Moss's arrival. Bourdzalis commanded a band of *andartes* with enough firepower among them to deal, for a few minutes at least, with any force likely to be out and about at that time of night. Once Leigh Fermor's team slipped away with the general, the *andartes* would break off the fight and disappear into the hills. Moss and Manoli agreed that Paddy should send a message summoning Bourdzalis.

That left the one perennial worry. Once the Germans discovered what had happened, reprisals became a certainty. The only way around that, Leigh Fermor believed, was to convince the German authorities that the raid had been carried out entirely by British forces that had been infiltrated for the specific purpose. Ironically, the airdrop fiasco on the Katharo plateau could prove useful in this regard. Rumor already had it that dozens of men had parachuted onto the island during those nights Moss and the others had spent buzzing around the plateau and dropping flares. Sixty, by an estimate that made the rounds in February. Forty, according to a more recent flurry of gossip. What Leigh Fermor needed was a way to encourage that line of thought. The scene of the crime, so to speak, had to be stamped with an imprint so British in character there would be no doubt about who had been there.

MEANWHILE, NEWS COMING out of Tom Dunbabin's intelligence network was beginning to suggest that the Germans might be losing their taste for the occupation. Reprisals were still commonplace, but they lacked some of their former ferocity. Dunbabin reported that a recent German raid in the Amari region had "dissolved amid the derisive laughter of the Amariots." Elsewhere raids were falling apart through sheer ineptitude. On April 1 another detachment of fifteen German soldiers marched into Gerakari—the center of SOE activity in the Lotus Land of the Amari—and entered a house where weapons had been found. "They attempted to blow up the house but the charge exploded in the face of one of the men, who left in disorder," or so Dunbabin had heard.

Everywhere there were reports of irresolute behavior on the part of the enemy. Hostages were being released or held briefly on merely trivial charges. Dunbabin had also spotted German soldiers reading propaganda flyers put out by SOE and had even heard fragments of his own misinformation repeated in conversations between Germans. If the enemy's resolve was beginning to waver, he believed, now was the time to strike. He envisioned a string of small-scale raids that would harass the enemy and limit their mobility on the island. "We want not so much to kill Germans as to terrify and bamboozle them," he recommended.

It was clear that he had Leigh Fermor's mission in mind as a part of this overall strategy.

To the east in the Lasithi district, Sandy Rendel was making preparations that could provide for submarine support of the raids Dunbabin called for. In the company of a local guide, Rendel slipped onto the island of Spinalonga, a former leper colony in the Bay of Mirabello, east of Áyios Nikólaos on Lasithi's north coast, and spent an afternoon in the shade of a carob tree, drawing a detailed map of the harbor and its defenses, which included a gun emplacement, a minefield, and sentries.

The RAF was doing its part too. Around noon on April 19, Leigh Fermor's band was treated to a spectacular show that spurred their morale as surely as it would dampen German spirits. From an outcrop above the cave, they watched as a flight of more than a dozen British bombers walloped the Kastelli airfield.

The next morning *Kapetan* Bourdzalis, wearing a spectacular pair of burgundy boots, arrived at the cave with his band of *andartes*. Even after an all-night march, the men entered the camp looking fierce, if poorly armed. Leigh Fermor noted that their weapons were of the same astonishing antiquity he had encountered again and again since the invasion. There were shotguns that must certainly have been fired in anger at the Turks. Bourdzalis admitted that until the previous day, a good part of his munitions had lain buried in out-of-the-way groves. This, he said, accounted for the fact that weapons were "a tiny bit rusty."

Over a lunch of potatoes and eggs, Leigh Fermor described the mission he wished Bourdzalis to support. By now it had become a kind of recitation that, like a Homeric poem, gained in detail each time it was told; the ambush would take place at the intersection of the Archanes and Heraklion roads, where the general's car would be flagged down as it slowed for the turn.

Leigh Fermor's men would subdue the driver and take control of the car. The *andartes'* role at this point would be strictly defensive. Leigh Fermor wanted them positioned on each of the three stretches of road leading to the intersection, where they could intercept any approaching traffic and give Paddy's team time to carry out the operation and make their escape with the general in tow. The plan was to drive north past the Villa Ariadne and into Heraklion, where they would make their way through the center of town and back out by way of the Chania gate and along the coast road in the direction of Rethymnon, eventually abandoning the car on a stretch of road near the sea and continuing southward over the mountains on foot. Bourdzalis and his *andartes* would later rendezvous with Leigh Fermor's company to help guide them over the mountains to a landing beach on the south coast.

As Leigh Fermor talked, Bourdzalis sat cleaning his nails with a dagger. But the casual pose did little to conceal his eagerness as the mission took shape before his eyes. Paddy had hardly finished when the *kapetan* leaped up and accepted the job. His men were ready, he said. They could set out as soon as darkness came. Leigh Fermor's men began packing their equipment and stores for the march to the village of Skalani, near Knossos, which would be their base for the operation. So long a kind of fantasy, the mission was now beginning in earnest.

Just after sundown, Leigh Fermor's team, which now included the two Russian escapees, filed down the goat path from their cave in the company of Bourdzalis and his men. They marched through the moonless night, crossing difficult terrain in utter darkness. "This sort of walking in Crete is really unpleasant," Moss felt, "like for ever going up or down a rickety staircase on which every third or fourth step gives way; and the staircase is as narrow as the slime-track of a snail, but it has no visible edges, and everything around you is black. You

Moss and Leigh Fermor (seated, center front) and their team with Athanasios Bourdzalis and his andartes. *Photograph © The Estate of William Stanley Moss—reproduced by permission*

can't even see your feet." But they pressed on. Near daybreak they were approaching the village of Kharaso, still thirty hard miles from their destination. It was decided to send a scout into the village to arrange a place to sleep and wait out the daylight hours. While the rest of the party stayed at a nearby house, Leigh Fermor, Moss, and half the men took shelter in a storage loft filled with olives and beans. They also discovered barrels of resinous wine, which were a little emptier by the time they left.

At ten o'clock the following night, after a dinner of mutton, greens, and snails provided by their hosts, the group struck out again, traveling roughly west toward Skalani. There they hoped to make contact with a man named Pavlos Zographistos, who had been recruited by Minoan Mike. It was his farm that would become their headquarters. Before they reached Skalani, however, their route took them through a number of slumbering villages, where the passage of such a large group of men would certainly be noticed. The danger, as Leigh Fermor knew, was that the villagers' curious talk about these goings-on in the night could alert the Germans. Remembering the trick he had used on the march the year before, Paddy soon had the men whistling "Lili Marlene" and barking German—or German-sounding—commands whenever they approached a village.

As the night wore on, Bourdzalis's men, who had been on the march for three nights in a row, began to show signs of exhaustion and their numbers gradually dwindled. By two o'clock the diminished party was drawing close to Skalani, and Leigh Fermor kept a lookout for a disused building near a dry riverbed where Mike had said the *andartes* could sleep. They soon found the place, which had once been a grape press, and Bourdzalis settled his men in for the night, while Leigh Fermor, Moss, Manoli, and George walked another half mile to the main house.

Pavlos, by the looks of him a successful young farmer in his early thirties, was waiting for them when they arrived. He gave the four tired men a warm welcome and escorted them into a remarkably tidy farmhouse, where he introduced them to his sister. The young woman did not appear to share her brother's enthusiasm for sheltering guerrillas in their house. "She is a strange person, attractively unattractive," was Moss's impression; "her looks depend upon which way the light catches her face." Even by lamplight she was clearly high-strung. It was hard not to worry about her reliability in the event of a mishap before the mission could be completed. But there was little to be done now. When they had finished the introductions, Pavlos showed the men through the ground-floor room, which served as a kitchen. A ladder led up to the second-story room where they would sleep.

Minoan Mike and his student friend Elias arrived the next morning from Heraklion. They brought with them chocolate and coffee to help restore the travelers after the long march from Kastamonitsa. More important, they had also smuggled two German military-police uniforms out of the city. Mike had acquired these from a member of his network whose brother was a tailor. Moss and Leigh Fermor would wear them when they flagged down the general's car. Elias had also done his homework on the car itself. Kreipe rode around in a fine new Opel, he said, and he now felt he could pick it out "among a thousand by day and recognize it by its headlights at night."

The German uniforms tipped Pavlos off to the fact that he was playing host to an operation with a bigger objective than just reconnaissance. When Mike and Leigh Fermor took him up to the loft and explained exactly what their mission entailed, the young man's enthusiasm drained away with the color in his face. Suddenly he looked as panicked as his sister. This was asking for trouble, he thought. Reprisals would surely come raining down on everyone living in the vicinity. Paddy calmed him down and assured him that it would be clear to the Germans that the British had staged the operation from outside Crete. Pavlos remained uncertain and said that he would like to speak with his father before he consented to let his house remain the headquarters for such an undertaking.

He was in the downstairs room preparing to leave while in the loft Leigh Fermor and Moss tried on the uniforms and Pavlos's sister sat stitching on insignia that would make them more convincing. Suddenly Pavlos appeared at the ladder hole with a look of terror on his face. Soldiers were approaching the house. "Germans, hide!" the sister cried.

But there was nowhere to hide. All three of them looked at Pavlos, whose head turned with a jerk as a clatter arose at the door downstairs. As the young farmer clambered down the ladder, Leigh Fermor and Moss waited above, holding their breath and fingering their Marlin guns. Pavlos asked who it was and stalled as long as he could before opening the door. By the time he let the men in, he had figured out that they were foraging for food. But he was still worried, since foraging was sometimes a cover that let a raiding party get a foot in the door without going to any trouble. Pavlos offered the men a drink but claimed there was no food in the house. For ten minutes Leigh Fermor and Moss listened as Pavlos and a German voice argued back and forth. At last they heard the door close. When their host reappeared, he looked edgier than before. As soon as he thought the coast was clear, he scurried off to meet with his father in a village half an hour's walk to the south.

On his way out Pavlos alerted Bourdzalis and his men to the presence of the German detachment, and the *andartes* posted lookouts to prevent another surprise visit. While their host was out of the house, Leigh Fermor and Moss sat down to compose a letter they intended to leave behind at the scene of the ambush in the hope of forestalling the reprisals Pavlos rightly feared. When they had finished, they added the date, April 23, signed their names—their actual names and ranks—and sealed the letter, pressing the signet rings they both wore into the wax for added effect. Moss's crest—with the griffin's head, sprigs of moss rose, and motto reading *Pro patria semper*—seemed especially apt. Most important, the crests marked the letter as incontrovertibly British.

In no time Pavlos returned, looking composed once again. The talk with his father had persuaded him to go on with his part in the operation. Although Pavlos's sister remained unconvinced, Leigh Fermor and Moss were free to go on with their preparations. Talking later that night to George and Manoli, with whom he had grown friendly, Pavlos was more candid. His father had been shocked to hear of his son's hesitation. The old man made no bones about it: if Pavlos did not do everything he could to help the Resistance, "he was not a man."

Soon after Pavlos's return, two men were spotted approaching the house, one of them wearing a police uniform. It turned

out, to everyone's relief—Pavlos's sister had nearly collapsed—
that they had been sent by Minoan Mike. The policeman was
named Stratis Saviolakis. Mike, recognizing that the police
uniform gave Stratis a freedom of movement the others did not
have, had sent him out to the intersection to go over the terrain in the daylight. Stratis had mapped out the hummocks
and bends that would best hide the *andartes* and the ambush
team. He had even picked out an almond tree that would conceal Elias's buzzer switch. The second man was a young villager
from Anogeia and would be a useful guide when the fleeing
kidnappers passed through the mountains there, provided they
made it that far.

Now it looked as if everything was in place. The following
evening, just after sundown, Leigh Fermor and his men would
be waiting in ambush on the Archanes road. Everyone in Pavlos's house went to bed that night with the knowledge that the
next twenty-four hours could change their lives, or perhaps
end them.

The next afternoon, April 24, Leigh Fermor and Moss put on
their German uniforms and went outside to have a photograph
taken. They both wore daggers on the belts that girded their
tunics. Paddy tucked his trousers into the high Cretan boots
he favored, while Moss made do with puttees. There was no
question that Leigh Fermor looked the part. He had shaved his
mustache and wore the corporal's uniform with a convincing
swagger. But the handsome Moss had more trouble vanishing
into the German disguise. To Paddy he looked like an Englishman rigged up in German costume for a fancy-dress party at a
London hotel.

Moss lit a cigarette and the two men waited for word from
Minoan Mike. At the grape press, Bourdzalis and the rest of the
party were preparing to take up their defensive positions as
soon as darkness permitted them to move through the coun-

Moss (left) and Leigh Fermor disguised as German soldiers. *Photograph © The Estate of William Stanley Moss— reproduced by permission*

tryside unseen. Around five o'clock Minoan Mike arrived at the farmhouse. He, Elias, and Stratis the policeman had been monitoring General Kreipe throughout the day. So far he had followed his usual schedule to the letter. If the pattern held, he would be leaving his headquarters as early as eight o'clock. By that time everyone would have to be in position. Elias was already at his lookout post and the buzzer wire lay strung and ready to operate. It was a good fifteen-minute march to the inter-section, and the sun would set around quarter to eight, so there would not be a minute to spare once they got moving.

Pavlos and his sister had worked through the afternoon to put together a hearty dinner for their departing guests, who now sat down to eat. They washed the meal down with glasses of mellow white wine, which Mike had procured for them on the black market. It was after seven o'clock, with dusk coming on, when Mike reappeared at the farmhouse with Stratis. This time it was evident from the Heraklion agent's face that something had gone wrong. Kreipe had altered his routine, he said. No one knew why. As Mike explained that the general had left headquarters early and by now had already reached the Villa Ariadne, the pallid face of Pavlos's sister reflected the worry on everyone's mind. The Germans must know! She told her brother that she thought the soldiers who had come under the pretense of looking for food had in fact been investigating rumors that must have been spawned by the movement of so many men to and from the farm. Pavlos had been thinking the same thing.

There was more, Mike said, turning to Stratis. The policeman informed them that a number of Bourdzalis's men had been careless about security—moving around in broad daylight—and he feared that they had been seen, if not by Germans then by villagers working in the fields. There would certainly be talk. And with the mission now delayed by Kreipe's unexpected change of habit, the *andartes* would quickly become even more of a liability. By the time Stratis finished talking, Pavlos's sister looked as if she expected to hear jackboots crunching up to the door at any minute.

Leigh Fermor and Moss knew they must act quickly, whatever course they took. It did not take them long to decide that they should proceed without Bourdzalis's band, risky as that might seem. The protection the *andartes* might have provided came at too great a cost. Manoli and George not only agreed but were also relieved. From the start neither of the two right-hand men had liked the look of Bourdzalis's men, who struck them as "an ill-assorted crew."

As the four of them talked over their options that night in the farmhouse, they all agreed that a small but utterly dependable force was preferable. (One of George's customary sayings made the point: "Too many cooks blow nobody any good!") With Bourdzalis out of the picture, they would still have, in addition to themselves, Stratis the policeman and the young guide who was familiar with the mountains above Anogeia. And for muscle they could rely on the seasoned old veteran Grigori Chnarakis and Wallace Beery, also an experienced guerrilla fighter.

There was also the nattily dressed Zahari to consider. Another gun or two would be comforting when the kidnappers fled toward the south coast, no doubt with German search parties nipping at their heels. But Zahari had not exactly impressed anyone on the march from Kastamonitsa. Moss recalled that the eager but inexperienced young man had twice mislaid his Marlin submachine gun, leaving the weapon behind when the party moved out after stopping for water breaks. The first instance had brought such a volley of derision down on him that he had been afraid to mention the blunder when it happened again. By the time he had finally spoken up, the whole band had been forced to stop for half an hour while he scurried back to retrieve the gun. In contrast, Ivan and Vassily had won everyone's admiration. Moss, whose grasp of their language brought him closest to the two Russians, not only liked them but had also come to rely on their discipline and sturdiness. But they had work to do on Crete, setting up an underground network for escaping Russian prisoners, and if they fled over the mountains with Moss and Leigh Fermor, there would be no one to guide them back to the cave that would be their headquarters. In the end, it seemed best to send them back to Kastamonitsa. And it was agreed that Zahari would make a capable guide for their return trip.

Around midnight, Leigh Fermor and Moss walked out to the grape press and broke the news to Bourdzalis. The *kapetan* himself took it hard, as they expected, but Moss noticed to his astonishment that a good number of Bourdzalis's men looked relieved. As the *andartes* rounded up their gear, Leigh Fermor handed each man a gold sovereign to thank them and smooth any ruffled feathers. Then he and Moss said good-bye to Zahari and the two affable Russians and watched as the whole band moved off down the trail that had brought them there two days earlier.

Soon after they returned to the farmhouse, Leigh Fermor sent off a letter to a man named Antoni Zoidakis, who Mike had learned was staying nearby. A policeman like Stratis by trade, Zoidakis was a hardened Resistance fighter from the Amari region. George Tyrakis told Moss that the man's "favourite recreation was throat slitting, and at this he appears to have had much practice." Later that night, Zoidakis arrived to join the team, along with two other reinforcements—Nikos Komis, a stocky, bearded young man from Thrapsano, and a dependable-looking fellow from Episkope named Mitsos Tzatzas—who had agreed to assist with the ambush.

Sometime before dawn, the freshly constituted ambush party slipped out of the farmhouse and made their way to a rock shelter at the head of a gully that lay not far away. Here they spent the next day and night, from time to time receiving updates from Minoan Mike that did nothing to reassure them. On the twenty-fifth Kreipe had remained at the Villa Ariadne all day. There was no way of knowing if this meant the Germans were onto their plan. One thing was certain, the local arm of the island's Communist resistance group had gotten wind of it, and they did not like what they heard. That afternoon the group's leaders sent a runner to the farmhouse with a letter, which the owner, Pavlos, carried to Leigh Fermor in the gully once the man had left. It threatened to expose the operation and hand Paddy's unit over to the Germans if they did not call it off and leave at once.

There was nothing to do but play for time. If the operation could be carried out the following evening, Leigh Fermor's men would disappear into the mountains with the general while the Communists still sat waiting for a decision. Leigh Fermor drafted an ambiguous reply and sent Pavlos back with it. That night, uneasy that they might be surrounded by Germans before daylight, the men rolled themselves in blankets and slept under a star-filled sky. When morning came, they were happy to find themselves still alone in the gully. Moss and Leigh Fermor spent the morning reading from the books they had carried from Cairo, trading passages from Robert Louis Stevenson, Shakespeare, and Saki as the sky darkened with storm clouds. Eventually the talk turned to Kreipe, and both men wondered what the general would be like. Moss captured the atmosphere in his diary: "Minotaurs, bull-men, nymphs of Ariadne, kings of Minos, and German generals—a splendid cocktail!" By the afternoon they were dodging snail hunters brought out by the rain that had begun to fall.

Though Leigh Fermor and Moss made the best of it, the waiting had begun to take its toll on some of the men. By the twenty-sixth the young guide from Anogeia had suffered all the uncertainty he could handle. "This morning, under the trees, he suddenly started frothing at the mouth and staring and gibbering," Moss recorded in his diary. As the day wore on, the young man's condition only declined. He refused help and would not even allow himself to be moved. In the end the others were forced to abandon him.

As it turned out, the anxious young man's wait would have ended soon enough, had he held on. By six o'clock the rain had stopped, and it was not much later when Elias, the student from Heraklion, came gasping up the gully with the news they had all been waiting for. Elias had been watching from a promontory above the Archanes road. That afternoon he had seen

Kreipe's car motor past, traveling from the Villa Ariadne to his headquarters, where he would be putting in his usual late-day round of work. It appeared that the general had clicked back into the groove of his usual routine. Elias immediately left to take up his watch again. The others ate a quick dinner, and then Moss and Leigh Fermor put on their German uniforms. When they were ready, the two lance corporals stood looking at each other for a moment. This was it.

IT WAS JUST before eight o'clock when the men reached the intersection, and they found themselves scrambling to take up their positions. Minoan Mike was on one end of the wire watching for a signal from Elias. The near end stretched to a point high on the bank flanking the intersection, where Mitsos, the young man from Episkope, waited with a flashlight. When Mitsos heard the buzzer, he would signal Leigh Fermor and Moss, who had taken cover at the far end of the eastern side of the road, with Manoli and the two veteran guerrillas, Wallace Beery and Grigori, nearby. George and the others crouched along the west side. Near the headquarters at Archanes, Elias was watching with his bicycle standing ready. When the general's car pulled out, he would pedal furiously to where Mike waited to activate the buzzer.

Waiting at the intersection, Leigh Fermor and Moss noticed more traffic on the narrow Archanes road than they had anticipated at this time of evening. A Volkswagen passed, then another. By nine o'clock they had watched a motorcycle and sidecar sputter by, as well as two large trucks. The general would ordinarily have been here by now. It was impossible not to wonder whether the Germans were wise to the ambush. Perhaps the vehicles going by were looking for Paddy's men.

Moss began to grow concerned. He fingered his sleeve back from his watch and checked the time. It was nine thirty on the

The abduction team.
Standing, left to right: Stratis Saviolakis, Manoli Paterakis, Antoni
Papaleonidas ("Wallace Beery"), George Tyrakis, Nikos Komis.
Seated: Grigori Chnarakis, Patrick Leigh Fermor, William Stanley Moss.
Photograph © The Estate of William Stanley Moss—reproduced by permission

dot. When he looked up again, a flash caught his eye. It was Mitsos's flashlight. It blinked three times. The signal meant that
Kreipe's car was approaching, and there was no escort to worry
about. In no time they heard the engine, and then the big Opel
could be seen ticking slowly around the corner. Leigh Fermor
and Moss stepped out onto the roadway. Leigh Fermor waved
a flashlight equipped with a red filter as Moss held up a German traffic paddle bearing a red circle that signaled "stop." At
the same time, Leigh Fermor called out, "Halt!"

As the Opel rumbled to a stop, he walked toward the passenger side. Through the window he saw an officer wearing the
Knight's Cross on his uniform. He saluted and asked politely to
see his papers, adding a polite *"bitte schön."* When Kreipe, with

a look of condescension, reached into his jacket, Leigh Fermor wrenched the door open. Moss did the same on his side, and their two flashlights illuminated the interior of the car, which suddenly shone like a flare on the dark road, calling the others into action.

Leigh Fermor wrestled Kreipe from the car, shouting "*Hände hoch!*"—"hands up." The muzzle of his pistol was now digging into the general's chest. On the other side of the car the driver went for his sidearm, and Moss swung hard with a blackjack, striking the man in the back of the head, leaving him slumped against the steering wheel. At this point George grabbed hold of the man and heaved him out onto the roadway, allowing Moss to slip behind the wheel. Manoli and Stratis shoved Kreipe, struggling, into the backseat. George slid in alongside them from the driver's side. As Mike came running up to see them off, Paddy climbed into the passenger seat and put on the general's hat. The engine was still humming, and the entire operation had taken little more than a minute.

Wallace Beery, Grigori, and Zoidakis were by now pulling the unconscious driver from the road. They were to take him overland, eventually meeting the others in the mountains. Elias and Mike would steal back into Heraklion the following day and "leak" the information that Kreipe had voluntarily defected to the British, as the Italian General Carta had done the year before.

With Manoli and Stratis poking their Marlin guns out the rear windows and George holding the general to the floor, Moss put the Opel in gear, edged out onto the Heraklion road, and tore off in the direction of the Villa Ariadne. They were hardly under way when a convoy of transport trucks filled with German soldiers motored by in the other direction. The sight of so many gray uniforms tempered the men's jubilant moods. Leigh Fermor turned and spoke to the general over his shoulder. "I am a British major," he explained, "and you are being taken as a prisoner of war to Egypt."

MINUTES LATER Moss spotted a red signal light waving and dipping just up the road. "Checkpoint ahead," he said. A sentry called out for the car to halt. Moss downshifted and the Opel slowed. But when the car drew close enough for the sentries to make out the steel staff pennants affixed to stays on the front fenders, they stepped back and presented arms. Leigh Fermor tossed the men a salute. Moss gunned the engine and the Opel surged past the checkpoint, quickly picking up speed again. "This is marvelous," he said.

A mile or two farther on, another checkpoint appeared. Now was the time to worry. If anything had looked amiss as they swept through the first outpost, the sentries would have notified the next one by telephone. But once again, Moss slowed and the German soldiers came to attention. Not much later, as the car approached the Villa Ariadne, Leigh Fermor and the others noticed the barriers that guarded the main gate being trundled open to receive the general's car, which Kreipe's sentries had no doubt been expecting for some time. Moss gave a few blasts from the horn and continued at speed in the direction of Heraklion.

At each checkpoint the Opel breezed by without incident, until they reached the eastern gate of the city itself. Here a roadblock barred the way. Moss again slowed and held his breath, letting it out as the bar swung up to let them pass. They were now within the Venetian walls of Heraklion itself, and the streets were clogged with German soldiers. The car was forced to inch along, while Moss tapped the horn to clear a path. Leigh Fermor remembered something Mike had warned him of—this was movie night for the German garrison. Paddy spoke softly to calm the others, reminding them that if they should be recognized, they were to abandon the general and use grenades and the Marlin guns to create a diversion that would allow them to escape into the labyrinth of side streets. But the German soldiers making their way to the cinema stepped aside as the Opel glided along, and soon they were out of the crowd and speeding toward the market square at the center of town, which they found completely empty. At the north end of the square Moss turned left onto a wide road leading to the Chania gate.

It was clear sailing until they reached the checkpoint at the gate itself. Here, where the road narrowed to barely a car's width, they encountered a sentry blocking the way. Moss slowed to give him time to see the staff pennants, but the soldier standing in the roadway with a red signal light did not move. As the car came to a stop, Leigh Fermor could see that there were a number of soldiers flanking the gate. A sentry walked toward the passenger side. Leigh Fermor heard clicks as Manoli and Stratis unlocked the safety catches on their Marlin guns. He rolled down the window and called out in as gruff a tone as possible, "Generals Wagen!"

To his relief, the sentry ahead immediately dropped his signal light and leaped to attention. The roadway was cleared and Moss gunned the engine. Leigh Fermor saluted and shouted, "Gute Nacht!" The Opel roared past the Venetian wall and motored into the night. Moss lit a cigarette, "which I thought was the best I had ever smoked in my life."

Seeing that German intervention was for the moment unlikely, Kreipe asked Leigh Fermor what he hoped to accomplish with "this hussar stunt," as he deemed it. He appeared especially distraught at having been duped by amateur soldiers. Leigh Fermor promised to explain their purpose tomorrow.

They drove on toward the west for more than an hour, climbing all the while into the foothills of Mount Ida. Around eleven o'clock Leigh Fermor and Stratis began to keep a lookout for a goat track that led south toward Anogeia. Fifteen minutes later Moss pulled the Opel off the road. It was not quite two hours since the buzzer had sounded on the Archanes road. In all they had passed twenty-two checkpoints. At five of these they had been forced to wait for a barrier to be raised.

Moss and Leigh Fermor got out to confer on the next step. Left alone in the backseat with George, Manoli, and Stratis, General Kreipe called out to the two British officers, begging them not to abandon him. Leigh Fermor told him to get out, then offered him a salute. Again he assured the general that he would be treated properly as a prisoner of war. He asked only Kreipe's cooperation in return. He explained that Captain Moss would lead the party escorting the general into the mountains, where he would himself join them soon.

GEORGE TYRAKIS slid into the passenger seat, and Moss watched as Leigh Fermor, who had very little experience with automobiles, settled himself behind the wheel. There was a knocking sound as he struggled with the hand brake, apparently mistaking it for the gearshift lever, and then came a blast that made them all flinch. Paddy had attempted to start the Opel by depressing the horn. Eventually he got the car started, and Moss heard the transmission grind into gear.

With a few lurching jolts Leigh Fermor steered the Opel back onto the road and drove on in the direction of Rethymnon, to the west. When they had covered almost a mile, he slowed the car. He and George watched the terrain sliding past the headlights on the northern shoulder. The darkness under a new moon made it hard to see beyond the roadside, but Leigh Fermor knew that somewhere along this stretch was a goat track that meandered three or four miles down through a ravine and eventually reached the sea at a peninsula called Peristeri, which was separated by a narrow channel from a small island called

Ketavati. A smaller island, which shared the name Peristeri, lay farther offshore.

The previous spring he had given himself a working vacation in the area. He had spent a few days swimming and getting to know the lay of the land. Before he left he had drawn a detailed map on a piece of silk cloth, showing that deep water stretched right up to the beaches that lay on either side of the promontory. His report to Cairo pointed out that the beach on the eastern side of the peninsula "is an ideal place for submarines or small craft." Not long after that, an SOE agent had in fact been put ashore here, and German intelligence had gotten wind of the fact that a submarine landing had taken place. Any German patrol that came across the general's car here might well assume the raiding party had made its escape by sea.

When the goat trail at last came into view in the sweep of the headlights, Leigh Fermor brought the Opel to a stop, leaving it on the road where it was sure to be discovered. They would have to work quickly. From his earlier reconnaissance he also knew that there was a German outpost at Almirou Potamou, which overlooked the goat trail and the beaches below from a vantage point high on the mountainside to the east. He added the stub he was smoking to a scattering of Player's cigarette butts that already littered the car's floorboards and tossed a British beret onto the seat. To ensure there was no mistaking the nationality of the kidnappers, he left behind a paperback Agatha Christie mystery as he and George climbed out. Then he pinned the letter he and Moss had composed a few days earlier to the driver's seat.

TO THE GERMAN AUTHORITIES IN CRETE

April 23, 1944

GENTLEMEN,

Your Divisional Commander, General KREIPE, was captured a short time ago by a BRITISH raiding force under

our command. By the time you read this both he and we
will be on our way to CAIRO.

We would like to point out most emphatically that
this operation has been carried out without the help of
CRETANS or CRETAN partisans, and the only guides
used were serving soldiers of HIS HELLENIC MAJESTY'S
FORCES in the Middle East, who came with us.

Your General is an honorable prisoner of war, and will
be treated with all the consideration owing to his rank.

Any reprisals against the local population will be
wholly unwarranted and unjust.

The letter closed with a farewell in German and a postscript:
"We are very sorry to have to leave this motor-car behind."

Leigh Fermor and George walked a hundred yards or so
down the goat path in the direction of the beaches, dropping
a few more clues to tempt German pursuers in that direction.
These included a British cigarette tin and a wrapper from a
Cadbury chocolate bar. The chocolate itself was too valuable
to waste. Then they scrambled back to the car, where George
paused to seize a souvenir of the operation. He pulled the general's pennants from the fenders and smiled. "Captured standards!" he said.

Leaving the car and clues behind, they struck out overland
toward Anogeia. It was hard going. With no trail to follow,
they bushwhacked their way through thickets and across rock-
strewn ravines. "The only people who saw us all night were two
boys with pine torches hunting for eels in a brook," Leigh Fermor recalled. "Every hour or so we lay down for a smoke. The
snow on Mount Ida glimmered in the sky and neither of us
could quite believe, in this peaceful and empty region, that the
night's doings had happened."

Just before dawn they began to hear the clanking of goat
bells and knew that they were nearing Anogeia. They entered

the village as the sun was coming up, and as they walked along the main street, Leigh Fermor noticed that the villagers were behaving strangely, falling silent as they passed or turning their backs. Anogeia was a Resistance stronghold, so the cold shoulder took him by surprise. Then it dawned on him that he was still wearing his German uniform. This, he told himself, must be what it feels like to be a German soldier serving in the occupation.

When he and George stopped off at the house of a friend, there was a tense moment before the man recognized them, but this quickly dissolved in laughter and a warm welcome. As word got out that "Major Livermore" had arrived, old friends dropped by to say hello and laugh at the "German soldier" in their midst. Leigh Fermor was able to recruit two runners to carry letters explaining the current situation to Sandy Rendel at his hideout in Males, some sixty miles to the southeast, and to Tom Dunbabin, who had a wireless station set up on the far side of Mount Ida.

That afternoon a German Fieseler Storch airplane flew low over the village dropping bundles of leaflets. "To All Cretans," the hastily printed notice read in Greek. "Last night the German General Kreipe was abducted by bandits. He is now being concealed in the Cretan mountains and his whereabouts cannot be unknown to the inhabitants. If the general is not returned within three days all rebel villages in the Heraklion district will be razed to the ground and the severest reprisals exacted on the civilian population."

CHAPTER 10

Bricklayer

AFTER A DIFFICULT MARCH of some four and a half hours, Moss and the others were closing in on the dry riverbed outside Anogeia where they were to rendezvous with Leigh Fermor. Without the nervous young guide who had suffered a breakdown before the ambush, they now had a hard time finding their way. For much of the distance there was no trail to follow, only more or less impassable stretches of overgrown and steeply undulating terrain. General Kreipe, in particular, found the walking difficult. His experience of the Cretan countryside up to this point had been gained largely from the passenger seat of his Opel as his driver chauffeured him to and from his headquarters. To make matters worse, his leg had been injured in the melee at the intersection and he was now walking with a pronounced limp. Moss and Manoli were forced to carry him over the most difficult portions of the route, ferrying his stout form over rivers and across ravines.

A little before dawn they stopped not far outside the village to sleep. When the sun came up, Stratis, finding the area more familiar in the daylight, led them to a stream where they settled in to wait for Leigh Fermor while the policeman walked into Anogeia to look for food and add messages from Moss to the letters bound for Dunbabin and Rendel. Moss was especially anxious that Rendel should take care of Ivan and Vassily, whom he

had come to think of as "my Russians." Around lunchtime a villager arrived carrying a sturdy basket filled with food and wine.
When they had eaten, Moss and the general both fell asleep.

Shortly after three o'clock, Manoli, his eyes wide with anxiety, shook Moss awake. A German search party was swarm-
ing up the hillside toward their position. The villager who
had brought their lunch led the fugitives to a cave farther up
the mountainside, where they hid for the next two hours as
enemy soldiers searched all around them. General Kreipe, who
seemed at first to think his deliverance was at hand, eventually
resigned himself to a bit more time in captivity and once again
fell asleep. Around five thirty Moss began to hear another drone
above the sound of the general's snoring. When he crept to the
cave entrance and looked out, he spotted a German plane and
watched as copies of the leaflets that had already fallen on Anogeia fluttered to the ground.

LEIGH FERMOR and George Tyrakis lay low in Anogeia until
the Germans, who had swept into the village while they were
eating lunch, finally left at six. When they were able to move
about again, they secured supplies for the long march over
Mount Ida and hired a mule and muleteer. Not long after dark,
Manoli arrived with word that Moss and the others were now
waiting just outside the village.

That night, after a supper of bread, cheese, and eggs, they
struck out toward the south, with General Kreipe now perched
atop the mule. The route followed a narrow, steep goat trail
that climbed the mountainside in a seemingly endless series
of switchbacks. Around two in the morning they paused at
the hut of a toothless old shepherd, who fed them cheese and
dried bread rusks called *paximadi* and kept a lookout while they
rested. Two hours later they pressed on.

By dawn they had reached their first way station, the cave

headquarters of the Anogeian *andarte* band. Here they were met by John Houseman, the SOE officer who had come ashore with Moss a few weeks earlier, and John Lewis, Tom Dunbabin's assistant. Dunbabin himself was holed up in the Amari district fighting a bout of malaria under the care of a local doctor. Word of the successful abduction had not yet reached him.

Houseman had the day before traveled over Ida along the route Leigh Fermor's band would now follow, and he had seen an unsettling amount of German aircraft activity. Fortunately, Houseman was on his way to set up a new wireless station near Heraklion and had a radio set and operator with him. The set was a godsend, since Leigh Fermor desperately needed to make contact with Cairo to arrange a rendezvous with the boat. But when the operator attempted to transmit the message, he found that the generator that charged the set was broken. The only way to get a message out was through the wireless sets at Sandy Rendel's headquarters farther east in the Lasithi district and at Fielding's old hideout in the west, where a major named Dick Barnes was now in charge. Once again Leigh Fermor sent runners scurrying in both directions.

That afternoon the veterans Wallace Beery and Grigori came bounding into the cave with Nikos and Zoidakis, after a long climb up from the plain below. They were full of news—German search parties were moving about all over the area. A motorized infantry detachment had nearly caught them in the foothills to the east. It was not until their excited voices finally paused for a breath that Leigh Fermor realized that there was no sign of General Kreipe's driver, who had been in their custody.

When he asked where the man was, none of them seemed to want to speak. The driver had grown unable to walk, they finally explained, perhaps because of the injuries he had received on the night of the ambush. When they encountered the German infantry patrol, they feared they might be overtaken, and the discovery of the driver would mean reprisals for all the villages on the slopes of Ida. Slowed down by the injured man, they had no chance of getting away, but they also could not leave him behind. It was Zoidakis, the accomplished throat slitter, who at last spelled out what had happened. They had done away with him as humanely as they knew how. "By surprise," he emphasized. "In one second."

Leigh Fermor consoled the men, telling them they had had no other choice, given the circumstances. But privately he regretted the blot on what was meant to be a bloodless operation. He and Moss made the decision to keep the information from the general.

That night, with the temperature in the mountainside cave dropping steeply after sundown, Leigh Fermor, Moss, and General Kreipe slept huddled together under the one blanket they had among them, pooling their feeble heat. Shortly after noon the next day, they set off on the steep climb over the top of Ida. At the point where the grade pitched up toward the summit, they found a band of *andartes* waiting to escort them. Leigh Fermor recognized their leader. It was none other than "Selfridge"— Giorgos Petrakogiorgos, the *andarte kapetan* who had been one of John Pendlebury's original henchmen.

By this time the gradient was growing too steep for the mule General Kreipe had been riding. There was no choice but to proceed with the general traveling on foot. It was slow going, and the Cretans, in particular, found the sluggish pace exasperating. When they reached the snow line, a freezing rain began to fall. It was near nightfall when they realized they must have crossed the summit without recognizing it. The south coast stretched out beneath the clouds somewhere below them. They took shelter in a dilapidated shepherd hut to wait for dark before moving on.

Tom Dunbabin arrived at the cave a few days after their

departure, worn ragged by the malaria and the long march and annoyed that he had missed Leigh Fermor and Moss. The news he had to give them was all bad. German troops were surrounding Mount Ida. His own headquarters had been ransacked and all the stores captured, he told Houseman, "and the Germans were threatening fearful reprisals."

AFTER DARK on April 29, Zoidakis set a match to the signal fire he had laid some distance down the southern slope of Mount Ida. The night before, Leigh Fermor had sent the fiery guerrilla ahead to scout the route down the mountain. The signal fire told the party lagging behind with the general that it was safe, for the moment, to proceed.

That evening the remainder of Leigh Fermor's band left the shelter of the hut and began their descent of the mountain. The night was pitch black and the air thin and cold. Despite the high altitude, the stumbling forced march that night marked a low point in their journey so far. "It took us two hours to reach the bottom of the snow-belt, and then we found ourselves groping between the wind-curved branches of stunted trees," Moss recorded. "Twigs would snap back into your face, and brambles would tear at your clothes and hands. The oaths and curses on all sides were a fitting mirror to the ugly mood of our companions, and there were times when Paddy and I felt seriously for the safety of the wretched German in our midst."

Once again they rested at a sheepfold in the middle of the night, and an hour or two before dawn a shepherd led them to a cave where they could spend the daylight hours. Although the mouth of the cave was on the small side, it opened into an extensive underground network of passages and stalactite-bristling chambers. Island legend had made it the birthplace of Zeus, but its more recent history was in line with Leigh Fermor's mission—the cave had housed a rebel army in the time of

Turkish rule. It served the same purpose adequately now, and most of the men fell quickly asleep.

When dawn broke on the morning of April 30, Leigh Fermor woke and went to the mouth of the cave to take in their new surroundings. He watched quietly as the morning sun began to glint off the snowcapped summit of Ida, which now lay behind them. General Kreipe was looking at it too, he noticed, and Leigh Fermor heard him saying something softly to himself. It took him a moment to realize that the general was speaking not German but Latin. "Vides ut alta stet nive candidum Soracte," he had said.

It was with a thrill of recognition that Paddy became aware of what he was hearing. *Do you see how Mount Soracte stands out white under deep snow?*—General Kreipe was reciting one of the odes of Horace! It was one he himself knew well.

His mother had given him a collection of Horace's odes when he struck out on his walk across Europe. And when that copy had been stolen, it had been thanks to one of his German hosts that the book had been replaced by a beautiful old duodecimo edition.

When the general's voice trailed off, Leigh Fermor picked up the verse and continued, also speaking in Latin. The poem called for dispelling the cold with logs on the fire, wine, and warmer thoughts. *Leave off asking what tomorrow will bring and count the days that fortune gives you as profit.*

General Kreipe turned toward him as he spoke, and their eyes met. When Leigh Fermor had finished, there was a lengthy pause, suffused with the silence of the mountain morning. At last the general spoke. "*Ach so*, Herr Major," he said. *Just right.*

"It was very strange," Paddy thought. "As though, for a long moment, the war had ceased to exist. We had both drunk at the same fountains long before."

It was a reminder that the war itself was the aberration,

interrupting something far more important and lasting. The moment of connection he and the general had just shared had sprung from a deep-running current of literature, art, and civility. It occurred to Leigh Fermor that what mattered was the history they shared, a story that transcended both time and national borders, which he had begun to detect signs of in the overlap of languages as he walked across Europe before the war.

Heinrich Kreipe was not a butcher like Müller, the predecessor who had ordered the massacres around Viannos the year before. Nor was he an aristocrat. By now Leigh Fermor had learned his story. The younger son of a Lutheran minister, Kreipe had come to the army not out of a sense of tradition but because the pay was good. Yet here was a German who, like Einer Heydte, the young baron Paddy had met in Vienna before the war, shared his interest in literature and history. Under

Moss and Leigh Fermor with their prisoner,
General Heinrich Kreipe (center).
Photograph © The Estate of William Stanley Moss—reproduced by permission

other circumstances they might well have become friends. Perhaps they still would.

WHEN WORD REACHED SOE headquarters in Cairo that the Germans had launched a leaflet campaign pinning blame for the kidnapping on the Cretans, Jack Smith-Hughes, the commander of the Crete Department, quickly set the gears in motion for an intelligence counterpunch. He had leaflets printed up that announced, in German and Greek: "Colonel General Heinrich Kreipe was captured by a party of British officers with no Cretan assistance whatsoever. Colonel General Heinrich Kreipe is safe and is no longer in Crete."

But leaflets on their own would not be enough. To Smith-Hughes it appeared that only one measure would have a chance of convincing the Germans that the British had already spirited Kreipe off the island. SOE would have to make contact with the BBC. If Smith-Hughes could somehow persuade the network to broadcast an announcement that independently confirmed the message of the leaflets, the ploy might pull the Germans off Leigh Fermor's trail. On the evening of April 30, the following coded telegram was transmitted from Cairo: "Essential, repeat, essential fullest possible broadcast all stations be made by midday tomorrow first, repeat, first May to effect that Kreipe captured by British, repeat, British party and already, repeat, already arrived in Cairo, repeat, Cairo. Matter most urgent as Cretan party report situation ugly, repeat, ugly."

When the request had finally wound its way through the twists and turns of bureaucratic machinery, it hit a snag. The powers that be at the BBC were squeamish about making a false report, even in the service of wartime strategy. In the end the broadcasters announced that news outlets in Cairo *were reporting* that the general had reached that city. Smith-Hughes hoped that would be enough to drain off some of the German zeal for the hunt.

LEIGH FERMOR was not the only one who was growing fond of the general. He noticed that Manoli had also taken an interest in Kreipe. Moss had seen this too. Although neither man spoke the other's language, Manoli and Kreipe could often be found near each other, cheerfully managing to converse in some makeshift fashion. They were a study in contrasts, the general a bullnecked, thickset man, Manoli hawk-faced and lanky. What's more, they came from completely different worlds. Yet they found something to talk about. "This attachment is a welcome event," Moss believed, "because hitherto the General has always grown anxious whenever Paddy and I have left him alone with the Cretans. I think he is slowly coming to realize that the island folk are not the barbarians he imagined them to be."

The general was content to be alone with Manoli while Leigh Fermor and Moss explored the deeper recesses of the cave later that morning. They might have hoped to find an escape route but instead found a labyrinth of interconnected tunnels worthy of the Minotaur. Before they turned back, Moss found himself recalling the story of Theseus, the Greek hero who had slain the monster. As he and Leigh Fermor fumbled their way back through the cave, Moss thought it would have been handy to have the thread Ariadne had given Theseus to keep him from losing his way in King Minos's labyrinth.

Just after lunch, a runner arrived with a message from Zoidakis, who was still some distance ahead scouting their route forward, and Manoli read the letter aloud. It warned that the Germans had all but surrounded Ida, with troops now massing in villages that ringed its foothills. Leigh Fermor's group was in danger of being trapped as the units closed ranks and swept up the lower slopes of the mountain, perhaps as soon as the following day. Zoidakis seemed to think their only chance was to slip through the German lines that same night. They would need to move as quickly and quietly as possible.

Just after dark, they struck camp once more and set out toward the southwest, in the direction of a village called Saktouria, near the point on the southern coast where Leigh Fermor's messages had asked Cairo to send a boat. With the grade beginning to slacken, the general was again able to travel by mule, and the party made better headway than on the previous leg of their journey.

A little after ten o'clock they reached the spot where they expected to rendezvous with Zoidakis. But there was no sign of him. Thinking they might have misjudged the location, Manoli and George went out in search of him but eventually returned empty-handed. By midnight he had still not shown. As Leigh Fermor began to grow concerned, it occurred to him to confirm the location in the message Zoidakis had sent. Concealing the glow of the flashlight under his coat, he opened the letter and began to read. It quickly dawned on him that there had been a terrible mistake. The letter said that under no circumstances should they try to make the journey that night.

With no way of knowing where Zoidakis was or when he might arrive to guide them to their next hideout, there was no choice but to wait where they were. When a steady rain began to fall sometime after daybreak, Manoli and George scouted out a gully overhung by trees that offered at least the appearance of shelter, though as the men sat hunkered among the rocks that afternoon, they were soon soaked to the skin. It was a sodden and miserable crew that Zoidakis stumbled across as he made his reconnaissance of the area the following morning.

From what he had seen, it appeared that the Germans had

some idea of where the general was being held, but for the moment moving was riskier than staying put. They would have to stick it out for another day in the miserable gully. Although Zoidakis proposed to bring them food that evening from his home village, which was nearby, the prospect of a delay at this point put a dreary cast on moods in the makeshift camp. It was not just the inclement weather or the living conditions that caused the trouble. The burst of adrenaline that had accompanied the ambush and the first days of the flight over the mountains had worn off. It was evident that the general, for one, was descending into a state of depression. And he was not alone in the gloom. "Paddy and I are feeling the anticlimax of this business acutely," Moss wrote in his diary. "It seems that we now have everything to lose nothing whatsoever to gain, and the only sort of excitement left to us is of the unpleasant kind. Ah me!"

AT 9:15 on the morning of May 1, Brian Coleman left Derna on the Libyan coast aboard *ML 842*, bound for Tobruk harbor, a hundred miles along the shore to the east, which he reached at 3:48 in the afternoon. The motor launch was hastily refueled, and Coleman placed his crew on standby while he awaited further instructions. He had received orders for an operation codenamed "Bricklayer," which called for one of two motor launches to extract Leigh Fermor's band from the south coast on the night of May 3 or May 4. The skipper of *ML 355*, R. A. Logan, made the first attempt, leaving Tobruk on the morning of May 3.

The signal for Coleman to proceed came through the next day. At 8:15 on the morning of May 4, he set sail for Crete. A few minutes after noon he spotted *ML 355* on its return voyage to Tobruk. Lieutenant Logan signaled that he had failed to make contact with the beach party the night before. Coleman thanked him for the information and sailed on. Almost half an hour later an aircraft was seen approaching the ship, coming in low, just a hundred feet off the water. It quickly closed to within two hundred yards. As the crew prepared to open fire, Coleman identified it as a Martin Baltimore, an American-built plane flown by the RAF. The pilot, apparently recognizing the motor launch to be friendly, veered off at the same time.

Without further incident the launch reached Paximadia Island, six or seven miles off Crete's south coast, at 11:20 that night. A little before midnight they were two thousand yards off the rendezvous beach below the village of Saktouria. The sea was calm, but a heavy fog and rain made it difficult to see anything of the shoreline. For the next two hours Coleman slowly patrolled the coast, keeping a constant lookout for a signal from the beach party. Having seen nothing, he turned back for Tobruk at 2:15. A little after noon the following day, he made visual contact with *ML 355*, now bound once again for Crete. By 3:20, Coleman's ship was anchored at Tobruk.

BETWEEN THE HIT-OR-MISS wireless transmissions and the need to use runners to get messages to and from Leigh Fermor, signals had gotten crossed. On May 2 Ralph Stockbridge, an old SOE hand who was known on the island as Mihali or Mike—since Ralph did not strike the Greeks as a proper name—received a message from Cairo saying that the boat would arrive the following night. The transmission also reported that the leaflets saying Kreipe was already in Cairo had been printed, but because of poor weather conditions the RAF had been unable to drop them. Boats would try the same beach on the four following nights. The Morse signal Leigh Fermor was to flash from the beach was "MK"—Monkey King. Headquarters attempted to transmit the same information to all the sets operating on Crete.

Stockbridge was not able to make contact again until

the next day. Meanwhile, he attempted to warn Cairo of the problem—"Cannot, repeat, not warn Paddy in time for boat on May 3/4. Have sent runner who will reach Paddy tonight. Believe Paddy will be able to reach beach only in time for boat night May 5/6 as will have to make all movements at night."

ON THE AFTERNOON of May 4, Moss came face to face with the eventuality he had dreaded since February, when he had watched Manoli and George suffer unalloyed boredom while they waited to be dropped into Crete. "I have completely run out of reading matter," he lamented, "so spend my day like any Cretan, contemplating." There was much to contemplate, and little of it was encouraging.

Although the rain had stopped and they were able to move to a more suitable camp, the weather appeared to be the only thing changing for the better. They had learned the day before that a force of some two hundred German soldiers had arrived at Saktouria, the village that lay just above the beach where they had hoped to meet the motor launch. Now they would have to find an alternate way out. Leigh Fermor had left with George just after dark that night to make his way quickly west into the Amari Valley and locate one of the wireless sets, so that he could better coordinate a new evacuation plan with Cairo. Meanwhile, Moss and the others would go to Gerakari, in the heart of the Amari's Lotus Land, to await their next move.

Since his arrival on Crete, Moss had been fixated on a series of coincidences that seemed to draw a pattern across his diary of the mission. They had left Cairo on January 4. Paddy had parachuted in on February 4. He, Manoli, and George had come ashore on April 4. Moss had hoped, almost expected, to leave for home on the fourth of May. Now it was clear that this would not happen.

AS THEY TRUDGED along toward the northwest the next day, Leigh Fermor and George began to hear the rumble of bomb blasts in the distance. It was hard to tell where the explosions were occurring, but some seemed to be coming from an area disturbingly close to the region they had just come through. Pressing on through the afternoon, they finally reached the village of Pantanassa, five or six miles north of Gerakari. Here they found a veritable *poste restante* office waiting for them. There were days-old letters from Dick Barnes and Sandy Rendel. Rendel's, which alerted them to the planned arrival of the boat at the beach now crawling with Germans, was not much help at this point. But the letter from Barnes gave Leigh Fermor the vital piece of information Ralph Stockbridge had been trying to relay to him: When they finally did make contact with a boat, the signal they were to use was the Morse letters "MK." The motor launch skipper would be looking for the signal beginning at 9:00 p.m.

Leigh Fermor and George now turned west and made their way within a few hours to Geni, where Ralph Stockbridge's letter finally caught up with them. In addition to the signal code, which they already knew, the letter told them that another SOE officer named Dennis Ciclitira had a wireless station set up in Asi Gonia, twenty-odd miles farther west. Ciclitira, who came from a British-Greek family and spoke the language fluently, had come ashore in December. He was scheduled to leave on a boat that was expected to land in a matter of days. Stockbridge thought Leigh Fermor and company might hitch a ride on the same boat. He said he would also relay their location to an SOE officer named Dick Barnes who was working farther to the west. Glad as he was to have this information, Leigh Fermor was almost equally pleased by a further development. Stockbridge had also sent him a map and a fresh supply of cigarettes.

DICK BARNES had in fact been trying since May 2 to make contact with Leigh Fermor. When Ralph Stockbridge's message reached him, he sent George Psychoundakis, Xan Fielding's longtime runner, to track Paddy down in Geni. Along the way, Psychoundakis recruited scouts to look for a new landing beach in the area directly to Paddy's south. By the time he arrived in Geni, he had also engaged Jonny Katsias to serve as a guide. Katsias, who had come from Cairo on the launch with Moss, reportedly knew every inch of the mountains to the west. He was also a quick hand with a gun and knife—in fact, he was accused of killing a number of men in various brawls and vendettas before the war—which could be useful if it came to a fight with the Germans. Leigh Fermor was reassured to have the services of Katsias, and he was still more pleased to see Psychoundakis, but the elfin runner was gone again almost as soon as he had arrived.

He returned the next day, May 7, accompanied by Barnes himself. The scouts he had recruited arrived not much later, bringing news that German troops had landed by sea just to the south. The beaches in that vicinity were now off the table as far as evacuation was concerned. But Barnes had another idea. The little village of Rodakino, twenty miles over the mountains to the southwest, was flanked by small beaches, and the Germans had been driven out by the locals some days earlier when they attempted to burn the village. It was worth a look. Leigh Fermor asked Jonny Katsias to scout out the beaches there.

Just when it looked like a plan was taking shape, another runner arrived with news from Barnes's wireless operator. It seemed that the commandos who had carried out the raids on the Kastelli airfield the previous summer were planning to crash General Kreipe's evacuation party. A raiding party of SAS troops was coming ashore on the ninth to find Leigh Fermor and his men and get them out. To Paddy and Barnes both, this sounded like a disastrous plan, given the size of the German force assembling on the beaches to the south. The SAS boys would be walking into a hornets' nest. This was one landing that had to be called off, if it was not already too late.

Meanwhile, runners were being kept on the move. While Leigh Fermor and George were still at Geni, another exhausted man arrived with a letter from Moss, explaining how matters in his vicinity had taken a turn for the worse. Moss told Paddy about the large contingent of Germans that had come marching up the valley above Saktouria, where he and the others had been hiding with the general. They had been forced to depart at once. Leigh Fermor also learned that the explosions he and George had heard on the trail the day before had come from a ring of villages that had been destroyed by the Germans. Fortunately, no one had been killed in the raids, but Moss had felt the German noose closing around him.

He and his party had slipped through the German cordon and reached Gerakari ahead of schedule. They had now moved on and were waiting about a quarter of a mile outside the village of Patsos, which put them closer at hand than Paddy could have hoped, less than ten miles to his east. For all the anxiety the German advance had caused, he quickly saw that the precipitate forced march had in fact come as a stroke of luck.

After nightfall on May 8, Leigh Fermor and George left Geni, walking east. It was not much later than midnight when they located Moss's hideout. It was in an ideal spot, a stone hut adjacent to a gurgling waterfall. Leigh Fermor found Moss sleeping and shook him awake. When his eyes came open, they had an alarmed look until Leigh Fermor cast the flashlight he was holding onto his own face and Moss recognized his tormentor. There was much to talk about, Paddy told him.

Moss stirred himself and produced a bottle of raki. For the next two hours they discussed the current situation and Moss filled Leigh Fermor in on developments in the camp. He and the general had suffered a falling-out when they exchanged heated words about the German destruction of the villages around Saktouria. A few prickly days had followed. But they were on speaking terms again now.

As Paddy told Moss about the SAS plan, he began to wonder if they should go down to the beach the following night with a band of *andartes*, so as to be on hand either to warn the raiding party off or to assist in the melee that would no doubt erupt if the SAS raiders came ashore. By the time they went to bed, he and Moss had concluded that this was indeed what they had to do. But then fate intervened. They had eaten breakfast the next morning and were preparing to break camp, when a runner arrived from Dick Barnes's cave. The message Barnes had sent to Cairo had gone through in time. The commando mission had been postponed.

Now, instead of backtracking to the SAS beach, they could push on west. Leigh Fermor wanted to make it as far as Foteinos, which would mean three or four hours through the mountains. This would allow them to reach the village of Vilandredo the following night—putting them just a hard day's march to the north of the beach below Rodakino. The men rested through the day, and when the moon was up that night, they helped the general onto a fresh mule and moved out.

They had not been on the march long when they passed through the ruins of one of the villages recently destroyed by the Germans. It was impossible not to be moved by this evidence of the war's impact on civilians. "It was a strange and ghostly feeling, walking through those skeletons of houses," Moss felt, "and there was something sickly about the smell which hung damply among the ruins." Though he had no way of knowing at the time, this was a scene that would become all too familiar by the time the war was over.

Shortly after midnight, they were met by a gang of *andartes* who turned out to be sentries from the Foteinos band, whose security perimeter seemed to extend a good two hours beyond their village. Under the command of a *kapetan* who must have been in his eighties, they formed an escort to ferry the general on to Foteinos, which the party reached around three in the morning, after a short, tense delay when the *andartes* took up positions to ambush an oncoming German patrol that turned out to be a late-arriving contingent of their own band.

Leigh Fermor, Moss, and the others spent the next day resting in an olive grove outside the village. At three in the afternoon, they were visited by a party of four Russians who had escaped from a prison camp in Rethymnon the previous week. Word of General Kreipe's abduction had already made it that far, and they were excited to see the man himself. When Moss had talked with the Russians, it was decided that one, an older man who was sick, would be evacuated to Cairo, while the other three, outfitted with Marlin guns and what clothing could be spared, would travel to Kastamonitsa with Grigori to join Ivan and Vassily. It seemed that Moss's private Russian army was growing.

The escaped prisoners left in the afternoon, and when night came, Leigh Fermor's group, now with the ailing Russian riding slumped atop a second mule, pressed on. As the party inched along the rugged mountain trail, the Russian swayed on his mule like a tree in a gale, looking as if any minute he would topple off. But it was in fact General Kreipe who took a fall. As his mule picked its way up a particularly steep pass, the general's saddle strap gave way, sending him crashing onto the rocks below. He landed on his shoulder and immediately cried out in pain. When Leigh Fermor and Moss rushed to help him, it appeared it was not just his collarbone but also his patience that had snapped. He writhed on the ground, shouting a blistering stream of curses at them. When he had calmed down, they helped him back onto the mule and assigned Stratis the policeman the job of keeping him upright for the rest of the journey. As the night wore on, General Kreipe seemed to repent of his uncivil behavior and from time to time offered apologies as he lurched along on the mule.

Sometime after midnight, the elderly leader of the Foteinos *andartes*, who had so far accompanied them, called a halt near an outlying hamlet. He explained that they had reached the point where his men would turn back to their village, and he pointed Leigh Fermor toward a small house where he would find another guide waiting.

When Leigh Fermor and Moss entered the modest building, it was Jonny Katsias who rose to greet them. At his side stood a pair of hardened men who turned out to be sheep rustlers whom Katsias had recruited to help guide the party through the mountains ahead. They were a rough-looking threesome, but between Katsias's innate ferocity and the sheep thieves' professional familiarity with little-used goat paths and out-of-the-way hideouts, the general's evacuation could not have been in better hands. "And so Jonny, a price upon his head, victor of numerous feuds and vendettas, killer of more than twenty men, who talks of his latest victim as though referring to a Last Duchess, is now responsible for our safe custody," Moss noted, "and we feel nothing if not safe in his hands."

Nearly four hours later Katsias brought the group to a rendezvous point near Vilandredo, where they were met by a pair of men who guided them on a difficult hourlong climb to the cave where Dennis Ciclitira had established his headquarters. When they reached the cave, they found a man with a dark, bushy beard lying in a corner, snoring outrageously. It was

Ciclitira. His wireless set was still operating at "Stubborn Corner," he told them—that is, only an hour away at Asi Gonia. Communications with Cairo would at last be more fluid.

Ciclitira told Leigh Fermor and Moss that they had missed a scheduled landing at the beach below Rodakino several nights earlier, but he assured them that their late arrival was fortunate. He and his band had gone down to the beach with Dick Barnes on the appointed night and flashed the appropriate signal for some three hours. At last, around midnight, they heard an engine rumbling in the darkness offshore. As they prepared for the landing they thought was at hand, things went terribly wrong. The vessel they had heard closed on the beach and opened fire on them with heavy machine guns. It was a German caïque. They beat a quick retreat into the mountains and managed to get away with no casualties. But it had been a narrow escape. It was when he returned to his headquarters the following day that Ciclitira had received the message telling him Leigh Fermor's group had been driven west by their pursuers and were headed into his territory.

After they had eaten and talked for a while, Ciclitira left for his wireless station, bearing messages for Cairo from Leigh Fermor. That night the men helped General Kreipe climb onto a rock ledge above the cave, where they all spent the evening eating and drinking wine provided by one of the villagers. After their long journey it was just the kind of banquet they had needed, and soon they were all singing. Leigh Fermor and Moss once again found themselves talking about literature—on this occasion the topic was the ne'er-do-well French poet François Villon—as they had in the days before the ambush. Even the general seemed restored and pleased that his ordeal, at least this part of it, would soon be over.

"Last night was beautiful, the sky filled with stars and the Milky Way looking like a scarf of sequins," Moss wrote in his diary the next day. "Good wine, Villon, that host of stars . . . and the war seemed a very long way off." But then, at five in the afternoon, the war caught up with them. One of the villagers who had been keeping the men provisioned since their arrival in the area burst into the cave looking distraught. Seven German transport trucks filled with troops—probably two hundred men altogether—had rolled into the nearby village of Argyroupoli, where the road stopped. By foot they were only an hour to the north.

Leigh Fermor and Moss posted lookouts and hurried everyone else into the cave, where they remained until dusk. Then, around seven o'clock, a runner brought them word that the Germans had moved west out of Argyroupoli, not south. They were making for Asi Gonia, where Ciclitira's wireless set was located. This was bad news for Ciclitira, who would have to dodge them, but it brought sighs of relief from the men in the cave.

That night Jonny Katsias's rustlers led the party to a safer location an hour farther south. When they reached the foot of the precipice where the new hideout was located, General Kreipe dismounted and started the climb on foot, perhaps fearing another mishap like the one that had injured his shoulder. A few minutes later, a terrifying noise split the night. Moss heard "a sudden hysterical shriek, followed by the sound of snapping branches and twigs and the thud of something falling." The general had lost his footing and pitched down the cliff face. Again Leigh Fermor and Moss scrambled down to help and found to their relief that he had landed on what might have been the only soft patch of ground for miles around. Miraculously, it was only his pride that was injured.

Around three in the morning they finally reached the opening in the cliff face where they intended to camp. It was a good hiding place but a wretched spot to sleep in. A spring that trickled through the cave made it uniformly cold and wet. The only thing to do was wait out the night and hope for good news after daybreak. "Think of those beasts back at Tara, dying of drink and happiness," Paddy whispered to Moss as they lay shivering on the damp rock.

First thing the next morning, they learned that their quick evacuation of their previous hideout, and the miserable night that followed, had been worth it. The Germans had come to the village after all and had made a thorough search of the vicinity. Leigh Fermor's men were much better off here. The messenger who brought the news had also carried food and raki up from the village. The latter made it possible, once the bottles had been emptied, to sleep in spite of the cold, wet ground that passed for beds.

When he awoke later in the day, Leigh Fermor found that some stiffness in his right shoulder, which had bothered him as he strained to help the general up the last pitch the night before, had grown worse. Sleeping on the damp rock had certainly not helped. A letter from Ciclitira soon put the discomfort out of his mind, however. In all likelihood a boat would arrive the following night, May 14. Ciclitira would be in touch again as soon as confirmation came from Cairo.

AN AMENDMENT to Brian Coleman's orders was issued on May 13, and the revised Bricklayer plan, designating the new landing beach near Rodakino, caught up with the skipper in Bardiyah, the harbor east of Tobruk where he had picked up Moss, Manoli, and George more than a month earlier. At 6:15 on the morning of the fourteenth, he sailed from Bardiyah on a course for Gavdos Island, off Crete's southwest coast. There was a light breeze stirring up only a slight swell, and visibility was good.

By ten o'clock that evening, Coleman was passing Gavdos, and he noted a light flashing from a peninsula on the north side of the island, facing Crete. This got his attention. A few weeks earlier he had spotted flashing lights, flares, and other shore activity while attempting to make a landing nearby and had later seen tracer shells being fired onto shore, from either an enemy vessel or a battery on Gavdos. Tonight, though, no further disturbance was evident. "Although a good lookout was kept, no answering flashes were seen on Crete," he noted in his log.

THE AFTERNOON of the thirteenth passed with no word from Dennis Ciclitira. Sometime around nine o'clock, Leigh Fermor and the others resigned themselves to another night in their dripping rock shelter and put themselves to bed. An hour or so later another man came stumbling into the pitch-black cave and woke them all up. For a moment there was confusion, until Paddy recognized the stranger's voice. It was Dick Barnes.

Barnes told them that the boat was indeed coming to meet them. He showed them on a map where to find the beach and gave them the Morse signal, which had now been changed from "MK" to "SB." He also had some warnings to offer about the area around the beach. The Germans had been patrolling there more regularly since a small detachment had been ambushed in Rodakino on April 29. Armed caïques had also become a problem along the shore, as he knew from experience, having been on the beach with Ciclitira the night he was fired upon. The most pressing enemy at the moment, Barnes added, was the clock. There was barely time to reach a hideout above the beach before daylight. It was decided that Moss should go by the most direct route with most of the men accompanying him. Jonny Katsias's rustlers would lead the way. Meanwhile, Leigh Fermor and Manoli would take the general by a more roundabout but safer path.

Moss and the others left immediately, and it was not until they had worn themselves ragged on the steeply undulat-

ing trail that they realized they had not paused to fill their
water bottles. The only thing they had to drink was raki,
which George had brought along. Nevertheless they were able
to move at an unbelievably rapid clip, thanks in large part to
Katsias's rustlers. "They knew every track and short-cut, and
never wasted a single moment in selecting the best and quick-
est route," Moss noted. "I found no difficulty in appreciating the
reasons for their having gone uncaptured while practicing their
nefarious profession." By dawn Moss and his men were perched
on a rock outcrop overlooking the beach.

TAKING THE LONG WAY around, Leigh Fermor, Manoli, and
the general marched through the night and into the next day.
The trail they followed ran over such steep terrain that General Kreipe was again traveling on foot. At several points he
required help from Manoli, who was by now watching over the
general like an old friend. Some hours into the march, Leigh
Fermor again became aware of the trouble with his right arm;
"there was no pain, but I could neither straighten it nor raise it
above my shoulder."

Shortly after ten o'clock, they began the final climb up to
the outcrop where they would rendezvous with Moss. As they
came out onto the promontory, the south coast opened up
below them. In the distance they could see a German outpost.
It was evident through binoculars that the garrison had no idea
they were being watched at such close range. Or else they did
not mind being seen playing leapfrog while their general was
being carried away by the enemy.

At eleven o'clock the two groups were back together again. A
few hours later they pooled the food they had carried through
the night and made a meager lunch. Then, between three and
four o'clock in the afternoon, they began to move in small, scattered groups down to the beach.

Leigh Fermor and Moss went first, accompanied by Jonny Katsias. Twenty minutes later, when no disturbance had been heard, Manoli and George made their way down with General Kreipe. The others followed at similar intervals.

When the group reassembled, they found themselves in a small, well-cultivated garden. This was a surprise, since the Germans had designated this area by the coast a forbidden zone. There was a fountain burbling out cool water, which they drank happily. Before long, a stooped old man came along and, barely taking note of the ragged band of visitors, went to work tending the plot. It seemed to Moss that the old gardener's quiet resolve reflected a way of life that would continue, in places like Crete, while wars and strife and conquering armies came and went, like the tides lapping at the adjacent beach. "He was still there, working on a row of beans, when at dusk we went on our way."

AS *ML 842* slipped past Gavdos Island, Coleman laid a course for the rendezvous beach, which lay thirty or so nautical miles to the north-northeast. At 11:45 he spotted a Morse signal coming from shore, at first flashing erratically, then eventually resolving itself into the "SB" he expected. By now a rising mist was making visibility difficult, but with the beach pinpointed, all that was left to do was to get close enough to send in the dinghies.

But as he began to close the distance to the beach, Coleman found that the ship's echo-ranging set, which had been giving him difficulties on previous attempts to reach Crete, would not function. When the launch was a thousand yards off the beach, he sent a man onto the bow to take soundings the old-fashioned way, and *ML 842* eased her way slowly forward. Ten minutes after midnight, they were a hundred yards offshore in two fathoms of water. Coleman gave the go-ahead, and rubber dinghies were lowered into the water. A detachment of commandos sent to provide security for the evacuation quickly slipped over the side of the launch and scrambled aboard the dinghies.

ON SHORE Leigh Fermor and Moss had run into difficulty. At nine o'clock, when they were to begin flashing the Morse signal out to sea, they realized that neither of them actually knew the entire Morse alphabet. After a few minutes of debate, they figured out that the SOS signal, which every schoolboy knew, would give them half the code they needed. That was the *S*. For the *B* they would improvise. They hoped that Brian Coleman, knowing who he was dealing with, would give them the benefit of the doubt.

When they finally heard engines rumbling offshore, they thought their plan had worked. But then the vessel seemed to be moving away again. They were scrambling to make themselves seen when Dennis Ciclitira came panting out onto the beach. Abandoning his besieged headquarters at Asi Gonia, he had marched through the day to reach the rendezvous. When Leigh Fermor and Moss confessed their problem, he took over the flashlight, snapped out the appropriate Morse letters, and quickly had Coleman's attention.

Leigh Fermor heard the sound of engines closing in again, "faint at first but gradually louder." And finally the ship came into view. "There was a slight coil of mist over the sea so it was not until she was quite close that we saw her," Paddy noted. "The chains rattled as the anchor went down and two boats were lowered."

The men stood watching on the beach as figures clambered into the boats. As they drew nearer, it was possible to make out the shapes of commandos clutching machine guns as the boats rocked their way ashore. When the boats at last crunched up onto the beach, the commandos leaped out and ran toward Leigh Fermor's group. He recognized their commander and quickly realized that they had expected to fend off Germans while the evacuation was under way.

Leigh Fermor assured them, to their disappointment, that there was no one to shoot at just now. But they could be helpful in another way. While his own party sat removing their boots, which were always left behind for the men who remained on the island, he persuaded the commando leader to donate the stores his detachment had brought with them. Soon they were emptying their rucksacks onto the beach.

Then began a round of good-byes, which lasted until a sailor told Leigh Fermor it was time to go. Minoan Mike and his student friend Elias had already departed, along with the Cretan Wallace Beery and Stratis the policeman. While Jonny Katsias, his two rustlers, and Antoni Zoidakis, who were staying behind, stood waving, Leigh Fermor and the others climbed into the remaining dinghy and steadied themselves as they were rowed away from the beach.

Looking back toward the shore, Leigh Fermor marveled at how quickly his comrades and the beach were lost against the looming silhouette of the island itself. Soon the dinghy came alongside the motor launch, and he watched as sailors leaned over the side to help the general up the swinging rope ladder that hung from the side of the vessel. Leigh Fermor, Moss, Manoli, and George followed, and soon they were all safely aboard. Brian Coleman came down from the bridge to greet them. "Then we were taken down to the wardroom, where we found English cigarettes, some rum, bunks with white sheets, and—a Coleman specialty—lobster sandwiches. It was wonderful," Moss thought.

When the boats had been hauled up, Coleman returned to the helm and wheeled *ML 842* around. Easing the engines into gear, he motored slowly away from the beach in order to avoid throwing sparks from the exhaust that would give away their

General Kreipe arrives in Cairo.
*Photograph © The Estate of William Stanley Moss—
reproduced by permission*

position. An hour later, wanting to be out of range of German aircraft by sunrise, he brought the speed up to sixteen knots. He hoped the weather, which had grown continually worse throughout the night, would keep the Stukas grounded in any case.

The morning of May 15 dawned over rough seas, and *ML 842* wallowed her way south throughout the day. At nine thirty that evening, Coleman steered into the harbor at Mersa Matruh, west of Alexandria. The next day Leigh Fermor and Moss flew with General Kreipe, his arm now in a clean white sling, courtesy of an RAF doctor, to the airfield outside Cairo. There they told the general good-bye and gave him a final salute as he disappeared into a waiting staff car.

"He smiled at us with a rueful though kindly expression,

and then he was gone," Moss noted. "Close at hand there was another car waiting for Paddy and me, so quickly we jumped into it. 'Tara!' we called to the driver, and he treated us to an enormous grin of understanding."

EPILOGUE

Ritterlich!

WHEN HE WAS questioned in Cairo on May 23, 1944, Heinrich Kreipe told British interrogators that the German garrison of Crete would fight "to the last cartridge" to hold the island. But he also confided that he believed General Bräuer, the commander of Fortress Crete, to be "a blockhead." Bräuer's critical mistake, as Kreipe saw it, lay in "regarding a quite substantial Partisan movement as nothing more than a few gangs of cattle thieves."

In the actual course of events, German troops withdrew from Heraklion in October, taking refuge in the area around Chania. Tom Dunbabin and a force of Cretan *andartes* occupied the Villa Ariadne, where John Pendlebury had once lived, the very house that General Kreipe had been trying to reach on the night of his abduction. It was here at the villa that the Germans, after a protracted stalemate, finally signed a surrender agreement in May 1945.

Following his interrogation, General Kreipe was sent to England. He was interned at a prison in Sheffield before being transferred to a camp in Canada. He remained in British custody until 1947. His countrymen who had overseen the occupation of Crete, Generals Bruno Bräuer and Friedrich-Wilhelm Müller, were both convicted by the Special War Crimes Tribunal in Athens in 1945. Both were executed by firing squad on

299

May 20, 1947, the sixth anniversary of the invasion of Crete. General Kreipe himself was never charged with any crime. To the end of his life he had mixed feelings about his wartime experience. Moss, who had taken on more of the day-to-day work of guarding the general, bore the brunt of his resentment. "I liked Paddy," Kreipe told an interviewer a few years before his death in 1976. "But Moss, always with his pistol," he said, pantomiming his prodding captor, "it was childish."

AMONG THE LIST of atrocities levied against Müller, who returned to Crete to replace Bräuer as commandant after Kreipe's abduction, was a string of brutal raids carried out in August 1944. German troops attacked more than a dozen villages, burning many to the ground. Hundreds of civilians were killed and the entire village of Anogeia was razed. The foremost historian of the war in Crete, Antony Beevor, concluded that the reprisals carried out that summer were unrelated to the Kreipe affair. He based this view on careful study of documents and evidence drawn from every level of British, German, and Greek command, and his judgment is persuasive.

Appearances on Crete at the time initially led Tom Dunbabin to consider a different conclusion. His field reports note that he saw no obvious cause to which the reprisals could be attributed. "No incident had taken place in this area," he wrote, "nor were there guerillas in the neighborhood." The reason offered by German command in a statement published in a local newspaper "was that Kreipe had passed through" the villages that were attacked "and was fed and concealed by the population." There was even a rumor afoot that said Kreipe had escaped from his captors and was himself taking revenge for the abduction.

In the end, however, Dunbabin concluded that while it was easy to point to the Kreipe abduction as a motive for the attacks, the truth was more complicated. He believed the reprisals were the result of mounting German fear of the Resistance movement in general and a panicked effort on the part of enemy commanders to combat defeatism in their own ranks. In the report he sent to Cairo at the end of August, he quoted a German soldier who put the matter in plain terms: "The war will end in two months' time and we shall all be ruined, but we mean to ruin you first."

As Leigh Fermor had hoped, the abduction of General Kreipe "hit the enemy hard on a different level," striking a blow at German morale. Stories that came trickling in through Dunbabin's intelligence network suggested that the impunity of the abduction raid had startled German commanders and led some to fear, only weeks before the Normandy invasion, that Crete was the target of the Allied offensive everyone had come to expect.

Even more important, Moss and Leigh Fermor's "hussar stunt" galvanized the already strong will of the Cretans. Buoyed by the success of the daring raid, the morale of the populace remained high even in the wake of subsequent German atrocities. After three years of occupation, the Cretans were again demanding arms so they could finish off the enemy they now perceived as weak. The Germans, for their part, showed no more inclination to fight "to the last cartridge."

The galvanizing effect of the mission could still be felt in the tense months that followed the end of the war. As the rest of Greece plunged into civil unrest—pitting factions of Communist partisans against each other and against various stripes of nationalists—Crete remained relatively calm. In large part this was due to the people's admiration for swashbuckling figures like John Pendlebury and Leigh Fermor, whose exploits lent credibility to the diplomatic campaign Tom Dunbabin waged throughout the war to foster cooperation among rival factions on Crete. Leigh Fermor and Dunbabin were both made honorary citizens of Heraklion in 1948, at a time when mainland Greece remained torn by civil war.

The Kreipe mission quickly assumed its place as an iconic episode in the centuries-long history of Crete's struggle against outside rule. Today a memorial stands at the intersection of the Archanes and Heraklion roads where the abduction took place.

WILLIAM STANLEY MOSS returned to Crete in the summer of 1944 with the intention of creating a sequel to the earlier mission by capturing General Kreipe's replacement. When circumstances made it impossible to carry out this plan, he considered mounting an outright attack on the headquarters at Archanes but decided instead to ambush German convoy traffic on the main road that ran along the north coast between Heraklion and Chania.

At three o'clock in the morning on August 8, he and George Tyrakis led a party of seven Greeks and six escaped Russian prisoners to a sharp bend in the road north of the village of Anogeia, where *andartes* had attacked an enemy column the previous day, leading him to expect the arrival of German reinforcements. Over the course of the next day, Moss and his men knocked out a half dozen German vehicles as they slowed for the turn, pushing each off a nearby precipice after it was destroyed in order not to alert the next that happened along. When an armored car arrived and opened fire on the party, Moss crept along a ditch, climbed onto the vehicle, and dropped a grenade down its turret. In total, the action killed thirty-five German soldiers and ten Italians and captured a dozen prisoners.

Once again Brian Coleman's motor launch picked him up from a craggy beach on the south coast. It was the last time he would ever see Crete. That fall he was sent to Macedonia, again taking Pixie's rubber ball along for luck. It was there that memories of the burned village he and Leigh Fermor had passed through during their escape from Crete came back to him, as he again encountered the "same nauseating smell" in one ruined town after another.

He returned to Cairo to find Sophie Tarnowska bedridden, with both legs in casts, following a serious automobile accident. Pixie had been seized by city authorities for "removing the trousers of a taxi boy who had been teasing him." By Christmas, however, the household was again together and in good health. The following April, Moss and Sophie were married in a ceremony witnessed by Prince Peter of Greece. Moss spent the rest of the war serving in Siam.

After the war, Moss wrote an account of the Kreipe kidnapping, based on the diary he had kept at the time. The book, *Ill Met by Moonlight*, was turned into a movie in 1957. It starred David Oxley as Moss and Dirk Bogarde as Leigh Fermor. Moss went on to write a string of books and mystery stories, including an inquiry into the disappearance of a substantial stockpile of gold during the collapse of the Third Reich.

Moss and Sophie Tarnowska split up in 1957, after which he traveled to New Zealand and Antarctica and sailed a small boat across the Pacific before finally settling in the West Indies. He was only forty-four when he died in 1965 in Kingston, Jamaica.

ALEXANDER RENDEL, David Smiley, and Julian Amery all published memoirs of their wartime exploits. Rendel donated the profits from his book to a Greek orphanage; he went on to become a respected diplomatic correspondent for *The Times* of London. Tom Dunbabin went back to archaeology and published books and articles on the ancient Mediterranean world. Rowland Winn, the Tara resident who had broken his ankle demonstrating parachute jumps, eventually received the transfer he wanted to SOE. He parachuted into Albania but landed hard in rugged mountain terrain and broke his ankle again.

"His leg was set in a splint by a horse doctor," his nephew would later recall, "and he rode through the mountains on a mule until he took part in something like a cavalry charge with the partisans and the mule fell on him and broke his leg a third time." Brian Coleman, skipper of *ML 842*, received a commendation following the Bricklayer mission citing "great skill, endurance and pertinacity in carrying out landings and embarkations in enemy controlled Crete." Cyril Fortune, the RAF pilot who dropped Leigh Fermor onto the Katharo plateau, later received the Distinguished Flying Cross. Whether he ever received the dagger Bandouvas had promised him is not recorded.

George Psychoundakis, the young man from Asi Gonia who served tirelessly as a runner for Xan Fielding and other British officers, wrote a memoir that was translated into English by Patrick Leigh Fermor and became one of the landmarks of World War II literature. Psychoundakis went on to translate Homer and Hesiod into the traditional Cretan form of epic verse.

Einer von der Heydte, who befriended Patrick Leigh Fermor in Vienna before the war and commanded a unit of German paratroopers during the invasion, was later named among the conspirators in a plot to assassinate Hitler. Heydte escaped arrest by the Gestapo because the papers implicating him misspelled his surname. Heydte too published an account of his experiences on Crete. Fritz, the young German Patrick Leigh Fermor befriended in 1935, was killed in fighting in Norway, perhaps in an engagement with a unit of Leigh Fermor's own regiment.

Xan Fielding transferred to the French section of SOE in the spring of 1944. That August, with orders that amounted to "You'll find out when you get there," he parachuted into southern France. Posing as an electric-company clerk, he set out to assist the Resistance but was soon captured by the Gestapo. He was later rescued from a death cell by Christine Granville, a Polish countess-turned-spy who was later said to have inspired the string of seductive female agents in Ian Fleming's Bond novels. After publishing his wartime memoirs, Fielding went on to make a name for himself as a writer. He was best known for his English translations of works by the French novelist Pierre Boulle, which included *The Bridge over the River Kwai* and *Planet of the Apes.*

DESPITE THE RISKS they continued to take after the Kreipe mission, George Tyrakis and Manoli Paterakis both survived the war. Both were recommended for Greek military honors. The final record sheet on Tyrakis summed up his service this way: "Brave, loyal, tireless, cheerful and enterprising. Cannot be praised too highly."

A letter of commendation sent by SOE to the Greek war ministry called Manoli Paterakis "certainly one of the bravest men in Crete." Successful as he had been as a soldier, Paterakis wished simply to return to the life he had known before the war. Many years later, he traveled to New York with Patrick Leigh Fermor at the invitation of the Cretan Union of America. When the two wartime friends rode to the top of the Empire State Building one evening to take in the panoramic view of the city, Leigh Fermor noticed that Paterakis had fallen silent. "I saw a pensive look on Manoli's face, and asked him what he was thinking of," Leigh Fermor wrote to a friend, "and he said 'I'm just thinking that back in Crete it would be just about time to go up to the folds and feed the ewes.'" Paterakis remained true to his heritage to the end. He was in his seventies when he fell to his death while stalking *agrimi*—the native wild goat—high in the White Mountains of western Crete.

BY THE TIME Patrick Leigh Fermor reached Cairo in the wake of the successful mission, it was clear that he was seriously ill. He spent the following three months hospitalized with rheumatic fever. After another month of sick leave in Syria, still not fully recovered, he was again infiltrated into Crete on October 26, 1944.

On the morning of December 8, a German detachment of seven tanks and four hundred infantry attacked the headquarters he had established near Suda Bay on the western end of the island. As the tanks rolled onto their streets, villagers took up positions in the surrounding hills and fired on the Germans. "During the day contingents from all the neighboring villages arrived and attacked the Germans with such spirit that at 1700 hours they were forced to retreat after having killed only four Cretans and destroyed only two houses," Leigh Fermor wrote in his final report to Cairo. German losses were far higher. "This was considered by everybody to be a signal triumph for Cretan arms and an illustration of the almost unvarying success of the guerilla tactics in guerilla country against vastly outnumbering forces."

Finding little work left to do on the island, he departed on December 23 aboard the destroyer HMS *Catterick*, hoping to reach Cairo in time to be transferred to the Far East. He landed in Alexandria on Christmas Eve. In fact, the war was all but over for him.

Leigh Fermor went on to become the most important British travel writer of the next half century. His first book, about travels in the Caribbean, came out in 1950. Books about Greece followed, but it was not until 1977 that he finally published the first volume based on his epic trek across Europe in the 1930s. A second volume appeared in 1986, and readers are still waiting hopefully for the third, on which he was working in the last months of his life. Taken together, Leigh Fermor's books created a literary genre that was distinctly his own—part memoir, part history, often lyrical, always precise. His writing was suffused with lightly carried erudition and infectious good humor. Having lived most of his life on the Mani peninsula in southern Greece, Patrick Leigh Fermor died in England in 2011 at the age of ninety-six.

IN 1972, Leigh Fermor was reunited in Athens with General Kreipe for a Greek television program. After the broadcast, the two men joined a group of Leigh Fermor's old Cretan allies at a nearby *taverna*. As he described the evening in a letter to a friend, it might have been a reunion of schoolmates rather than former enemies: "Lots of Cretan songs and dances, a few German folk songs sung by the General and me, after much wine had flowed." When local journalists heard what was going on, they crashed the party. "One asked the General how I had treated him when he was my prisoner in the mountains and the Gen said—wait for it!—most energetically: '*Ritterlich! Wie ein Ritter!*'"

Chivalrously. Like a knight.

Acknowledgments

The Ariadne Objective owes its inception to Geraldine Gesell and the Department of Classics at the University of Tennessee, who together made my first trips to Crete possible and nurtured my interest in Aegean history, both ancient and modern, introducing me to the events of the story presented here and to the landscape on which it unfolded. That the book now has a second life in this new edition is thanks to the staff at Paul Dry Books— among them Maude de Moll Kushto, Mara Brandsdorfer, and Julia Sippel—who have encouraged the *Ariadne* project from an early stage, and helped me improve upon the earlier edition.

I am deeply grateful to my friend McKay Jenkins, who helped in innumerable ways to launch me on the path to this book, not least by introducing me to the ideal shepherd for the project in the person of my agent, Neil Olson.

Without the memoirs and field reports written by those who took part in the history recounted here, the book would simply not have been possible. I am indebted to the work of Patrick Leigh Fermor and William Stanley Moss, as well as Julian Amery, Harry Brooke, Thomas J. Dunbabin, Xan Fielding, Friedrich August Heydte, John Houseman, George Psychoundakis, and A. M. Rendel, among others. I owe a similar debt to the writers who have told parts of the story from different angles, in particular Antony Beevor, Imogen Grundon, Dylis Powell, and Andrew Tarnowski. Thanks to Tim Todd, author of a website devoted to the Kreipe abduction mission (illmetbymoonlight.

info), who early on sent me tips on locating SOE-related holdings in the National Archives, and to Tom Sawford, whose blog (patrickleighfermor.wordpress.com) is a rich and constantly evolving resource on the subject. Artemis Cooper, whose biography of Patrick Leigh Fermor was published in the UK not long after I completed the manuscript, deserves special acknowledgment, both for her history of wartime Cairo, without which I could not have written the chapters set at Tara, and for graciously answering my questions about Leigh Fermor.

I am especially grateful to the families whose assistance brought the book's subjects to life. Gabriella and Hugh Bullock were both kind and helpful beyond description, giving me access to photographs and diaries as they shared their memories of Gabriella's parents, Billy Moss, and Sophie Tarnowska. Sandy Rendel's son and granddaughter, Robert Rendel and Tamsin Rendel, were similarly welcoming and unfailingly generous with their archives and their memories. Talking and corresponding with them all was one of the deepest pleasures of writing the book.

I would like to thank the staff and librarians of the National Archives of the United Kingdom, the Imperial War Museum, the Firestone Library of Princeton University, the Yale University Library, and the Sarah Lawrence College Library.

Many thanks are also due to editors of the first edition: Charles Conrad, who saw the manuscript through the revision process, Kevin Doughten, who carried it on to publication, and John Glusman, who first brought the book to Crown. Janice Benario, Miriam Chotiner-Gardner, Bill Deresiewicz, Ben Downing, Paul Dry, David Findlay, John Kulka, Alan Levenstein, C. E. Mamalakis, Claire Potter, Hilary Roberts, Pat Willis, and Ben Yagoda all provided important help along the way, as did my parents, who offered encouragement at every step.

Most of all, thanks to my wife, Jessica, who makes everything doable and, along with our daughters, Willa and Alice, worth doing.

Notes

Prologue: Whimsical

xix **Its code name . . . was Whimsical:** Details and dialogue from the parachute mission are derived from Cyril Fortune, "Sortie Report," Feb. 4/5, 1944, AIR 23/1443, National Archives of the UK, and from records in AIR 27/996.

xx **gold sovereigns:** Patrick Leigh Fermor, "Afterword," in W. Stanley Moss, *Ill Met by Moonlight* (London: Folio Society, 2001), 204.

xx **the Katharo plateau:** Leigh Fermor and others have used the name Omalos to refer to the plateau in question. In the years following the war, maps showed both names, Omalos for the southwestern arm of the plateau, Katharo for the northeast. The coordinates given in archival material relating to the drop place are on the Katharo side of the plateau, and I have used that name to distinguish the area from both the so-called Little Omalos to the south and the larger and better known Omalos plateau on the western end of the island.

xxii **"if he wished to drop":** AIR 23/1443.

xxii **"There was some terrible finality":** W. Stanley Moss, unpublished diary, Documents.13338, Private Papers of Major I W S Moss MC, Department of Documents, Imperial War Museum.

xxiii **"Captain found he was":** AIR 23/1443.

xxiv **"Well," he wrote, "here we are":** Patrick Leigh Fermor to Annette Crean, Feb. 9, 1944, Documents.6433, Private Papers of Mrs A Street, Imperial War Museum.

Chapter 1: Shanks's Mare

3 **"Nice weather for young ducks":** Patrick Leigh Fermor, *A Time of Gifts* (New York: New York Review Books, 2005), 22.

4 **"I would travel on foot":** Ibid., 19.

4 **"Hallelujah I'm a Bum":** The passport episode is recounted in *A Time of Gifts* at pages 20–21.

5   **"a universal smell of rotting timber":** Ibid., 24.

5   **"the *Stadthouder* was twanging":** Ibid.

5   **"Leave thy home":** Ibid., 20.

5   **"The kingdom had slid away":** Ibid., 25.

6   **"an out-and-out naturalist":** Ibid., 10.

6   **the elder Leigh Fermor's work:** H. Crookshank and J. B. Auden, "Lewis Leigh Fermor: 1880–1954," *Biographical Memoirs of Fellows of the Royal Society* 2 (November 1956): 101–16.

6   **The snowflake discovery:** Leigh Fermor also recalled that his father had once had a mineral named after him. Sadly, in 2010 fermorite was reclassified as a variety of another mineral and renamed Johnbaumite-M.

6   **"Rose of Simla":** Charlotte Mosley, ed., *In Tearing Haste: Letters Between Deborah Devonshire and Patrick Leigh Fermor* (London: John Murray, 2008), 149.

7   **"simultaneously writing plays":** Fermor, *A Time of Gifts*, 9.

7   **"navigable birdsnests in a gale-wind":** Ibid.

7   **"I was left behind":** Ibid., 6.

7   **"farmer's child run wild":** Ibid.

7   **"Those marvelously lawless years":** Ibid., 7.

8   **"rise at 5 o'clock each morning":** Crookshank and Auden, "Lewis Leigh Fermor," 101.

9   **gardener's "fearfully pretty" daughter:** Mosley, *In Tearing Haste*, 250.

9   **"a mixture of a rather dog-eared romanticism":** Fermor, *A Time of Gifts*, 87.

9   **Bicycling a few miles:** Alan Watts, *In My Own Way* (New York: Pantheon, 1972), 100.

10   **"I knew that plants":** Ibid., 23.

10   **shoot the tobacco out of a cigarette:** Ibid., 19.

10   **"in his black gown and mortarboard":** Ibid., 43.

10   **"the only really interesting boy":** Ibid., 102.

10   **"a fine poet, a born adventurer":** Ibid.

11   **"like ectoplasm":** Fermor, *A Time of Gifts*, 12.

11   **"When utterly oppressed":** Watts, *In My Own Way*, 102–3.

11   **"swift and flexible sanctions":** Fermor, *A Time of Gifts*, 13.

11   **"was constantly being flogged":** Watts, *In My Own Way*, 103.

12   **"He is a dangerous mixture":** Fermor, *A Time of Gifts*, 13.

12   **"a ravishing, sonnet-begetting beauty":** Ibid., 14.

12   **"a comely brunette":** Watts, *In My Own Way*, 103.

12   **"we were sitting in the back-shop":** Fermor, *A Time of Gifts*, 15.

12 **"It was the formal start":** Ibid., 26.

13 **"Thank God I had put":** Ibid., 30.

13 **"thanks to an effortless mastery":** Ibid., 126.

13 **"atrocity stories, farmhouses on fire":** Ibid., 45.

14 **In the summer of 1919:** In *A Time of Gifts*, Leigh Fermor gives the date as June 18, but he makes it clear that the celebration marked Peace Day, which fell on July 19.

14 **"Black, white and red":** Ibid., 36–37.

16 **"They looked less fierce":** Ibid., 41.

16 **"It was charming":** Ibid.

16 **"She was very pretty":** Ibid., 50.

18 **"Adolf Hitler will change":** Ibid., 70.

18 **"They were amusingly dressed":** Ibid., 75.

19 **"How do you do":** Ibid.

19 **"Halfway up the vaulted stairs":** Ibid., 103.

20 **"in those minutes":** Ibid., 114.

21 **"It was the Odes":** Ibid.

21 **"long winters, early nightfall":** Ibid., 123. See also Patrick Leigh Fermor, *Roumeli* (New York: New York Review Books, 2006), 196.

21 **"I used to punch the heads":** Fermor, *A Time of Gifts*, 133.

22 **"a thimble full of the cold":** Ibid., 146.

22 **"lapping whiskey and soda":** Ibid., 189.

23 **"Wildish nights and late mornings":** Ibid., 218.

23 **Nazi who was badmouthing the Church:** For Heydte's biography, see James Lucas, *Hitler's Enforcers* (London: Cassell, 1996), 26–39.

24 **"how the progress":** Friedrich August, Freiherr von der Heydte, *Daedalus Returned*, trans. W. Stanley Moss (London: Hutchinson, 1958), 15.

24 **"perhaps as a scholar":** Ibid.

25 **"It seemed to hit the nail":** Patrick Leigh Fermor, *Between the Woods and the Water* (London: Penguin Books, 1988), 197.

25 **When the conversation turned:** Ibid., 198.

26 **"A promise of the Aegean":** Patrick Leigh Fermor, *Words of Mercury*, ed. Artemis Cooper (London: John Murray, 2004), 30.

26 **he glimpsed a cluster of beehive huts:** See Fermor, *Roumeli*, 7–9.

26 **"Jarred and shaken":** Fermor, *Words of Mercury*, 30.

27 **"Good evening, Good evening!":** Ibid., 30.

27 **"They were wild looking men":** Ibid., 32.

28 ***"Lordos Veeron!":*** Ibid., 38.

28 **"There was much to think about":** Ibid.

29 **"For though it was possible":** Henry Cary, *Herodotus: A New and Literal Version from the Text of Baehr, with a Geographical and General Index* (New York: Harper, 1889), 421.

30 **"all women, all female animals":** Jacques Valentin, *The Monks of Mount Athos*, trans. Diano Athill (London: A. Deutsch, 1960), 87.

30 **"of a faith where all the years have stopped":** Robert Byron, *The Station* (London: Century Publishing, 1984), 256.

30 **"fierce-whiskered, brigand-faces":** Patrick Leigh Fermor, *A Time to Keep Silence* (New York: New York Review Books, 2007), 13–14.

31 **"so that even Calypso's isle":** Leigh Fermor quotes from Basil's letter in *A Time to Keep Silence* at page 96.

31 **"'Light,' 'peace' and 'happiness'":** Ibid., 95.

31 **The first job, he knew:** Fermor, *Roumeli*, 55–56.

33 **"It was the most extraordinary thing":** Quoted in James Owen, "Rotterdam to Istanbul by Foot," *Daily Telegraph*, February 19, 2000.

33 **Once the shooting stopped:** Fermor, *Roumeli*, 54.

33 **"the nearest any of us":** Ibid.

33 **"watched them jingle away":** Ibid., 55.

33 **"reached the windowsills":** Fermor, *Words of Mercury*, 44.

34 **"It had been a happy day":** Ibid., 53.

34 **"Recruit Leigh-Fermor!":** William Stanley Moss, *A War of Shadows* (New York: Macmillan, 1952), 64.

35 **"it was the obsolete choice":** Fermor, *A Time of Gifts*, 5.

Chapter 2: Sword Stick

36 **"the most bogus Vice-Consul":** Dilys Powell, *The Villa Ariadne* (London: Hodder & Stoughton, 1973), 113.

36 **"the heir apparent":** S. R. K. Glanville, *Journal of Egyptian Archaeology* 28 (December 1942): 63.

36 **"a wonderful country—much richer":** Powell, *Villa Ariadne*, 68.

37 **"It was a soft darkish blue":** Mary Chubb, *Nefertiti Lived Here* (London: Libri, 1998), 65.

37 **"Have just got a Cretan costume":** Powell, *Villa Ariadne*, 81.

38 **"Greece behaving grandly":** Imogen Grundon, *The Rash Adventurer: A Life of John Pendlebury* (London: Libri Publications, 2007), 253. Leigh Fermor was captivated by the leather-bound sword stick. See Patrick Leigh Fermor, *Words of Mercury* (New York: New York Review Books, 2006), 188.

39 **"Send everything as quick":** Grundon, *Rash Adventurer*, 3.

39 **"I went up to town on Monday":** John Pendlebury to Herbert Pendlebury, quoted in ibid., 238.

39 **"I think it is going to be great fun":** John Pendlebury to Hilda Pendlebury, quoted in ibid., 239.

40 **"I've forgotten all about being an archaeologist":** Powell, *Villa Ariadne*, 109.

40 **"an especially resolute traveller":** Ibid., 110.

40 **"hocuspocus":** Nicholas Hammond, quoted in Grundon, *Rash Adventurer*, 240.

41 **hop the Orient Express:** The train Pendlebury and his friends hoped to catch was the Simplon Orient Express that ran from Paris to Istanbul in the 1920s and included a spur line to Thessaloníki and Athens.

41 **"fresh as a daisy":** Quoted in Grundon, *Rash Adventurer*, 120.

41 **"learning the tricks of the trade":** Powell, *Villa Ariadne*, 111.

42 **"poring over the latest maps":** Grundon, *Rash Adventurer*, 240.

42 **"would be the ideal weapon":** Powell, *Villa Ariadne*, 111–12.

42 **"could hardly wait":** Hilda Pendlebury to Dilys Powell, quoted in ibid., 110.

43 **"He is a very dignified old gentleman":** John Pendlebury to Herbert Pendlebury, quoted in Grundon, *Rash Adventurer*, 248.

43 **"Bandouvas is a good man":** Ibid., 266.

43 **When the corporal called Pendlebury "un-Captainlike":** Ibid., 257. The corporal was Maxwell Tasker-Brown.

43 **"a somewhat rickety wardrobe":** Mike Cumberlege to Herbert Pendlebury, undated, quoted in ibid., 298.

44 **"*pente dodeka,* 512" :** Grundon, *Rash Adventurer*, 257.

44 **"It took a few visits":** Ibid., 258.

44 **"Pendlebury would sometimes saunter in":** Patrick Savage, quoted in ibid., 259.

44 **"He told me about his hill men":** Maxwell Tasker-Brown to Imogen Grundon, quoted in ibid., 258.

45 **"We also checked out look-out points":** Tasker-Brown, quoted in ibid., 269.

45 **"It worked quite well":** Tasker-Brown to Imogen Grundon, quoted in ibid.

45 **"nothing to the savages":** John Pendlebury to Hilda Pendlebury, quoted in ibid., 269–70.

46 **"The Uncrowned King of Crete":** Tasker-Brown, quoted in ibid., 279.

46 **"At present we seem as safe":** John Pendlebury to Hilda Pendlebury, quoted in Powell, *Villa Ariadne*, 119.

46 **"Love," the messaged concluded:** John Pendlebury, cable to Hilda Pendlebury, quoted in ibid., 120.

47 **"Keen as mustard":** Grundon, *Rash Adventurer*, 287.

47 **"May be against rules of war":** John Pendlebury, private note-book, quoted in ibid. (The notebook was later captured by the Germans.)

48 **"under more or less perpetual":** Alan Clark, *The Fall of Crete* (London: Cassell, 1962), 22.

48 **Corpses floating in the water:** See ibid.

48 **One of his students:** Antony Beevor, *Crete: The Battle and the Resistance* (London: John Murray, 1991), 27.

49 **"havoc of a spectacular and enjoyable kind":** Peter Fleming, quoted in ibid., 34.

49 **"a bald-headed giant":** Grundon, *Rash Adventurer*, 299.

49 **"He breathed blood and slaughter":** Ibid.

50 **"He had already driven":** Nick Hammond, quoted in ibid.

50 **"like the roof of the world":** Lawrence Durrell, *The Greek Islands* (New York: Viking, 1978), 86.

50 **"an amazing buccaneerish figure":** Patrick Leigh Fermor, *Three Letters from the Andes* (London: John Murray, 2005), 105.

51 **"It was going to be a terrific party":** Grundon, *Rash Adventurer*, 298.

51 **"Pendlebury was confident":** Ibid., 303.

53 **"like bees in a bee-garden":** George Psychoundakis, *The Cretan Runner*, trans. Patrick Leigh Fermor (London: Penguin Books, 1998), 42.

53 **"We've eaten them up":** Ibid.

53 **"For the villagers had kept":** Ibid., 41.

53 **"Stand still, Turk":** Ibid., 43.

53 **One New Zealand soldier:** D. M. Davin, *Official History of New Zealand in the Second World War, "Crete"* (Department of Internal Affairs, War History Branch, 1953), 235; reproduced in Clark, *Fall of Crete*, 138.

53 **"You cuckolds!":** Psychoundakis, *Cretan Runner*, 42.

54 **women took to the fields:** Ioannis Spanakis, in Costas N. Hadjipateras and Maria S. Falios, *Crete 1941 Eyewitnessed* (Athens: Efstathiadis Group, 2007), 107.

54 **"He too wanted to go and fight":** Theoharis Mylonakis, in ibid., 94.

54 **"The first German I bandaged":** Theoharis Mylonakis, in ibid., 95.

55 **"Let them go and see the fighting":** Winston Churchill to Chief of the Imperial General Staff, October 30, 1940, quoted in Winston Churchill, *Their Finest Hour* (Boston: Houghton Mifflin, 1949), 473.

55   **Paddy was still in the hospital:** Beevor, *Crete*, 9–10.

55   **"an astonishing repertoire":** Ibid., 10.

55   **atmosphere at the Grand Bretagne:** Ibid., 12.

56   **"a country within sight of Italy":** Gibbon is quoted in Patrick Leigh Fermor, "Foreword," in David Smiley, *Albanian Assignment* (London: Chatto & Windus, 1984), x.

56   **"It was a fierce mountain state":** Ibid.

56   **"hardy and courageously independent":** Ibid.

58   **"When the roar of our guns":** Fermor, *Words of Mercury*, 189.

59   **"The short May night was illuminated":** Patrick Leigh Fermor, *A Time of Gifts* (New York: New York Review Books, 2005), 220.

59   **"He had a Cretan guerilla":** Leigh Fermor, personal communication, quoted in Grundon, *Rash Adventurer*, 307.

60   **"smiled obligingly, drew it":** Fermor, *Words of Mercury*, 188.

62   **"I could not see the adjutant's face":** Friedrich August, Freiherr von der Heydte, *Daedalus Returned*, trans. W. Stanley Moss (London: Hutchinson, 1958), 145.

62   **"What was the point":** Ibid., 146.

63   **"You ought to be with Bob":** Evelyn Waugh, *The Diaries of Evelyn Waugh*, ed. Michael Davie (Boston: Little, Brown, 1976), 490.

63   **"He was wearing shorts":** Ibid., 499. This story is told from a different perspective in Beevor, *Crete*, 195.

64   **"Just below us was":** Waugh, *The Diaries of Eveyln Waugh*, 502.

65   **"that he wished to surrender the town":** Heydte, *Daedalus Returned*, 167.

65   **"He was the last British soldier":** Ibid., 170.

66   **"In a monastery one should":** Ibid., 178.

66   **"Only a few days later":** Ibid., 180.

66   **"we had encountered for the first time":** Ibid., 181.

67   **"the Black Watch leaves Crete":** Major Alastair Hamilton, quoted in Beevor, *Crete*, 207.

67   **"All at once":** Fermor, *Words of Mercury*, 190–91.

67   **"My child," the old *andarte*:** Ibid., 191.

68   **"stench of decomposing dead":** Captain Tomlinson, quoted in Maria Hill, *Diggers and Greeks* (Sydney: University of New South Wales Press, 2010), 227.

69   **"just as Daedalus had done":** Heydte, *Daedalus Returned*, 186.

70   **"the western edge of the town":** Captain Gerhard Schirmer, quoted in Grundon, *Rash Adventurer*, 309. Schirmer was at least partly wrong in crediting the strong defenses to the English.

71   **"We saw that machine-guns":** Nick Hammond, quoted in ibid., 311.

72 **"The great thing was":** Patrick Leigh Fermor, quoted in ibid., 307.

72 **"We also tried to drop a wireless":** Beevor, *Crete*, 142.

Chapter 3: Oak Apple Day

74 **"a silent sad-eyed man":** Xan Fielding, *Hide and Seek* (London: Secker & Warburg, 1954), 54.

75 **"an electric torch, a small automatic":** Ibid., 28.

76 **"only succeeded in making me look":** Ibid.

77 **"an absurdly pejorative term":** Ibid., 13.

77 **"I had little money":** Ibid., 14.

77 **"I might have made a decent escape":** Ibid.

77 **a frail Oxford-trained anthropologist:** Fielding's friend was Francis Turville-Petre. He had spent most of the 1930s living the life of an eccentric, largely nocturnal, hermit on this tiny Greek island. His peculiar habits had attracted the attention of the poet W. H. Auden, who wrote a play about him. Auden's friend and sometime collaborator Christopher Isherwood was the previous occupant of the room Fielding moved into at the end of September 1939.

78 **"I was not afraid":** Ibid.

78 **"But what good do":** Ibid., 16.

78 **"Now, for the first time":** Ibid., 12.

79 **"Bearded men wielding breach-loading muskets":** Ibid., 12–13.

80 **"Have you any personal objection":** Ibid., 23.

80 **"For three days I was initiated into the mysteries":** Ibid., 27.

80 **"We were in enemy country":** Ibid., 112.

81 **"I lost count of them":** Ibid., 65.

81 **"to talk to people":** Details are derived from HS 5/728, National Archives of the UK.

82 **"To say that we were old friends":** Fielding, *Hide and Seek*, 87.

82 **"Though we all wore":** Ibid.

82 **"wishing success to the mission":** Ibid., 88.

84 **"By the time the raki":** Ibid.

84 **Fielding's zone was known to be the more difficult:** HS 5/728, Field report, April 1943, National Archives of the UK.

84 **"a holiday between . . . areas":** HS 5/732, National Archives of the UK.

85 **"a motley rabble":** This and other details are derived from HS 5/732.

85 **"a dark burly man":** Fielding, *Hide and Seek*, 194. Fielding had said the same thing in one of his reports from the field: "'The struggle

needs blood' is Bo-Peep's favourite catch-phrase" (HS 5/725, National Archives of the UK).

86 **"any coast you can 'smell out' ":** HS 9/458/1, National Archives of the UK.

87 **"A very keen and penetrating mind":** Ibid.

87 **"He has an excellent knowledge of Greek ":** Ibid.

87 **"When I arrived the food":** HS 5/728.

88 **"His memory turned all":** Patrick Leigh Fermor, *Words of Mercury*, ed. Artemis Cooper (London: John Murray, 2004), 190.

88 **"Little in these crags":** Patrick Leigh Fermor, *Roumeli* (New York: New York Review Books, 2006), 137.

88 **"Onions, garlic and tomatoes hung":** Ibid., 137–38.

88 **"was a sequence of insurrections, massacres":** Ibid., 134.

88 **"the moonlit jigsaw of roofs":** Ibid., 137.

89 **"changed what was before":** David Roessel, *In Byron's Shadow* (New York: Oxford Univerity Press, 2002), 110.

89 **"goat-folds and abandoned":** Fermor, *Roumeli*, 139.

89 **"active, lean, spare, hawk-eyed men":** Ibid., 53.

90 **"They are virtually weaned":** Ibid., 135.

90 **"Never fear, my child":** Ibid., 140.

90 **"seeing as much of the Huns":** HS 5/728.

90 **"I feel that if I had managed":** Ibid.

91 **"We want to go home":** Ibid.

91 **"of royal blue broadcloth lined":** Fielding, *Hide and Seek*, 126.

91 **"I, for example, affected":** Ibid.

92 **"Though it was now too cold":** Ibid., 127.

92 **"Since I was in full view":** Ibid., 127–28.

92 **"You come with us":** Ibid., 128.

93 **"It was easy for me":** Ibid., 129.

93 **"With a final unconvincing cry":** Ibid.

93 **"They seemed so gullible":** Ibid., 129–30.

94 **"I am a poor man":** Ibid., 132. The Vicar was Father John Alevizakis.

94 **"What is it?":** George Psychoundakis, *The Cretan Runner*, trans. Patrick Leigh Fermor (London: Penguin Books, 1998), 135.

95 **"who escaped," Dunbabin reported:** HS 5/723; National Archives of the UK.

95 **"came streaming down again":** HS 5/728.

96 **"The Changebug did not reappear":** Ibid.

96 **"I am now in an elfin grotto":** Ibid.

97 **"Sancho . . . and Changebug . . . have been":** Ibid.

97 **"The Vicar has been loyal":** Ibid.

Chapter 4: The Fishpond

99 **"squareheads":** HS 5/728, Field report, April 1943, National Archives of the UK.

99 **"heavily armed as pirates":** Ibid.

100 **"The result was perfect":** Ibid.

100 **"loyally and unwearyingly":** HS 5/723, National Archives of the UK.

100 **He was admired for his discretion:** HS 8/657, SOE liquidation reports, National Archives of the UK.

100 **"He is a grand chap":** HS 5/728, April 1943.

100 **"Man Friday":** W. Stanley Moss, *Ill Met by Moonlight* (London: Folio Society, 2001), 27.

100 **"Working in this area":** Ibid.

101 **"Work in my present area":** Ibid.

102 **German morale had fallen to a low point:** HS 5/723, February 1943, p. 9. The number of troops comes from appendix D.

102 **As Dunbabin told headquarters:** HS 5/723, February 1943, p. 18.

102 **"I think the chance of success":** Ibid.

102 **"The larger vessels withdraw":** HS 5/728, April 1943.

103 **code-named Tweedledee:** The SOE agent who bore this code name was Konstantinos Kastrinogiannes.

103 **"Once inside, we all heaved a sigh":** HS 5/728, April 1943.

103 **"When the time came to go":** Ibid.

103 **"I do not want to discuss":** Ibid.

104 **"Chief of Francs-Tireurs":** Ibid.

104 **"Crete must be set free":** Ibid.

104 **"He is the most admired":** HS 5/728, May–June 1943.

105 **"of an imaginary Cretan":** Ibid.

106 **"could drink everyone under the table":** Leigh Fermor recalls Micky Akoumianakis's (Minoan Mike's) remark in "John Pendlebury," *Words of Mercury*, ed. Artemis Cooper (London: John Murray, 2004), 186.

106 **"a splendid chap":** HS 5/728, May–June 1943.

106 **"over under or through":** Ibid.

106 **"The cop and I":** Ibid.

107 **"Shooting . . . started next day":** Ibid.

108 **Lamonby sent one of his men:** The man was Lance Corporal Richard Holmes.

109 **"The fact that he could not":** Quoted in David Sutherland, *He Who Dares* (Annapolis: Naval Institute Press, 1999), 109. It would come out later that Lieutenant Lamonby had indeed been wounded and died in the Heraklion hospital.

109 **"I'm afraid there is no":** HS 5/728, September 1943.

110 **"I hope the service":** HS 5/728, July 1943.

Chapter 5: Spaghetti and Ravioli

111 **"*Viva Inghilterra!*":** HS 5/728, National Archives of the UK.

112 **"Italian nonsense":** HS 5/728, April 1943.

112 **"The German authorities":** Ibid.

113 **"Ravioli . . . sent out Lieut. Spaghetti":** Ibid.

113 **"spiritual matters":** Ibid.

114 **"We are ready to defend ourselves":** Ibid. Here and following, Lieutenant Tavana's communications with the British, which took place for the most part in French, are quoted or paraphrased in French, and sometimes English, in the field reports Leigh Fermor sent to Cairo.

114 **"because the Greeks can":** Ibid.

114 **"Spaghetti was in a":** Ibid.

115 **"He is very Latin and nervy Italian":** Ibid.

115 **"mixed" . . . "dummy executions":** Ibid.

115 **"one or two dark patches":** Ibid.

116 **"We took them to their barracks":** Ibid.

117 **"the strangest of plain clothes":** Ibid.

118 **"kissed him on both cheeks":** Ibid.

118 **"This struck him as a good idea":** Ibid.

118 **"disappointed and apologetic":** Ibid.

118 **"I am bound by military honor":** Ibid.

119 **general's position was a "delicate" one:** Ibid.

119 **"to liberty and peace" . . . "Spaghetti nearly wept":** Ibid.

120 **"Oh, mon Capitaine":** Ibid. Leigh Fermor's communications with Carta are quoted or paraphrased in the field reports Leigh Fermor sent to Cairo.

120 **"be ready to take advantage":** Winston Churchill, *Closing the Ring* (Boston: Houghton Mifflin, 1951), 204.

120 **"This is no time":** Winston Churchill, message to General Pug Ismay, quoted in ibid.

122 **"godmothers" . . . "The poor thing was christened":** HS 5/728.

123 **"liquidated" . . . "Three 'rubbings out'":** Ibid.

124 **"take up positions":** HS 5/723, National Archives of the UK.

125 **four hundred men:** This was Harry Brooke's estimate. HS 5/722, National Archives of the UK.

125 **"joyfully" launched a clutch of flares:** HS 5/728.

126 **"Large numbers are now in bush shirts":** Ibid.

126 **"Long live Paddy . . . Long live England":** Harry Brooke, HS 5/722.

126 **"It was like Bo-Peep's birthday":** HS 5/728.

127 **"Mon general . . . What an honor":** Ibid.

127 **"My dear friend," his letter began:** Ibid.

128 **"is very unlike my present appearance":** Ibid.

128 **"The cigars were excellent":** Ibid.

128 **"Please excuse my scrawl":** Ibid.

129 **In each case a donkey was accepted:** Tom Dunbabin reports this as a "Silly Story": HS 5/723, report 5, p. 7.

131 **Bandouvas believed the British were preparing:** George Harakopos, *The Abduction of General Kreipe*, trans. Rosemary Tzanaki (Heraklion, Greece: V. Kouvidis–V. Manouras, 2003), 38.

132 **"He was dressed in":** HS 5/728.

132 **"This was the result":** Ibid.

133 **"He is plump, rosy":** Ibid.

133 **"their old comradeship of arms":** Ibid.

134 **Anyone caught destroying or trafficking:** Ibid., appendix: "General Order to All Italian Troops in Crete by the German General Muller."

135 **"an uncomfortable half hour":** HS 5/728.

135 **"I found him beaming":** Ibid.

136 **"arms had been landed by parachute":** Ibid.

136 **"fuss and anxiety":** Ibid.

137 **they killed or captured every last man:** HS 5/723. Later accounts differ on the outcome of this firefight.

139 **"regaled . . . with lively anecdotes":** HS 5/728.

139 **"They landed right at our feet":** Ibid.

139 **"The Italian General Carta":** HS 5/728, "Translation of a German leaflet printed in Greek, Italian and German."

139 **"Carta," Paddy noted, "was very amused":** HS 5/728.

140 **"lean and chastened":** HS 5/723.

140 **"The behaviour of this force":** Ibid.

141 **The fiction he devised:** Harokopos, *Abduction of General Kreipe*, 56.

141 **"arrested our mule":** HS 5/723.

142 **with a radio operator:** Rendel's radio operator was George Dilley.

142 **what he called "soft jobs":** A. M. Rendel, *Appointment in Crete* (London: A. Wingate, 1953), 8.

142   **"wound itself with sickly":** Ibid., 7.

142   **"in some intelligence job":** Ibid.

143   **"There were plenty of letters":** Ibid., 7–8.

143   **"doing nothing at all":** Ibid.

143   **"scrambling about at night":** Ibid., 9.

143   **"Well I'd better tell you something":** Ibid.

144   **"But Tom . . . if you go":** Ibid.

144   **"Spy . . . an ugly word":** Ibid.

145   **"sentimental and unreal":** Ibid., 15.

145   **"must be a person entirely":** Ibid., 14.

145   **"Didn't you get covered":** Ibid., 11.

145   **"by hook or by crook":** Ibid., 16.

146   **"On the march," he thought:** Ibid., 28.

146   **"How good the Cretans were to you":** Ibid., 19.

147   **"The supplies were usually":** Ibid.

147   **"What about the salad dressing?":** Ibid., 20.

147   **"It shot low and I saw":** Ibid., 34. Years later Rendel was still moved by this recollection and remarked that it was strange to recall the fury of that morning in such a different setting, "from the depths of an armchair with my wife sewing quietly at the other side of the fireplace" (ibid).

148   **"Bob Young himself, looking":** Ibid., 35.

148   **"a tall fair-haired boy":** Ibid.

148   **"The old cliché about":** Ibid., 36.

149   **"Bob Young signaled that we":** Ibid., 38.

149   **"suitably down-at-heel":** Ibid., 50.

149   **"looked cold and distant":** Ibid., 22.

150   **"he called many times":** Ibid., 56.

151   **"would be carried out from the land":** HS 5/723.

152   **"It should be easy to kidnap":** Ibid.

Chapter 6: Fleshpots

155   **"I am sure I can be useful":** HS 5/728, National Archives of the UK.

156   **interrogators, who were particularly:** KV 3/319, National Archives of the UK.

156   **"I am in Egypt":** Angelo Carta, quoted in G. Harokopos, *The Abduction of General Kreipe*, trans. Rosemary Tzanaki (Heraklion, Greece: V. Kouvidis–V. Manouras, 2003), 56.

157   **"while there was still time":** Winston Churchill, *Closing the Ring* (Boston: Houghton Mifflin, 1951), 207.

157 **loyalty of Germany's remaining allies:** Ibid., 208.

158 **"There was death and tragedy in Europe":** Suzy Eban, "A Cairo Girlhood," *New Yorker*, July 15, 1974, 64.

158 **"Dickens would have had no need":** Christopher Sykes, *A Song of a Shirt* (London: Derek Verschoyle, 1953), 11.

158 **"What was so remarkable":** Margaret Pawley, *In Obedience to Instructions* (Barmsley: Leo Cooper, 1999), 60.

158 **"an atmosphere of permanent holiday":** Eban, "Cairo Girlhood," 64.

159 **"the most magnificent sports grounds":** Artemis Cooper, *Cairo in the War* (London: Hamish Hamilton, 1989), 37.

159 **then dinner and dancing:** Annette Crean, unpublished memoir, Documents.6433, Private Papers of Mrs A Street, Imperial War Museum, 38.

159 **"The air we breathed":** Pawley, *In Obedience to Instructions*, 62.

159 **"Hope you're enjoying the fleshpots":** Xan Fielding, report 12, HS5/725, National Archives of the UK.

160 **"keep alive the tradition":** Robert St. John, *From the Land of Silent People* (Garden City, NY: Doubleday, Doran, 1942), 331.

160 **"The hot dusty streets":** Pawley, *In Obedience to Instructions*, 57.

160 **"The food was good":** Julian Amery, *Approach March* (London: Hutchinson, 1983), 317–18.

161 **known as Hangover Hall:** Cooper, *Cairo in the War*, 285.

161 **"charming figure, with his":** Patrick Leigh Fermor, "Afterword" in W. Stanley Moss, *Ill Met by Moonlight* (London: Folio Society, 2001), 203.

162 **"He always did it":** Moss, *A War of Shadows* (New York: Macmillan, 1952), 3.

162 **"Most of the rickshaw":** Ibid., 2.

164 **"We are in the soup":** W. Stanley Moss, Diary 1939, Estate of I. W. Stanley Moss.

164 **"It had been wonderful":** W. Stanley Moss, unpublished diary, Documents.13338, Private Papers of Major I W S Moss MC, Department of Documents, Imperial War Museum, 18.

165 **"lovely feeling of advancing":** Ibid.

165 **"The floods of tears":** Moss, *War of Shadows*, 1.

167 **"No, I can't possibly":** Andrew Tarnowski, *The Last Mazurka* (London: Aurum Press, 2006), 216.

168 **"Mrs. Khayatt is so sorry":** Ibid., 217.

169 **"rude comments about the Mother Superior's body odor":** Ibid., 62.

169 **"Goodbye—Sophie":** Ibid., 63.

170 **"They were going so low":** Quoted in ibid., 96.

170 **"Hurrah," he called out:** Ibid., 96–97.

173 **"Altogether it is a bit of a fairy tale":** Ibid., 172.

174 **"A throne, a throne":** Ibid., 184.

174 **"This is like being in heaven":** Quoted in ibid., 182.

175 **"I'll be damned":** Ibid., 182.

176 **"the best looking couple":** Fermor, "Afterword," 205.

Chapter 7: Tara

177 **"made the air of summer":** Suzy Eban, "A Cairo Girlhood," *New Yorker,* July 15, 1974, 64.

178 **"thronged assemblies of all":** Standish O'Grady, *The Story of Ireland* (London: Methuen, 1894), 51–52.

179 **"the mule who-riding-man-is-having-gone":** Xan Fielding, *One Man in His Time* (London: Macmillan, 1990), 13.

179 **"He struck me as a":** Ibid., xxii.

179 **"I'm damned if I'm leaving":** Ibid., 38. The fellow officer was Peter Kemp, who had met Julian Amery when both took cover in the same ditch during the Spanish civil war and later told him this story.

180 **"After the breakthrough at Alamein":** David Smiley, *Albanian Assignment* (London: Chatto & Windus, 1984), 2.

180 **"In Palestine I had":** Ibid., 3.

181 **"We studied German and Italian":** Ibid., 4.

181 **"my dirty tricks course":** Ibid., 7.

181 **weakness for what he called "smells":** W. Stanley Moss, unpublished diary, Documents.13338, Private Papers of Major W S Moss MC, Department of Documents, Imperial War Museum, 15.

182 **"perhaps he was happier with the sword":** Patrick Leigh Fermor, "Foreword," in Smiley, *Albanian Assignment,* xii.

182 **"Smiley lived for action":** Julian Amery, *Approach March* (London: Hutchinson, 1983), 328.

182 **"You bloody communist":** Moss, unpublished diary, 14.

183 **Paddy thought him "quixotic":** Fermor, "Foreword," xi.

184 **As Pixie grew by leaps and bounds:** W. Stanley Moss, *A War of Shadows* (New York: Macmillan, 1952), 149.

185 **"Oh, it's nothing":** Andrew Tarnowski, *The Last Mazurka* (London: Aurum Press, 2006), 215.

185 **"It so happened that I":** Ibid., 222.

185 **"Life at Tara was":** Amery, *Approach March,* 319.

187   **"She reclined on the pillows":** Ibid.

188   **"Were such a thing possible":** Patrick Leigh Fermor, "Afterword," in W. Stanley Moss, *Ill Met by Moonlight* (London: Folio Society, 2001), 202.

189   **"A sort of road was here":** Quoted in Tarnowski, *Last Mazurka*, 219.

190   **"Not yet," he replied:** Fermor, "Afterword," 203.

191   **"would be a dead giveaway":** Annette Crean, unpublished memoir, Documents.6433, Private Papers of Mrs A Street, Imperial War Museum, 48.

191   **"During a parachute course":** Lawrence Durrell, *The Greek Islands* (New York: Viking, 1978), 92.

192   **"is undeniably contrary":** Amery, *Approach March*, 328.

192   **"As the roar of the engines":** Ibid., 329.

193   **"the full horror of falling":** Ibid.

194   **"He used to lock ladies into boxes":** Fermor, "Afterword," 206.

195   **"The air of sorcery":** Moss, *War of Shadows*, 13.

196   **"as though I were a witch's bowl":** Ibid.

196   **the ether knockout drops:** This was the experience, for instance, of an SOE captain named Arthur Reade in November 1943. HS 5/730.

197   **"Most of the day it had rained":** A. M. Rendel, *Appointment in Crete* (London: A. Wingate, 1953), 120.

198   **move his radio station to a spot near Kritsa:** When I talked to villagers in a rural area east of Kritsa in 2009, they still recalled hearing about a British wireless station that had been set up nearby during the war, though they believed the set had been kept in a hollow tree. Whether the story reflects Rendel's station is impossible to know.

199   **"a stately old hawk":** Moss, unpublished diary, 16.

200   **"but before they had made":** Patrick Leigh Fermor to Moss, quoted in Moss, unpublished diary, 15.

202   **"Is this the last time?":** Moss, unpublished diary, 3.

203   **"staring wistfully at Paddy":** Ibid., 4.

203   **"Everyone in the canteen":** Ibid., 5.

204   **"like triangles cut out":** Ibid.

Chapter 8: Moonstruck

205   **coordinates chosen for the drop:** These and other details of Leigh Fermor's parachute drop are drawn from Squadron 148 Sortie Reports, AIR 23/1443.

206   **"Perhaps I have been":** W. Stanley Moss, unpublished diary, Documents.13338, Private Papers of Major I W S Moss MC, Department of Documents, Imperial War Museum.

207 **so full of mishaps:** Details of Fortune's earlier mission are drawn from AIR 23/1443.

207 **"hit a colossal bump":** AIR 23/1443.

210 **"Sometimes he finds something":** Moss, unpublished diary, 8.

211 **"It has rained a great deal":** Ibid., 12.

211 **"Western wind, when wilt thou blow":** Anonymous 16th-century lyric, reproduced in James J. Wilhelm, *Lyrics of the Middle Ages: An Anthology* (New York: Garland), 294.

212 **One day Manoli arrived:** Moss, unpublished diary. The Scottish adventure novel Leigh Fermor read was *The New Road* by Neil Munro.

212 **and thought it "flawless":** Ibid.

213 **Leigh Fermor thought the production:** Patrick Leigh Fermor, "Afterword," in W. Stanley Moss, *Ill Met by Moonlight* (London: Folio Society, 2001), 207.

213 **"Paddy had a strange":** Moss, unpublished diary, 23.

214 **"They're exactly like our cheese huts":** Fermor, "Afterword," 207.

214 **"an eastern priest bowing":** A. M. Rendel, *Appointment in Crete* (London: A. Wingate, 1953), 130.

215 **"How filthily artificial":** Ibid., 131.

215 **"The plane flew on":** Ibid.

216 **"Mr. Leigh Fermor, I presume":** Ibid.

217 **"still low above us":** Ibid., 132–33.

218 **"As time went on":** Ibid., 137.

218 **"I could hardly have":** Ibid., 133.

218 **"I have been a guest":** HS 5/728.

219 **"And in your boat":** Rendel, *Appointment in Crete*, 134.

220 **"No Germans should have":** Ibid., 138.

221 **"We were contemplating a telegram":** Ibid., 139.

222 **"which was partly flat":** Moss, unpublished diary, 25.

222 **"Unfortunately I was due":** Ibid., 25–26.

222 **"they 'acquired' a couple sheep":** Ibid., 26.

222 **"Of course there wasn't a boat":** Ibid.

223 **"a bitter, sneering man":** HS 5/728.

224 **"we had stowed the stores":** Rendel, *Appointment in Crete*, 140.

224 **"had begun to advise the party":** Ibid.

225 **"When they had climbed level":** Ibid., 140–41.

225 **"a young, spectacled, alert":** Patrick Leigh Fermor, "Afterword," 210.

226 **"We could see them":** HS 5/728.

226 **"If they would have":** Rendel, *Appointment in Crete*, 149.

227 **"The actual pilot, W/O Fortune":** This and the following quotations are from Patrick Leigh Fermor, field report, HS 5/728.

228 **"Hope Billy and the lads arrive":** Ibid.

229 **"Might go fishing with explosives":** Moss, unpublished diary, 27.

229 **"as soon as possible":** Details of Coleman's mission are drawn from ADM 199/889.

230 **"the sea rougher than before":** Moss, unpublished diary, 27.

230 **"As I write I can smell:"** Ibid., 28.

231 **Dermatos Beach, east of the village:** The orders Lieutenant Coleman received from the Office of Commander Coastal Forces, Eastern Mediterranean, give the coordinates of the point off the beach: N 34°58', E 25°19'30". HS 5/677. Other versions of Coleman's orders also refer to Dermatos explicitly. In the log of operations for the unit as a whole, the latitude was mistakenly transcribed as 35d 58m N, a point in the Aegean far north of the island of Crete. The mistake perhaps accounts for some later confusion about the precise location of the beach where Moss's party came ashore.

232 **In all, forty-five people:** A number of the thirty-nine Greek men in the party later complained about the treatment they received at the other end of the voyage. In Cairo, according to an M Branch memorandum dated April 7, they were examined by an Indian medical officer who took an extreme approach to delousing: "This officer appears to have ordered all the Greeks to have their heads shaved, stating that the hair would grow back in a fortnight; he also ordered four Greeks to shave other parts of their anatomy." HS 5/677.

233 **"Some of the men stood":** Moss, *Ill Met by Moonlight*, 33–34.

233 **"You friend Paddy?":** Ibid., 34–35.

234 **"He wore a smart moustache":** Moss, unpublished diary, 34.

234 **"We sat, chatted and smoked":** John Houseman, HS 5/727.

234 **"And after three hours":** Ibid.

Chapter 9: The Intersection

236 **"I haven't washed":** W. Stanley Moss, *Ill Met by Moonlight* (London: Folio Society, 2001), 42.

236 **"Xan and I like them to think":** W. Stanley Moss, unpublished diary, Documents.13338, Private Papers of Major I W S Moss MC, Department of Documents, Imperial War Museum,, 34.

237 **"It was a pity":** Moss, *Ill Met by Moonlight*, 44.

238 **"a gay rogue":** Ibid.

239 **His father was an old friend:** Zahari's father was Kimon Zographakis.

241 **"the guards, the barbed wire":** Patrick Leigh Fermor, "How to Steal a General," in Part 68, *History of the Second World War* (Marshall Cavendish, 1974), 1900.

241 **"the risks which she took":** HS 8/692.

244 **"We have given them":** Moss, *Ill Met by Moonlight*, 61.

245 **"Christ is risen—Bang!":** Patrick Leigh Fermor to W. Stanley Moss, quoted in Moss, unpublished diary, 44.

247 **"dissolved amid the derisive laughter":** HS 5/724.

247 **"They attempted to blow up":** Ibid.

247 **"We want not so much":** HS 5/724.

248 **"a tiny bit rusty":** Moss, *Ill Met by Moonlight*, 71.

249 **"This sort of walking":** Ibid., p. 72.

251 **introduced them to his sister:** Moss, in *A War of Shadows*, calls this young woman "Maria," but SOE records give her name as Anna E. Zographistos.

251 **"She is a strange person":** Moss, *Ill Met by Moonlight*, 77.

252 **"among a thousand by day":** G. Harokopos, *The Abduction of General Kreipe*, trans. Rosemary Tzanaki (Heraklion, Greece: V. Kouvidis–V. Manouras, 2003), 116.

252 **"Germans, hide!":** Ibid., 118.

253 **"he was not a man":** Ibid.,119.

256 **"an ill-assorted crew":** Moss, *Ill Met by Moonlight*, 71.

257 **"Too many cooks":** W. Stanley Moss, *A War of Shadows* (New York: Macmillan, 1952), 27.

258 **"favourite recreation was throat slitting":** Moss, *Ill Met by Moonlight*, 87.

259 **"Minotaurs, bull-men, nymphs":** Ibid., 90.

259 **"This morning, under the trees":** Ibid., 91.

261 **called out, "Halt!":** This and the following dialogue are from Fermor, "How to Steal a General," 1900.

262 **"I am a British major":** Ibid.

263 **"This is marvelous":** Ibid.

264 **"Generals Wagen!":** Ibid.

264 **"Gute Nacht!":** Moss, *Ill Met by Moonlight*, 102.

264 **"which I thought was the best":** Ibid., 103.

264 **"this hussar stunt":** Fermor, "How to Steal a General," 1901.

266 **"is an ideal place for submarines":** HS 5/728.

267 **"We are very sorry":** HS 5/728. Moss's published account in *Ill Met by Moonlight* recalls the postscript slightly differently.

267 **"Captured standards!":** Fermor, "How to Steal a General," 1901.

267 **"The only people who saw":** Ibid.

268 **"To All Cretans":** Ibid.

Chapter 10: Bricklayer

271   **the Anogeian *andarte* band:** This was a group led by a *kapetan* named Mihale Xilouris. HS 5/727.

272   **"By surprise," he emphasized:** Patrick Leigh Fermor, "How to Steal a General," in Part 68, *History of the Second World War* (Marshall Cavendish, 1974), 1901.

272   **crossed the summit without recognizing it:** It is easy to imagine that Leigh Fermor and Moss were reminded of Wordsworth's account, in *The Prelude*, of discovering to his surprise that he had crossed the Alps.

273   **"and the Germans were threatening fearful reprisals":** HS 5/727.

273   **"It took us two hours":** W. Stanley Moss, *Ill Met by Moonlight* (London: Folio Society, 2001), 126.

274   **It was with a thrill:** The Horace episode is recounted in Patrick Leigh Fermor, *A Time of Gifts* (New York: New York Review Books, 2005), 86.

276   **"Colonel General Heinrich Kreipe":** HS 5/732. Note: These documents seem to have been misfiled in this National Archives folder.

276   **"Essential, repeat, essential":** HS 5/418.

276   **news outlets in Cairo *were reporting*:** HS 5/418. In *Ill Met by Moonlight*, Moss says the broadcast claimed the general *was leaving* the island, which would not have done much to dissuade German search parties. Communications on file in the SOE archives tell the story somewhat differently, and I have followed that documentary evidence.

277   **"This attachment is a welcome event":** Moss, *Ill Met by Moonlight*, 136.

279   **"Paddy and I are feeling":** Ibid., 131.

281   **"Cannot, repeat, not warn Paddy":** HS 5/732. Note: These documents seem to have been misfiled in this National Archives folder.

281   **"I have completely run out":** Moss, *Ill Met by Moonlight*, 137.

283   **Dick Barnes had in fact been trying:** HS 5/722.

285   **"It was a strange and ghostly feeling":** Moss, *Ill Met by Moonlight*, 153.

287   **"And so Jonny, a price":** Ibid., 158.

288   **The vessel they had heard closed on the beach and opened fire:** This account of Ciclitira's close call is in HS 5/722.

288   **"Last night was beautiful":** Moss, *Ill Met by Moonlight*, 162.

289   **"a sudden hysterical shriek":** Ibid., 165.

290   **"Think of those beasts":** Ibid., 166.

290 **landing beach near Rodakino:** Coleman's orders point to a position just off the beach: N 35º10'24", E 24º18'24".

290 **A few weeks earlier he had spotted:** ADM 199/899.

291 **"Although a good lookout":** ADM 1/29697.

291 **with Ciclitira the night he was fired upon:** HS 5/722.

292 **"They knew every track":** Moss, *Ill Met by Moonlight*, 170.

292 **"there was no pain":** Fermor, "How to Steal a General," 1901.

293 **"He was still there":** Moss, *Ill Met by Moonlight*, 176.

294 **"faint at first but gradually louder":** Fermor, "How to Steal a General," 1904.

295 **"Then we were taken down":** Moss, *Ill Met by Moonlight*, 180.

296 **"He smiled at us":** Ibid., 185.

Epilogue: *Ritterlich!*

299 **"to the last cartridge":** WO 208/4208.

300 **"I liked Paddy":** Dilys Powell, *The Villa Ariadne* (London: Hodder & Stoughton, 1973), 177.

300 **"No incident had taken place":** HS 5/729.

301 **"The war will end":** Ibid.

303 **"same nauseating smell":** W. Stanley Moss, *Ill Met by Moonlight* (London: Folio Society, 2001), 153.

303 **"removing the trousers":** W. Stanley Moss, *A War of Shadows* (New York: Macmillan, 1952), 149.

304 **"His leg was set":** Andrew Tarnowski, *The Last Mazurka* (London: Aurum Press, 2006), 225.

304 **received a commendation:** ADM 1/29697.

304 **the papers implicating him:** "Instead a major called von der Heyde was arrested, and later freed by the Russians." Antony Beevor, *Crete: The Battle and the Resistance* (London: John Murray, 1991), 76.

304 **killed in fighting in Norway:** Patrick Leigh Fermor, *A Time of Gifts* (New York: New York Review Books, 2005), 71.

304 **"You'll find out when you get there":** Xan Fielding, *Hide and Seek* (London: Secker & Warburg, 1954), 225.

305 **"Brave, loyal, tireless, cheerful":** HS 8/729.

305 **"certainly one of the bravest":** HS 8/657.

305 **"I saw a pensive look":** Mosley, *In Tearing Haste*, 236.

306 **"During the day contingents":** HS 5/728.

307 **"*Ritterlich! Wie ein Ritter!*":** Mosley, *In Tearing Haste*, 121.

Credits

Grateful Acknowledgement is made to the following for their permission to reprint previously published and unpublished material:

The Estate of Patrick Leigh Fermor: Excerpts and sketch from a February 9, 1944, letter by Patrick Leigh Fermor to Annette Crean. Reprinted with permission by the estate of Patrick Leigh Fermor.

The Estate of William Stanley Moss: Excerpts from "W. Stanley Moss, unpublished diary, Documents 13338 Private Papers of Major I W S Moss MC, Department of Documents, Imperial War Museum," copyright © the Estate of William Stanley Moss. Excerpt from "W. Stanley Moss, Diary 1939," copyright © the Estate of William Stanley Moss. Reprinted by permission of the Estate of William Stanley Moss.

Hodder & Stoughton Limited: Excerpt from *A Time of Gifts* by Patrick Leigh Fermor, copyright © 1977 by Patrick Leigh Fermor. Reprinted by permission of Hodder & Stoughton Limited.

Imogen Grundon: Excerpt from *The Rash Adventure: A Life of John Pendlebury* by Imogen Grundon (Libri Publications, 2007). Reprinted by permission of the author.

Paul Dry Books, Inc., and the Estate of William Stanley Moss: Excerpts from *Ill Met by Moonlight* by W. Stanley Moss, copyright © 1950 by W. Stanley Moss. Reprinted by permission of Paul Dry Books, Inc., www.pauldrybooks.com, and the estate of W. Stanley Moss.

Paul Dry Books, Inc.: *Hide and Seek* by Xan Fielding (Secker & Warburg, 1954). Reprinted by permission of Paul Dry Books, Inc., www.pauldrybooks.com.

Robert Rendel: Excerpt from *Appointment in Crete: The Story of a British Agent* by A. M. Rendel (Allen Wingate, 1953). Reprinted by permission of Robert Rendel.

List of Illustrations

Patrick Leigh Fermor. © *Imperial War Museum (HU 98922)*, 35.

John Pendlebury takes target practice. *Col. Stephen Rose, courtesy of Imogen Grundon*, 38.

Xan Fielding sights a Lee-Enfield rifle. © *Imperial War Museum (HU 66049)*, 81.

Leigh Fermor in civilian disguise on Crete. © *Imperial War Museum (HU 66084)*, 83.

Manoli Bandouvas and two of his *andartes*. © *Imperial War Museum (HU 66051)*, 85.

Manoli Paterakis. © *Imperial War Museum (HU 66057)*, 101.

Sandy Rendel in uniform. *Rendel Family Archive*, 146.

Sandy Rendel in civilian disguise on Crete. *Rendel Family Archive*, 146.

William Stanley Moss. © *Imperial War Museum (HU 66053)*, 167.

Sophie Tarnowska. *Photograph © The Estate of William Stanley Moss—reproduced by permission*, 167.

Billy Moss on Crete. © *Imperial War Museum (HU 66085)*, 235.

George Tyrakis, Antoni Papaleonidas ("Wallace Beery"), Manoli Paterakis. *Photograph © The Estate of William Stanley Moss—reproduced by permission*, 238.

Moss and Leigh Fermor (seated, center front) and their team with Athanasios Bourdzalis and his *andartes*. *Photograph © The Estate of William Stanley Moss— reproduced by permission*, 250.

Moss (left) and Leigh Fermor disguised as German soldiers. *Photograph © The Estate of William Stanley Moss—reproduced by permission*, 255.

The abduction team. Standing, left to right: Stratis Saviolakis, Manoli Paterakis, Antoni Papaleonidas ("Wallace Beery"), George Tyrakis, Nikos Komis. Seated: Grigori Chnarakis, Patrick Leigh Fermor, William Stanley Moss. *Photograph © The Estate of William Stanley Moss—reproduced by permission*, 261.

Moss and Leigh Fermor with their prisoner, General Heinrich Kreipe (center). *Photograph © The Estate of William Stanley Moss—reproduced by permission*, 275.

General Kreipe arrives in Cairo. *Photograph © The Estate of William Stanley Moss—reproduced by permission*, 296.

Selected Bibliography

Published Sources

Amery, Julian. *Approach March.* London: Hutchinson, 1983.

Beevor, Antony. *Crete: The Battle and the Resistance.* London: John Murray, 1991.

Benario, Janice M. "Horace, Humanitas and Crete." *Amphora* 2, no. 1 (spring 2003): 1-3.

Byron, Robert. *The Station.* London: Century Publishing, 1984.

Chubb, Mary. *Nefertiti Lived Here.* London: Libri, 1998.

Churchill, Winston. *Closing the Ring.* Boston: Houghton Mifflin, 1951.

———. *Their Finest Hour.* Boston: Houghton Mifflin, 1949.

Clark, Alan. *The Fall of Crete.* London: Cassell, 1962.

Cooper, Artemis. *Cairo in the War.* London: Hamish Hamilton, 1989.

Crookshank, H., and J. B. Auden, "Lewis Leigh Fermor 1880–1954." *Biographical Memoirs of Fellows of the Royal Society* 2 (November 1956): 101–16.

Downing, Ben. "A Visit with Patrick Leigh Fermor." *Paris Review* 165 (Spring 2003), 165–226.

———. "Philhellene's Progress: Patrick Leigh Fermor." *The New Criterion,* vol. 19, January 2001, 9.

Durrell, Lawrence. *The Greek Islands.* New York: Viking, 1978.

Eban, Suzy. "A Cairo Girlhood." *The New Yorker,* July 15, 1974, 62–73.

Elliot, Murray. *Vasili: The Lion of Crete.* London: Century Hutchinson, 1987.

Fermor, Patrick Leigh. "Afterword." In W. Stanley Moss, *Ill Met by Moonlight* (London: Folio Society, 2001), 193–211.

———. *Between the Woods and the Water.* London: Penguin Books, 1988.

———. "Foreword." In David Smiley, *Albanian Assignment* (London: Chatto & Windus, 1984), ix–xii.

———. "How to Steal a General." In Part 68, *History of the Second World War* (Marshall Cavendish, 1974): 1900–1904.

———. *Mani.* Middlesex: Penguin Books, 1984.

———. *Roumeli.* New York: New York Review Books, 2006.

———. *Three Letters from the Andes.* London: John Murray, 2005.

———. *A Time of Gifts.* New York: New York Review Books, 2005.

———. *A Time to Keep Silence.* New York: New York Review Books, 2007.

———. *Words of Mercury.* Edited by Artemis Cooper. London: John Murray, 2004.

Fielding, Xan. *Hide and Seek.* London: Secker & Warburg, 1954.

———. *One Man in His Time.* London: Macmillan, 1990.

Fox-Davies, Arthur Charles. *Armorial Families,* vol. 2. London: Hurst & Blackett, 1929.

Grundon, Imogen. *The Rash Adventurer: A Life of John Pendlebury.* London: Libri Publications, 2007.

Hadjipateras, Costas N., and Maria S. Falios. *Crete 1941 Eyewitnessed.* Athens: Efstathiadis Group, 2007.

Harokopos, George. *The Abduction of General Kreipe.* Translated by Rosemary Tzanaki. Heraklion, Greece: V. Kouvidis–V. Manouras, 2003.

Herodotus. *Herodotus: A New and Literal Version from the Text of Baehr.* New York: Harper & Bros., 1889.

Heydte, Friedrich August, Freiherr von der. *Daedalus Returned.* Translated by W. Stanley Moss. London: Hutchinson and Co., 1958.

Hill, Maria. *Diggers and Greeks.* Sydney: University of New South Wales Press, 2010.

Kokanos, N. A. *The Cretan Resistance 1941–1945.* Iraklion, Greece: Manouras G.–Tsintaris A., 2004.

Lucas, James. *Hitler's Enforcers.* London: Cassell, 1996.

MacNiven, Ian. *Lawrence Durrell: A Biography.* London: Faber & Faber, 1998.

Mosley, Charlotte, ed. *In Tearing Haste: Letters Between Deborah Devonshire and Patrick Leigh Fermor.* London: John Murray, 2008.

Moss, W. Stanley. *Ill Met by Moonlight.* London: Folio Society, 2001.

———. *A War of Shadows.* New York: Macmillan, 1952.

Pawley, Margaret. *In Obedience to Instructions.* Barnsley, UK: Leo Cooper, 1999.

Phillips, Gene D. *Evelyn Waugh's Officers, Gentlemen, and Rogues.* Chicago: Nelson Hall, 1975.

Powell, Dilys. *The Villa Ariadne.* London: Hodder & Stoughton, 1973.

Psychoundakis, George. *The Cretan Runner.* Translated by Patrick Leigh Fermor. London: Penguin Books, 1998.

Rendel, A. M. *Appointment in Crete.* London: A. Wingate, 1953.

Roessel, David. *In Byron's Shadow.* New York: Oxford Univerity Press, 2002.

Smiley, David. *Albanian Assignment.* London: Chatto & Windus, 1984.

St. John, Robert. *From the Land of Silent People.* Garden City, NY: Doubleday, Doran, 1942.

Sutherland, David. *He Who Dares.* Annapolis: Naval Institute Press, 1999.

Sykes, Christopher. *Evelyn Waugh.* Boston: Little, Brown, 1975.

———. *A Song of a Shirt.* London: Derek Verschoyle, 1953.

Tarnowski, Andrew. *The Last Mazurka.* London: Aurum Press, 2006.

Valentin, Jacques. *The Monks of Mount Athos.* Translated by Diano Athill. London: A. Deutsch, 1960.

Watts, Alan. *In My Own Way.* New York: Pantheon, 1972.

Waugh, Evelyn. *The Diaries of Evelyn Waugh.* Edited by Michael Davie. Boston: Little, Brown, 1976.

———. *Officers and Gentlemen.* Boston: Little, Brown, 1955.

Unpublished Sources

National Archives of the UK

ADM 1/29488
ADM 1/29697
ADM 199/889
AIR 23/1443
HS 5/418
HS 5/456
HS 5/677
HS 5/722
HS 5/723
HS 5/724
HS 5/725
HS 5/727
HS 5/728
HS 5/729
HS 5/730
HS 5/731
HS 5/732
HS 8/403
HS 8/405
HS 8/461

HS 8/478
HS 8/571
HS 8/577
HS 8/657
HS 8/690
HS 8/692
HS 8/698
HS 8/729
HS 8/765
HS 9/317/2
HS 9/458/1
HS 9/760/1
KV 3/319
WO 208/4208

Imperial War Museum

Crean, Annette. Memoir. Documents.6433, Private Papers of Mrs A
    Street, Imperial War Museum.
Moss, W. Stanley. Diary. Documents.13338, Private Papers of Major
    I W S Moss MC, Department of Documents, Imperial War
    Museum.
———. Diary 1939. Estate of I. W. Stanley Moss.
Rendel, A. M. Papers of Alexander Meadows Rendel, Rendel Family
    Archive, London.

Index

Note: See pages xvii–xviii (A Note on Names) for an explanation of the author's use of surnames, code names, and nicknames. The abbreviation "PLF" refers to Patrick Leigh Fermor.

Leonidas (SOE collaborator, Dr.), 113, 118

Logan, R. A. (motor launch skipper), 279–80

Lollards (Communist partisans), 98, 111, 258–59, 301

"Lord Rakehell" (PLF nickname), 168

"Lotus Land" (pro-British safe area), 81, 91, 95, 111, 247, 281

Ludovici (Italian captain), 138

"Manoli the Cop." See Paterakis, Manoli

Maskelyne, Jasper (SOE tradecraft expert), 194–96, 226

McLean, Billy (SOE officer), 178–83, 187, 199–200, 202

Menasces, Denise, 201

"Micky." See Akoumianakis, Mihali

Middle East Command, 45, 50, 54, 80

"Mihalaki"/"Mihali." See Brooke, Harry

"Mihali"/"Mike." See Stockbridge, Ralph

"Mihali"/"Paddy." See Fermor, Patrick Leigh

"Minoan Mike." See Akoumianakis, Mihali

"Minoan Minnie," 116

Moss, Edward, 162–63

Moss, William Stanley and Natalie (parents), 161

Moss, William Stanley (SOE officer)
aborted air-drop onto Crete, xix–xxiii, 205–08, 214–18
awaiting assignment, 160–61
childhood and education, 161–63
Cretan disguise, 236
departure for Crete, 198, 200, 201–04
early missions, 178, 189–91
engagement to Patsy, 165–166, 186
enlistment and training, 164
final departure from Crete, 302
parachute training, 191–92
post-war activities, xv–xvi, 303

relationship with Sophie, 166–67, 176, 200–01, 211, 222, 303
rental of "Tara," 166–68, 177–78
return to Crete, 200–02, 229–35, 302
service in North Africa, 164–65
Tara nickname "Mr. Jack Jargon," 168

Mount Athos, 5, 29–32

Mount Dikti, 124–25, 139, 188, 191, 194, 196, 185

Mount Ida, xvi, 50, 67, 85–86, 264–65, 267–68, 270, 273

Mount Soracte, 274

"Mr. Jack Jargon" (Moss nickname), 168

Müller, Friedrich-Wilhelm (German general)
disarmament of Italians, 132–35
living in Villa Ariadne, 116
massacre at Viannos, 137–38, 152, 156–57
plans for kidnapping, 152, 187–89, 197, 227–28, 236–37
replacement by Kreipe, 228, 237–40
war crimes conviction, 299–300

Mussolini, Benito, 45, 113, 118–19

Nazism. See also Hitler, Adolf
1933, presence in Germany, 14–16
German attitude toward, 17
PLF encounters with, 14–15, 18, 19–20, 21–22

Negroni (Italian general), 155–56

"Never-Never Land," 158. See also Crete

Normandy, Allied invasion, 301

North Africa
Battle of El Alamein, 143, 161, 176
British Middle East Command, 45, 50, 54, 80
British military operations, 144, 164–65, 195, 213
German Afrika Korps, 84, 174, 176, 180

Wes Davis is the author of *American Journey: On the Road with Henry Ford, Thomas Edison, and John Burroughs* and editor of *An Anthology of Modern Irish Poetry*. He served for two years as an assistant to the director of excavations at Kavousi in Eastern Crete, not far from the plateau where Patrick Leigh Fermor parachuted onto the island during WWII. He holds a Ph.D.

photograph by Alice Ensor Davis

in English Literature from Princeton University and is a former assistant professor of English at Yale University. Davis has written for many publications including the *New York Times*, *Wall Street Journal*, and *The Nation*. He lives outside New York City.